A MODEL OF THE MIND

A MODEL OF

explored by hypnotically controlled

psychodynamic implications

The University of Michigan and Fellow, Center for

in collaboration with:

JUSTIN L. WEISS, Massachusetts Mental Health Center and Harvard University

ABRAM MINKOWICH, Hebrew University (Israel)

ANN L. VROOM, St. Christopher's Hospital for Children (Philadelphia, Pennsylvania)

John Wiley & Sons, Inc.,

THE MIND

experiments and examined for its

by **GERALD S. BLUM,** Professor of Psychology,

Advanced Study in the Behavorial Sciences (1959-60)

GERALD A. MENDELSOHN, University of California
(Berkeley)

SIDNEY I. PERLOE, Yale University

IRVING W. WOLF, General Electric Company (Syracuse,
New York)

ROBERT H. GOLDSTEIN, University of Rochester

New York • London

Prologue

SETTING THE STAGE

This book is calculated to be controversial on a number of counts. It advocates a *general* yet *detailed* theory of human thought, feeling, and action—probing phenomena from perception to psychodynamics, from sensation to symptoms. It stresses those mental functions occurring *between* stimulus and response, and pursues them in the laboratory with the aid of techniques like hypnosis, galvanic skin recordings, and introspection. Its approach is cast in the form of a model which is neither neurophysiological nor mathematical but purely *conceptual.* It appraises some significant problems posed by psychoanalysis, at the same time shaping a different theoretical base. The guiding framework is acknowledged to be unfinished, requiring much additional structure from empirical research. And finally, the experiments suggested by the model often tend to be rather unorthodox in design as well as execution.

With so many potential affronts to the established scientific community, it is only natural for the author to convince himself that he is writing his "one world of psychology" theme primarily to make an impact upon the still "uncommitted peoples," the rising generation of students whose theoretical biases have not yet hardened under the molding hands of their elders. Actually, though, several encouraging signs have already appeared in psychology's sometimes zany *Zeitgeist* since our group undertook its conceptual model of the mind in 1955. Miller, Galanter, and Pribram (30) have recently issued an eloquent plea for a "subjective behaviorism" linked to computer analogy. Though devoid of data and offering for future research only the advice that investigators listen to what experimental subjects have to say, their book has nevertheless evoked favorable reaction from such stalwarts as E. G. Boring * and D. O. Hebb.† The latter, during a presidential address to the American Psychological Association in 1960 (22), himself emphasized the necessity for a "behavioristic analysis of the thought process" and listed "mind and consciousness, sensations and perceptions, feelings and emotions" all as intervening variables or constructs properly part of a behavioristic psychology. A noted biologist, S. S. Kety, goes so far as to state: ". . . denying the existence or the importance of mental states merely because they are difficult to measure or because they cannot be directly observed in others is needlessly to restrict the field of the mental sciences and to curtail the opportunities for the discovery of new relationships" (27). In short, the stage may be better set for our production than we think.

CUES FOR THE READER

The model concerns principles of processing in the Mental System— ways in which inputs interact with existing memory traces to produce cognitive, affective, and motoric outputs. Though developmental features are given some attention, it is primarily a *contemporary* rather than a genetic approach to thought, feeling, and action.

Chapter 1 of Part A provides the background and rationale for the current form of the model. Chapter 2 treats the conceptual scheme in broad overview, intending to familiarize the reader with the general framework as a prelude to the presentation of specific experiments. Those readers who prefer to peruse initially a more detailed exposition of the model are advised to skip directly from Chapter 2 to 10, which spells out structural and functional characteristics, and then return to the experiments.

Part B reports a series of twelve experiments. These are labeled in descriptive terms rather than the technical language of the model in

* Address delivered at Western Psychological Association meeting, San Jose, California, 1960.
† Review in *Contemporary Psychology*, 1960, 5, 209–211.

order to facilitate communication. The studies, relevant to a variety of fields (as a glance at the table of contents will confirm), can be examined independently of the model. However, it must be borne in mind that each of them did grow out of considerations during various phases of the model's evolution, and the laboratory findings in turn contributed significantly to theoretical formulation.

While going over the experiments, some readers may find themselves obsessed by such methodological questions as "How do we know the subjects weren't simulating under hypnosis?" or "Can the galvanic skin response be relied upon as a measure of anxiety?" These and related issues are discussed in the Epilogue to Part B but, if anyone's patience is too sorely tried before that point, he is urged to turn immediately to pp. 103–107.

Lastly, Part C expands the model in the context of perception and learning, and then explores its power to generate new light that can be cast on diverse psychodynamic phenomena, e.g., anxiety, defenses, hypnotic compliance, amnesia, prelogical thinking, and therapeutic alterations. Here the reader is cautioned not to expect reviews of the literature bearing on these topics, or systematic comparisons between our theory and all others. Tasks of such magnitude are beyond the scope of the present endeavor.

ACKNOWLEDGMENTS

Wherever I employ the first-person plural, it is not a perfunctory use of the "editorial we." The research program was a group effort in every sense and the persons listed as collaborators on the title page all made important contributions. Their affiliations with the project are listed below. In addition, they offered many suggestions for revision of the manuscript.

Justin L. Weiss: Research associate, 1956–59.
Abram Minkowich: Research assistant, 1956–58; associate, 1958–59.
Ann L. Vroom: Research assistant, 1957–59.
Gerald A. Mendelsohn: Research assistant, 1958–59.
Sidney I. Perloe: Research assistant, 1956–58; consultant, 1959.
Irving W. Wolf: Consultant, 1955–59.
Robert H. Goldstein: Research assistant, 1956–58.

Financial support for the program was provided by grants from two sources: The National Institute of Mental Health (Grant M1286) and the Ford Foundation, the former for the three-year period 1956–59 and the latter for five years beginning in 1956. A fellowship at the Center for Advanced Study in the Behavioral Sciences, 1959–60, made available ideal facilities for preparation of the manuscript.

Several colleagues at the Center were kind enough to read and comment upon the material: J. A. Deutsch, G. Adrian Horridge, William Kessen, George Mandler, Ernest Nagel, and especially David T. Lykken, who donated hours of discussion and constructive criticism. At the University of Michigan, J. D. Birch participated in a number of group meetings during 1957–58; Wilbert J. McKeachie read portions of the manuscript; and several graduate students—Kalman Benyamini, Carol J. Reverski, Sheila G. Siebert, and Charles G. Stewart—also gave helpful editorial reactions. Finally, Ernest R. Hilgard of Stanford University was the source of invaluable advice for improving the presentation.

Three other persons deserve special acknowledgment. Mary Lee Pierce worked as project secretary for several years; Anna C. Tower typed most of the first draft of the manuscript; and Helen E. Sherman transcribed all the tape-recordings of our experimental sessions and also typed portions of the manuscript.

Permission to quote or reprint material from their publications was graciously extended by the following: Springer Publishing Company, Journal Press, American Association for the Advancement of Science, University of Wisconsin Press, Psychological Corporation, American Psychological Association, *The New Yorker* magazine, Henry Kimpton, and Hogarth Press.

GERALD S. BLUM

Ann Arbor, Michigan
September, 1961

Contents

PART A

CONCEPTUALIZING THE MIND

Evolution and revolution of a conceptual approach

1

The temptation to begin at the end is admittedly great. The finally orbiting product of several years of intensive work is bound to be seen as more of an accomplishment than its inadequate predecessors destroyed shortly after having left the ground. But to view our conceptual model of mental activity as though it had been launched full-scale in its current form would be quite misleading. Instead I shall try to describe enough of its development to make readily apparent the fact that our formulations and experiments have undergone a number of overhauls before attaining the present path.

Originally we consoled ourselves that reaching for the moon has always been a vexing business. But lately even moons seem to have acquired an encouraging degree of accessibility. Our particular moon is a comprehensive theory of human thought, feeling, and action which is capable of encircling psychology's vast and scattered realm of facts. The reader will have to make his own estimate of how many thousands of miles our efforts are off course. From our vantage point the goal appears much less remote than it did at first.

The venture commenced in truly fortuitous fashion during the Christmas vacation of 1955. The author, a psychologist engaged in the preparation of a class lecture, showed the following passage in

Freud's "A Note Upon the Mystic-Writing Pad" to his brother-in-law, an engineer,* and called attention to its radar-like character:

> On the Mystic Pad the writing vanishes every time the close contact is broken between the paper which receives the stimulus and the wax slab which preserves the impression. This agrees with a notion which I have long had about the method in which the perceptual apparatus of our mind functions, but which I have hitherto kept to myself. I have supposed that cathectic innervations are sent out and withdrawn in rapid periodic impulses from within into the completely pervious system Pcpt-Cs. So long as that system is cathected in this manner, it receives the perceptions (which are accompanied by consciousness) and passes the excitation on to the unconscious mnemonic systems; but as soon as the cathexis is withdrawn, consciousness is extinguished and the functioning of the system ceases. It would be as though the unconscious stretches out feelers, through the medium of the system Pcpt-Cs, towards the external world, and these are hastily withdrawn as soon as they have sampled the excitations coming from it. Thus I attributed the interruptions, which with the Mystic Pad have an external origin, to the discontinuity in the current of innervation; and the place of an actual breaking of contact was taken in my hypothesis by the periodic non-excitability of the perceptual system. I further suspected that this discontinuous method of functioning of the system Pcpt-Cs lies at the bottom of the origin of the concept of time. (17, p. 180)

The ease with which the engineer was able to diagram Freud's description of perceptual and memory processes re-kindled a nearly dead spark in the psychologist—the possibility of systematizing psychoanalytic theory. Though a long-time proponent of experimental testing of psychoanalytic concepts, I had never come to grips with the problem of the total theory more than to realize its shortcomings, which Freud himself keenly recognized. An electronic scheme spelling out in detail the functions of Id, Ego, and Superego suddenly seemed attractive.

Throughout the remaining week of what was turning into an odd vacation, the two of us proceeded to draw up a series of block diagrams, like those used for electronic systems, and plugged in as many psychoanalytic notions as we could. The result was a complicated contrivance, replete with energy storage systems, idea generator, scanners, alarms, modulator, monitor (no merrimac), amplifiers, etc. The next phase, back at the University of Michigan, saw the scheme exposed to the critical appraisal of psychology graduate students and colleagues. The clinically oriented were aghast at what seemed a defection from their ranks and smiled condescendingly; the few gadgeteers were mildly intrigued but decided the machine would never fly; most were dutifully polite and offered helpful comments. In this

* Irving W. Wolf, Electronics Division, General Electric Company.

period Forms B and C (the latter containing relatively minor alterations) came into existence. The major changes from Form A were
the addition of detailed analogues of the various psychoanalytic mechanisms of defense, a simplification of the Id's operations, and a com-
plication of Memory's.

Work began in earnest, as it inevitably does in this marvelous age
of science, with the advent of money in the fall of 1956. Both the
National Institute of Mental Health and the Ford Foundation gen-
erously contributed to the establishment of a long-term research program (dignified by the title "Research in Psychoanalytic Behavior
Theory") involving the joint efforts of the collaborators listed on the
title page. From that time on we functioned as a closely knit group,
whose frequent meetings were characterized by lively (at times almost violent), free exchanges of ideas as we grappled with the problems of model, psychoanalysis, psychology, and research.

The project soon undertook several large-scale experimental investigations designed to illuminate controversial issues raised in our discussions of early forms of the model. During this period the conceptual scheme itself was being modified regularly. Forms D and E
saw central emphasis placed on decision-making functions of the Ego,
broken down according to levels of awareness (unconscious, preconscious, and conscious). The Id by now was reduced solely to the
status of an energy source and the Superego was absorbed into a
general memory storage. Some of the mechanisms were openly pro-
vocative; witness the teasing remark of a fellow symposiast at the
International Congress of Psychology in July, 1957: "Tell me, have
you caught anything in your *Trap* (one of the model's parts at the
time) this morning?" But jibes were not hard to take because the
worth of our endeavor was to be judged in terms of the research
it generated (as this same critic pointed out in his public comments)
and we were confident of the model's heuristic value from the very
first. The task which we had set for ourselves—detailed specification
of model functions—continually raised questions requiring empirical
answers. Our problem has always been to select, from among the
many studies suggesting themselves, those upon which to concentrate.

Forms F and G, evolved early in 1958, departed markedly in several respects. Data were already filtering in and we began to question
some of our basic assumptions. For example, it became clear to us
that we could account for experimental results and psychoanalytic
observations without postulating a fixed amount of energy available
in the system at any one time. Having freed ourselves from the
restrictions implicit in Freud's notions of psychic energy and the prin-

ciple of economy governing its distribution, we were able to eliminate a series of energy storage functions. The model suddenly became simpler instead of more complex, reversing the earlier trend. We found ourselves, too, paying less attention to electronic feasibility of our conceptualizations, though it should be stated that from the outset we deemed psychological considerations to be primary. The machine was always designed to fit the theory.

But the real revolution coincided with the advent of Form H. In the publication of Form F (2) we had spelled out overall research strategy and had included some illustrative experiments. Our approach sought:

> . . . to integrate within a systematic framework the concepts of academic psychology and psychoanalysis. We have set our sights on the understanding and prediction of human behavior, studied at the individual psychological level, with special concentration on dimensions of personality as they relate to behavior in a variety of domains. For a particular domain we aim to specify in detail the conditions bearing on the complex processes which occur between original stimulus and final response. Put in the jargon of electronic computers, our hope is to "write the program" by which human beings process information from input to output. (pp. 107–108)

Steps in our strategy for developing a behavior theory had been outlined as follows:

I. A comprehensive working model is constructed from general background material drawn from academic psychology, psychoanalysis, and to some extent physiology.
   A. Such a framework, although tentative, points systematically to problem areas where research is needed.
   B. The working model later provides a structure within which to incorporate principles suggested by research findings.
II. A miniature behavioral system with known inputs and outputs is analyzed.
   A. Selection is made of a diversified sample of domains of behavior where the behavioral output can be clearly related to the stimulus input.
   B. Operational measures are developed to tap each domain.
   C. With precise knowledge of inputs (Stage 1) and outputs (Stage 4), it is then possible to attack Stages 2 and 3.
      1. Stage 2, the mapping of stimulus-relevant memory traces, involves the best estimation of memory traces existing prior to experimental stimulus inputs plus recording of new traces formed after presentation of experimental stimulus inputs.
      2. Stage 3, the derivation of principles according to which activated memory traces are processed, constitutes the crux of the problem. These principles are to be inferred by filling in the

gaps which follow Stages 1 and 2 and precede Stage 4, all of
which are now known.
  D. The working model is next revised to fit the principles inferred in
     Stage 3.
III. The revised model is applied to the prediction of Stage 4 within the
     miniature behavioral system.
  A. Knowledge of Stages 1, 2, and 3 is utilized to predict output.
  B. These predictions are then checked against the actual recorded
     output.
  C. Further revision and refinement of the model is made as necessary.
IV. The model is finally tested for its ability to predict a wide range of
     behaviors outside the miniature system.
  A. Extensions are made to a variety of stimuli other than those al-
     ready employed.
  B. Extensions are made to domains other than those already sampled
     (pp. 109–110)

Having committed ourselves in print as to our conceptual approach
and mode of research (a "long-range perspective"), it was fittingly
ironical that we should deviate on both fronts shortly thereafter. The
shift in research tactics will be described in Chapter 3. The approach
veered after some intensive soul-searching. It was apparent that the
conceptual scheme contained much more of us than it did of Freud.
More often than not when we looked to psychoanalytic theory for an
answer none was forthcoming and we were forced to improvise.
"Theory" became more and more of a misnomer for psychoanalysis
as we pushed our detailed inquiries farther along. Why not, then,
give up the psychoanalytic ghost and pursue a more general theory,
still capable of encompassing the vital phenomena to which Freud
called attention but no longer seeking to conform to his speculations?
We did, and have never regretted the parting.

As a consequence Forms H through P (the currently stabilized version) were neither obviously electronic nor psychoanalytic. Rather
they portrayed general mental functions hypothesized to operate
between stimulus inputs and response outputs. The gradual evolution of these revisions, which took place mostly during the academic
year 1958–59, reflects the conclusions from a substantial number of
experimental investigations (to be presented in Part B) and from an
extensive review of concepts drawn from many diverse areas of psychology (discussed in Part C).

But enough of the history of our earlier probes. After some comments concerning the philosophy underlying the approach proposed
in this book, we shall be ready to give intrepid readers a whirl through
the mind's inner space as we now conceive it.

On page 3 the ultimate objective of our quest was stated to be a theory of "human thought, feeling, and action." The regression from psychology's customary "science of human behavior" definition is deliberate. Concentration on the prediction of overt acts has, in our opinion, stunted the growth of the discipline. A steady diet of pellets, relieved occasionally by the tingle of electric shocks, tends to make one overlook the richness inherent in human thought and feeling. Stimulus-Response psychology has filled the alphabet soup with S's and R's, but even the O which now and then bobs up between them provides little more nourishment than if it were a zero. Although one can arbitrarily define "behavior" broadly enough to include just about everything, its connotation is so tied to observable action that we feel the need to specify these other aspects as well. Thought and feeling, admittedly communicated by acts of speech and gesture, should occupy prominent places on the psychologist's bill of fare.

Behind the above terminological quibble lies the strong conviction that more attention should be focused on the processes which intervene *between* stimulus and response. The *mind* must again become a matter of central concern for psychology, as it was in the early days of the science. Inquiry has to be made into the intricate sequence of events by which sensory inputs are translated into behavioral outputs. Such molecular preoccupations are typically delegated to the neurophysiologist and physiological psychologist, who seem to be making some exciting advances. To rely exclusively on them for answers, though, is a serious error in strategy. Recent discoveries have served to highlight the complexity of neural processes and the distance still to be traveled before brain and behavior can be joined in more than a superficial conjunctive relationship.

Ultimately the central nervous system has to be fully comprehended, at which time psychological theorizing must be consistent with physiological knowledge. Meanwhile it seems appropriate for psychologists to seek a conventional solution to congested routes, namely, a bypass. An alternate road, possibly even a shortcut to the understanding of mental functions is available via conceptual models. McCulloch (29) makes this point strikingly when he bemoans the staggering complexity of the mathematics of actual neural transmission upon which he and his colleagues have been working for a number of years. Conceptual approaches are clearly needed, but we hasten to add that several cautions must accompany their construction.

The first caution in devising a conceptual scheme is to avoid incompatibility with currently well-established physiological findings. At the same time it is unwise to lay one's formulations too squarely upon a still shaky biological foundation. Hebb's (23) theorizing, which has had such a strong impact on contemporary psychology, seems vulnerable to the latter hazard. Cell assembly and phase sequence are attractive concepts weakened by their ties to the assumed growth of synaptic knobs in learning. We advocate periodic downward glances to check on the neurophysiological footing, but a keen, searching gaze must be directed toward human thought processes.

Next, a working model of the mind should be laid out with enough vision to permit detailed inspection of the various fields of psychology. Perception, cognition, motivation, learning, etc. must all be readily accessible from this conceptual highway. Theories which seek to traverse one field and avoid the others inevitably lead to dead-ends. Those which fit the facts of cognition may fail utterly when applied to motivation. Unsurpassed in narrowness is the well-known theory which predicts with admirable precision the behavior of white rats, in a particular type of learning situation, in one section of the alley of a maze (43). Thus, the piecemeal theories, whose exponents deliberately seek access to limited paths, tend to foster short-sightedness. Apart from the possibility that approaches of this sort may never lead into a freeway at all, there are built-in hazards since small sections cannot easily be roped off for exclusive traffic. Studies of perception, for example, tend to involve other areas like cognition, motivation, or action, whether the experimenter is aware of the fact or not. In this sense the comfort a small-scale theorist derives from the ease with which he thinks he can survey the boundaries of his path may be quite unfounded.

The opposite extreme, of course, is psychoanalysis with its virtually unlimited horizons, but whose royal roads are likely to turn up mirages the closer one gets to the enchanting scenery. Freud's great frustration, according to Jones (26), was over the fact that he was unable to put his insightful concepts together into a firm, well-cemented theory. Nevertheless his observations are so compelling that any newly emerging psychological model must perforce reckon with them and the phenomena they seek to explain. The absence of psychodynamic considerations is virtually a landmark of contemporary psychological theories, though the road signs indicate new directions may be opening up. An eminent cognitive mapper, for example, talked more and more about repression in his last formulations (44). The history of our own reckoning with psychoanalysis has already been sketched briefly and psychodynamic phenomena will be discussed in detail later on.

So far we have stressed the necessity for the science of psychology to be "re-minded" by way of a comprehensive, dynamically oriented conceptual scheme, not incompatible with known physiology. The most vital caution in following such an approach is to insure full flexibility of interaction between conceptualization and research. A sound model of mental activity must be prolific in generating hypotheses for experimental test and also responsive to changes suggested by the findings. The continuous interplay of model and data is essential. Two noteworthy attempts to reformulate psychoanalysis, by Rapaport (40) and Colby (13), have fallen short of the mark when measured in terms of their stimulus-value for research.

Now that our goals and biases have been written into the record we can proceed with the business at hand: an overview of the working model, followed by sections on research explorations and reflections on some of the contents in diverse fields of psychology.

Overview
of the
working
model   2

Lest the reader have the impression from the preceding chapter that conceptual models are a dime a dozen in our research program, I hasten to the defense of Form P to be described below. "Currently stabilized" has for us the implication that this latest version incorporates all the experimental findings to date, and has withstood the test of intense exposure to a multitude of psychology's facts. Although the model does *not now* represent a complete, tightly knit body of theory permitting an elaborate set of unequivocal deductions, we view such a lofty state as definitely attainable. Actually the *rigor* of its present form is quite uneven—at some places leading to precise predictions, at others simply blocking out unknown areas which require exploration. The experiments to be reported in the next section reflect this quality of unevenness. A number serve to test hypotheses explicitly suggested by the model; others were included to guide further detailed development of the scheme itself. The level of *vigor* inherent in the working model is in our opinion consistently high if we appraise its heuristic potential for generating original research topics and offering new explanations of existing phenomena.

But the question "Why foist a 'working' model upon the public?" can still be legitimately asked. The answer is that our efforts have now progressed to the point where we ourselves are convinced of the ultimate feasibility of an all-embracing, detailed theory of the mind's operations—in other words, the working model shows distinct promise of being able to *work*. This book is written in the hope of converting at least some readers to the same conviction, and some researchers to similar pursuits.

Curiously the prevailing winds of psychological opinion do not often blow in this direction. A thoroughly conventional reaction is to label such an approach "monolithic" and thereby assume that it must vanish into thin air (an unlikely prospect when one contemplates the adjective in its full, massive, stony connotation!). In neurophysiology, on the other hand, comprehensive brain models are all the rage. Doesn't it seem logical that human behavior, mediated by man's unified central nervous system, should also adhere to an integrative framework? In short, we feel that our program is far enough along, and our cause sufficiently just, to warrant exposing the current product to public scrutiny.

The technical language of Form P at first (or even afterward) may seem a curious melange of terms borrowed from psychology, electronics, physiology, and plain everyday English. We chose them primarily for their descriptiveness. Along with electrical labels like "circuits" and "signals" there is a sprinkling of physiologically diluted terms such as "facilitation" and "inhibition," all mixed with the traditional psychological designations "cognitive," "affective," and "motoric." Our attempt at semantic neutrality, in an era when words get so easily attached to red flags (try "libido" on an old-line experimental psychologist), obviously stresses coverage rather than consistency!

The electrical undercurrent should not convey that we are potential machine-builders. The observation has been made that engineers are looking to psychologists to tell them how to construct their mechanical brains, and psychologists on their part are waiting for bigger and better computers to furnish clues as to how the human brain might work. We do not subscribe to either of these positions. Instead we are geared to laboratory experiment with human subjects as a technique for improving easily disposable, dittoed diagrams. It is possible that an engineer might be able to use the conceptual scheme as a point of departure, but we have purposely refrained from involvement with details of electronic construction per se. For example, the concept of "signal strength" is not committed specifically to either amplitude characteristics or number of repetitions. In another sense, though, the electronic language is particularly appropriate because the model functions in an automatic, highly mechanistic fashion. Inputs are processed without the aid of little men lurking about and decisions are not made by the force of conscious deliberation. The course of action is directed via the circuitry within the system itself.

The brief description of the model which follows is very general and intended primarily to acquaint the reader with the type of conceptual approach. The details will be furnished later in appropriate contexts, especially in Chapter 10 of Part C. In Figure 1 we begin with an overview of the Mental System, consisting of cognitive, affective, and motoric subsystems.

Inputs to the Mental System are coded sensory signals based on stimuli originating either internally or externally to the organism. Internal inputs, mediated by interoceptors and proprioceptors, arise from visceral needs, such as hunger, and from glandular and muscular discharges. External events, e.g., visual and auditory, impinge upon the exteroceptors. Whatever the source, all these sensory inputs vary in intensity and thereby contribute to variation in strength of the cognitive activities which they instigate.

The coded signals transmitted from sensory elements make contact with the cognitive subsystem through specific links designated as *components* (see Figure 2). These sensory-cognitive connections between elements and components reflect the past experience of the individual. Each cognitive component possesses storage, reception, and transmission properties, so that a stored signal conveying characteristic content is released by arriving sensory input. Components contiguously discharging repeatedly over time are interconnected and form a *circuit*. At a still more molar level, circuits which are activated many times together become hooked up into a *network*. The latter may involve more than one subsystem or be contained solely within the cognitive.

To illustrate these hypothetical levels of structure, let us take the example of a traffic light turning red just as a driver crosses the beginning of a policed intersection. The external stimulus, the red light, eventuates in the transmission of signals from a number of sensory elements which, upon reaching the Mental System, trigger a variety of cognitive components having to do with shape, hue, brightness, etc. The fact that these particular components have frequently discharged together means that there is a well-established red-light circuit, pre-

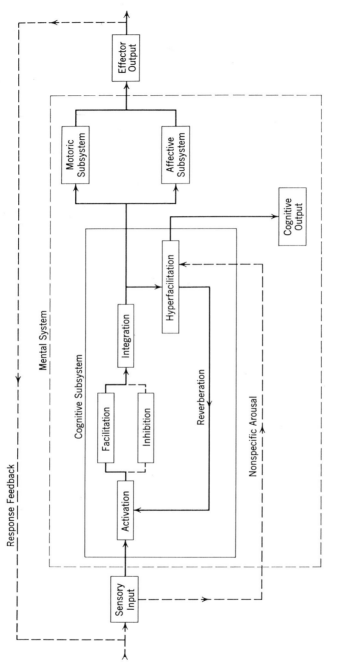

FIGURE 1. Overview of a conceptual model of mental functions (Form P). [*Note:* Arrows indicate the direction of signal passage. Signals from the external world or response feedback always pass (by way of sensory input) through the cognitive subsystem before reaching the motoric and affective subsystems. Effector output is by way of the latter subsystems, whereas cognitive output refers to the products of hyperfacilitation in the cognitive subsystem.]

14

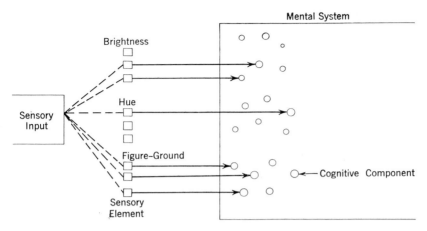

FIGURE 2. Impingement of sensory stimulation upon the Mental System. [*Note:* Coded stimuli (broken lines) release signals from sensory elements (solid lines), which in turn activate linked cognitive components. Cognitive circuits, consisting of connected components, evolve from repeated contiguous activation of components.]

sumably with connections to many other cognitive circuits. In this example the environment not only provides the presence of the red-light stimulus but also the timing of its appearance with respect to the position of the car in the intersection. All these cognitive circuits likely have been coupled with certain motoric and affective circuits in the past, so that a fairly complex network becomes salient throughout the system—producing cognitive outputs such as thoughts about stopping and concern over being apprehended by the police; and effector outputs like incipient motor movements, physiological manifestations of anxiety, and so on.

Returning to the mental functions shown in Figure 1, activation of a connection anywhere in the system automatically strengthens that connection, making it less resistant to subsequent signal passage. This process of *facilitation* by activation takes place among components within a circuit and also at the intercircuit or network level. The neurophysiological analogue is described in an excerpt from Bullock:

For example, many junctions manifest the property known as *facilitation*. This means that successively arriving impulses in the presynaptic pathway cause larger and larger synaptic potentials in the postsynaptic neuron. The excitability of the postsynaptic membrane may be said to have increased—although there may be no change whatever in the level of membrane potential after one synaptic potential has passed off and before the next has begun—from the corresponding level at an earlier stage, when the excitability was lower. . . . (10, p. 1000)

(At this point a parenthetical note must quickly be inserted to remind the reader that our approach, while favoring compatibility with known physiological facts, does not intend to equate parts of the Mental System with parts of the brain. Components, for example, bear no necessary correspondence to neurons.)

It is assumed that facilitation can be increased only to some asymptotic point, beyond which repeated activation has no appreciable effect. When red lights have been encountered daily over a period of years, no increment in facilitation of that circuit can be expected. At the other extreme, protracted absence of activation permits a connection to dwindle gradually until it no longer remains functional. Thus the strength of a circuit's discharge at any one time depends partly on the pre-existing state of facilitation among its connected components. Other determinants are the intensity of arriving sensory signals, and the number of components specifically triggered by that sensory input.

The next step in the cognitive subsystem is *integration,* by which the separate signals discharging from components of a circuit are put together locally into a composite signal. The existence of mechanisms to perform such functions is taken for granted by those who work in brain physiology, but relatively little is known about them. Jasper speculates as follows:

The highest level of integration must occur in that system of neurons with the greatest number of confluent disparate convergent afferent and efferent connections. Integrative processes depend upon spaciotemporal impulse patterns processed at various levels, including cortex, and then some significant signal projected to the centrencephalic system of the brain stem for final coordination with signals from multiple simultaneously active systems to give coherent unity or direction to behavior and conscious mental life. The brain stem reticular system seems to possess many of the required properties for such a system of neurons with central integrative functions. (25, p. 59)

Since the model makes provision for concurrent integrations of all simultaneously discharging circuits, some mechanism is required to account for the phenomenon of attention to certain mental events and exclusion of others. Here we introduce the notion of *hyperfacilitation,* which functions to amplify the strongest composite signal from among those momentarily active. As the signals of new circuits emerge in integrated form the hyperfacilitation shifts automatically to the strongest circuit of the moment, a process corresponding to changes in the focus of conscious attention.* The amplifying mechanism is presumed to be regulated by its own nonspecific sensory input, the degree of amplification being in direct proportion to the amount of nonspecific arousal. On such points the neurophysiological footing appears somewhat more sure. Magoun and Jasper offer these pertinent comments respectively:

> From a number of recent studies, conceptions of brain organization have been enlarged by identification of nonspecific neural mechanisms lying between the sensory and motor systems of classical neurophysiology and richly interconnected with them. Reciprocal ascending and descending connections between these nonspecific neural mechanisms in the brain stem and wide areas of the hemispheres, including both neo- and paleo-cortex, are involved in arousal to wakefulness and alerting to attention. Further study of these nonspecific neural mechanisms may be expected to be rewarding in relating brain organization and behavior. (28, p. 33)

> The ascending reticular system, that portion intimately related to the cerebral cortex, seems to be most closely associated with what we generally recognize as conscious behavior. This is manifest in relation to states of coma or sleep in contrast with wakefulness, and in relation to attention in the waking individual. Attention seems most likely to be a further differentiation of the gross generalized arousal mechanism permitting focused "arousal" in restricted assemblies of neurons with momentary exclusion of the rest. (25, p. 58)

The magnitude of hyperfacilitation in turn determines the intensity with which the integrated and amplified signals reverberate throughout the subsystem. *Reverberation* is conceived as a positive feedback loop which reactivates the originating cognitive circuit and spreads to other circuits in the same network. In this way continuity of thought processes is sustained until new sensory inputs take over. Generally a circuit discharging after reverberation transmits weaker signals than one whose discharge is instigated directly by sensory stimulation. In the event of temporal competition for hyperfacilitation, therefore, the sensory-supported will win out. It is nevertheless possible for the reverse to occur, that is, for reverberatory-triggered signals to gain the amplification, if weak sensory signals arrive at a minimally facilitated circuit simultaneously with strong reverberation to a maximally facilitated one. Also, in the absence of new

---

* Though we are interested in accounting for conscious phenomena, like attention, the model does not incorporate consciousness as an explanatory concept. Instead consciousness is seen as lying beyond the scope of the Mental System, corresponding to outputs of the cognitive subsystem shown in Figure 1.

inputs, reverberation can greatly strengthen a circuit's cognitive output by leading to repeated hyperfacilitation of its composite signal.

The cognitive subsystem is master in our working model. Affective and motoric subsystems, highly complex in their own right, are set into motion by inputs from the cognitive. Integrated cognitive signals trigger their connected affective and motoric circuits, whose discharged output signals in turn are decoded at the effectors to enable activation of appropriate muscles, glands, etc. In terms of the nervous system, affective and motoric circuits are themselves central and exert peripheral influence. The strength of a circuit's discharge in these two subsystems depends upon the pre-existing state of facilitation among its own components, the original intensity of the transmitted cognitive signal, and the resistance encountered by the latter along its path. Finally, the consequent effector action itself provides positive feedback to the Mental System. Such *response feedback* undergoes sensory coding and becomes a source of input along with external and other internal stimuli. Movements of the driver in stopping his car, for example, are conveyed back to the system as input by way of the proprioceptors.

The last function to be described in this brief overview is *inhibition,* which is assigned a key role. The fact of inhibitory action in the central nervous system is unquestioned, though details of its operation are still obscure. According to Bullock (10), the firing of the same neuron under the same conditions may, at one junction, be facilitated whereas at another junction it may be diminished. Complicating the process even further are "aftereffects," which refer to periods of after-inhibition or afterdischarge once the input has ceased. So it is apparent that almost any conceptual use to which inhibition may be put will be unlikely to exceed the bounds of possible neurophysiological speculation.

An inhibition mechanism, located in the cognitive subsystem, is ascribed the special capacity to interfere with transmission. Signals discharged from such a mechanism *increase* the resistance in pathways—a function opposite to facilitation, which represents a *decrease* in resistance. Linked closely to a network of anxiety (which includes circuits in both cognitive and affective subsystems), inhibition can also impede transmission in any network whose circuits happen to be discharging contiguously. Apart from a ceiling on inhibitory output itself, the amount of interference depends both upon strength of the cognitive signals triggering inhibition and upon degree of facilitation already existing between the inhibition mechanism and the target networks.

Though details of the model's operations have not yet been supplied, the reader no doubt has already detected some familiar parts lying about: the description of circuit connections brings to mind associationistic theories; contiguity is recognizable as the basic principle of learning in the system; evolution of circuits and networks from sensory input has a distinct Hebbian cast; the central role of inhibition, intimately related to anxiety, is reminiscent of psychoanalysis; nonspecific arousal has acknowledged physiological antecedents; the concept of positive feedback is borrowed from engineering; and so on down the line. In sum, the model, as well as its language, is quite eclectic. But eclecticism runs the risk of not pleasing anyone more than a little and offending everyone quite a lot, so it is best that we proceed at once with a demonstration of the model's heuristic value in areas of research. Accordingly we can view the hasty sketch given in this chapter as a backdrop and turn our attention next to the center of the stage where real, live people are asked to dramatize mental functions in a series of laboratory experiments.

PART B

EXPERIMENTS
DESIGNED
TO EXPLORE
MENTAL
FUNCTIONS

Research
tactics,
subjects,
and
setting   3

It is understandable that academic psychology has tended to overlook what happens between stimulus and response. Mental functions
do present elusive targets for experimental scrutiny. Consequently
the domain has been dominated by clinicians, in psychiatry and psychology, who argue that by studying their patients with well-trained
eyes they can discern the inner workings of the human mind. I contend (and here I part company with some members of our research
group) that clinical observation has already passed the point of dim-
inishing returns even as a source of hypotheses. Psychodynamics are
not being viewed very differently than they were by Freud before his
death, which is not surprising since contemporary viewers have in-
herited the spectacles previously worn by the deceased. Major advances (here our members all agree) are more likely to come from
carefully controlled laboratory experiments which deliberately seek to
explore underlying processes. With faith in this conviction and liberal
recourse to imaginative use of techniques, one can continue to be
amazed by the accessibility of what seem to be most baffling methodological problems. Specifically, a technique which lends itself singu-
larly to the pursuit of mental functions is hypnosis. But before going

on to procedural aspects of our hypnotic endeavors, it might be well to fill in a bit of the immediately antecedent research setting.

RESEARCH TACTICS

Our initial approach, which preceded the work described in the present volume, required the construction of a miniature behavioral system, including known inputs and outputs and the mapping of stimulus-relevant memory traces (see pp. 6–7). Methodologically, the system revolved about the use of Blacky Pictures (7) as stimuli in a variety of experimental tasks. Twenty-eight male and 34 female college students were each seen for a total of approximately ten hours over a series of several individual sessions and one small-group meeting. They were asked to tell spontaneous stories about the dog's actions and feelings in the eleven cartoons; to describe experiences of their own which corresponded to Blacky's; to indicate pictures disliked the most; to ruminate over their self-insights in the various psychosexual areas of the test; and to fill out the Defense Preference Inquiry (4). From these measures and accompanying GSR (galvanic skin response) records a large number of possible indices of anxiety were set up and factor-analyzed. The major resulting factor enabled us to compute "anxiety potential" scores, for each individual on all eleven pictures, which were employed in several studies growing out of early forms of the model.*

Among these was an experiment by Perloe (37, 38) testing two theories of perceptual defense—direct inhibition versus competing response explanations—by means of an intricate design involving tachistoscopic presentation of the Blacky stimuli at very rapid speeds. Goldstein (21) investigated the stress effects of experimental arousal of anxiety on performance in tasks of sensory discrimination, sensory-motor coordination, reasoning, rate of associative verbal output, and preconscious decision making. An extensive analysis of correlates of superego functions, also operationalized in the context of Blacky dimensions, was conducted by Minkowich (32). In another experiment (2) attempts were made to predict the recall of Blacky pictures using the variables of vividness, similarity, and anxiety. These and other studies were all intended to assist in building an integrative

---

* Further details pertinent to this initial approach are available in Chapter 5 of *Perspectives in Personality Research* (H. P. David and J. C. Brengelmann, Eds.), New York, Springer, 1960 (2).

model by utilizing an interlocking base of memory traces formed from the subject's experiences in areas tapped by the cartoons.

However, the problem of mapping memory traces, though feasible, was proving to be extremely tedious. How much simpler if we could deposit traces according to our own specifications! We found the solution in the technique of hypnosis, which led to a revolution in our research tactics corresponding to the change in conceptual strategy already described in the opening chapter. The remainder of the present chapter is devoted to the procedures involved in selecting and training good hypnotic subjects, and to a description of the research setting.

SUBJECTS AND SETTING

First some mention of the primary source of recruitment of subjects for this new phase of our research is in order. During registration period for the University of Michigan summer session of 1958, the project secretary set up headquarters at the end of the line, alongside a placard reading "Psychology Experiments—$1.25 an hour—Sign Up Here." Those who expressed interest were immediately told that the work would entail hypnosis (this did not seem to deter anyone!) and would typically require 4 to 6 hours of their time each week for a couple of months. Other selection criteria were that they be over 21 years of age and not have taken more than one course in psychology. Approximately 30 names were collected very quickly and all but a handful of these individuals appeared at a group session to which they were invited a week later.

In this group meeting the two faculty members * connected with the project made a few introductory comments stressing the confidential nature of the task; the fact that detailed feedback would be supplied upon completion of the experiments; etc. Then two suggestibility tests were administered to the group—inability to unclench clasped hands and falling backward (into the waiting but unseen arms of an assistant) at instruction. Observers noted reactions among the various individuals and a list of the best prospects was compiled immediately afterward.

Preliminary hypnotic work was undertaken with 13 persons, most of whom were drawn from the above pool (toward the end of the

* Justin L. Weiss and the writer, both trained as clinical psychologists, shared equally in conducting hypnotic procedures through all phases of the research.

year the list of prospects was supplemented by a few referrals from
subjects already taking part). Each was asked, at the start of his
first session, to sign a "volunteer" form for participation as a hypnotic
subject and to certify his age, freedom from any kind of diagnosed
heart ailment, and that he had never undergone treatment for mental illness. Arrangements had previously been made for the services
of a consulting physician, but no occasion ever arose for him to be
called.*

The first few hours were spent in assessing the subject's ability to
enter a sufficiently deep trance. For our purposes it was necessary
that he be capable of complete amnesia, execution of posthypnotic
suggestions, speaking freely without having the trance lighten, and
moving around the laboratory without awakening. Ten of the 13
met these requirements and were subsequently carried through to
completion. The other three, although hypnotizable, failed in one or
more of these respects. In view of the fact that we planned to do
intensive, exploratory work on a small sample, we chose to concentrate on one sex, namely, males. But halfway through the series of
subjects we could not resist the advice "cherchez la différence" and
did include one female along with nine males. All these numbers
have bearing, of course, on the generality of research findings and
will be discussed later (Epilogue to Part B).

Table 1 contains some biographical data provided by the subjects
on a personal history questionnaire. Within the restriction of being
young adult college students, the group seems fairly heterogeneous.
On other items, all describe their parents as belonging to the "middle
class" except Max, who checks "working class." Grade-point averages
vary between C and B+. Additional information collected on physical complaints reveals a number to be suffering from various types
of allergy, and a few who report frequent headaches, sleeping difficulties, speech problems, and weight fluctuations. Half the group
wears glasses all or part of the time.

The laboratory setting is depicted in Figures 3 to 5. The experimental room is electrically shielded and sound deadened, though not
air-conditioned. (In fact it was occasionally necessary to suggest to
the hypnotized subject that he was feeling cool and comfortable,
which left only the experimenter miserable.) It is furnished with a
couch, chairs, carpet, art prints, and a table on which rests a Ger-
brands tachistoscope. A one-way mirror permits observation from
outside and a two-way telephone enables experimenter (E) and

---

* See appendix B for detailed set of regulations governing our use of hypnosis.

TABLE 1. Biographical Data Supplied by Subjects

Project Identi- fication Name	Age	Sibling Position	Place of Birth	Population of Town Where Reared	Father's Occupation	Recent Annual Family Income	S's Religious Affili- ation	S's Marital Status	Field of Specialization in College
Ned	24	Middle of 5	Michigan	Under 10,000	Supervisor in large organization	$5,000–7,000	Methodist	Single	Spanish (G) *
Victor	21	Older of 2	New York	Over 1 million	Professor	$15,000–20,000	None	Single	Electrical engineering (U) †
Tom	23	Middle of 3	Michigan	Under 10,000	Owner of small business	Over $20,000	Episcopal	Married (1 child)	English (G)
Laura	22	Older of 2	Michigan	Under 10,000	Agricultural inspector	$3,000–5,000	Dutch Reformed	Single	Nursing (U)
Joe	23	Second of 4	Michigan	100,000–1 million	Vice President of small company	$9,000–11,000	Episcopal	Single	Architecture (G)
Max	25	Fourth of 6	Germany	Under 10,000	Machinist	Under $3,000	None	Single	Physical educa- tion (U)
Steve	26	Youngest of 4	New York	10,000–50,000	Factory foreman	(Parents deceased)	None	Married (2 children)	Sociology (G)
Rudy	25	Oldest of 3	Pennsylvania	Over 1 million	Manager of small shop	$9,000–11,000	Catholic	Single	Linguistics (G)
Harold	21	Youngest of 3	Michigan	Over 1 million	Factory foreman	$5,000–7,000	Lutheran	Single	Chemical engineer- ing (U)
Fred	21	Only child	Michigan	10,000–50,000	Skilled laborer	$9,000–11,000	Unitarian	Married (no children)	Industrial design (U)

* G = graduate student.
† U = undergraduate student.

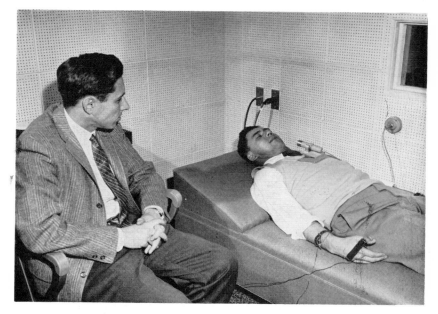

FIGURE 3. Interior of experimental room showing S reclining.

machine operator (O) to converse when necessary. The subject (S) always wears a microphone around his neck and typically is hooked up to the GSR or EMG apparatus or both. In Figure 3 a posed S (if actual subjects remained so obviously tense, hypnosis would be difficult indeed!) has the zinc GSR electrodes placed on the palm and forearm. The wall cable connects to a Fels Dermohmmeter * (being adjusted by O in Figure 5) and EMG equipment † in the exterior room. Figure 4 shows EMG electrodes set to pick up eye movements while looking in the tachistoscope.

The technique for inducing hypnosis approximated the method described by Friedlander and Sarbin (20). S, reclining on the couch, was told to stare up at the center of a light in the ceiling (controlled by a dimmer switch) and to listen carefully to what E was about to say. Appendix A contains a verbatim transcription of an initial induction for one of our subjects. Once training had pro-

* Manufactured by the Yellow Springs Instrument Co., Yellow Springs, Ohio.
† Electromyographic apparatus manufactured by the Edin Co. of Worcester, Mass. Primary EMG record integrated by equipment from the Medical Electronics Development Corp. of Great Neck, N. Y.

gressed sufficiently, it was possible to abbreviate the procedure, in some cases even to the simple commands "Sleep!" and "Wake up!"

In summary, hypnosis permitted us to shape the memories of our "normal" subjects to fit the requirements of experimental designs growing out of the conceptual model. Our interest in the method, therefore, does not lie in the process itself, which has many intriguing aspects, but rather in its unique capacity for attaching specifiable properties, especially affective ones, to a variety of stimuli. In most of the experiments the desired antecedent conditions were built in during the trance and the tests themselves executed in the waking state.

A potential hazard, well-documented by Orne (34), is that the

FIGURE 4. Interior view showing S seated at tachistoscope.

FIGURE 5.   Exterior control room.

highly suggestible individual may "catch on" to the purpose of the
research and subsequently produce the "right" responses. To check
on this possibility, inquiries encouraging S to guess the intent were
conducted after every study, in both waking and hypnotic states. Insight was uniformly absent. Apart from the fact that the investigations were often exploratory and not geared to a "right" answer, the
designs themselves were usually so intricate that discerning professional colleagues, observing the experiments, were at a loss to know
what was going on until told. The reader can form his own opinion
on this issue in the next six chapters, which present the studies in
detail.

Facilitation and hyperfacilitation 4

One of the knottiest problems in constructing conceptual schemes is the selection of an appropriate unit of analysis. Where should we saw off segments of the Mental System in order to have them serve as efficient building blocks? The answer, we feel, has to be dictated by one's research strategy. Given the avowed goals of doing laboratory experiments on "human thought, feeling, and action" and deliberately searching for details of the "intricate sequence of events" between inputs and outputs, the unit must be both manipulable and more molecular than those of available behavior theories. It must be as small as possible within the limits of susceptibility to experimental control.

The hypothesized structural unit of the model is a component, but such elements are too tiny to be identifiable when dealing with the cognitive complexity of the mind. Nor can the next larger segment, the circuit consisting of a series of connected components, be easily isolated for study. The network level, though, does offer real promise for our purposes. By using appropriate manipulations, it *is* possible to establish a clearly delineated network whose specific activation can result in the characteristics of its coupled circuits becoming salient among all ongoing events in the Mental System. Thus the *activated network,* varying in size according to the requirements of each task, qualifies as our functional unit—one whose operations can be specified and submitted to experimental scrutiny. An illustration of these functional units is provided by the first experiment described below.

Experiment 1. Facilitation of Associative Recall without Awareness

Facilitation is a general term by which we refer to the strengthening of connections, including component connections within a circuit and couplings between circuits, as a result of activation. Connections get strengthened automatically by the passage of signals, independent of conscious awareness. This reduction of consciousness to the status of an innocent bystander troubled our group (though perhaps not the reader) enough to make us want to try the following experiment suggested by the model.

Under hypnosis S was asked to open his eyes and look at a list of three pairs of letters which he was told to learn. After the letters had been correctly paired for several consecutive trials, he was then instructed to put the list "temporarily out of mind" before being shown a second. List 2 was next learned perfectly, whereupon E said: "Now both lists are available in your memory but when you're awake you won't remember the fact that you learned them." The lists contained these letter pairs:

W L	W R
K R	K F
N F	N L
List 1	List 2

Let's pause for a moment to analyze what has taken place thus far. E has introduced into S's memory a series of interconnections between letters. Conceiving of each letter as a simple circuit we can diagram the network in this fashion (see top of next page):

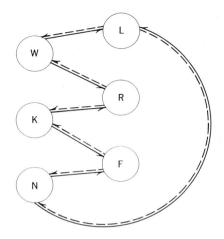

W, for example, has been connected both to L (List 1) and to R (List 2). The reverse connections, L to W and R to W, are drawn in dotted lines to indicate that they are probably not as strong as the forward ones because of the order of presentation. Of course other connections among the letters may have been formed sheerly by physical contiguity, and previously existing connections to letters not shown may also have been activated. We tried to minimize the latter possibility by pairing letters which have low associative value in combination. In general, though, the diagram can be said to portray accurately the salient features of the network.

Upon awakening, S was queried to be certain the amnesia instruction was effective. E then said:

What I'm going to do now is show you some slips of paper, each of which is going to have two letters on it. I want you to tell me the first letter that pops into your mind. Just let your mind be a complete blank, look at these letters, and tell me what comes to mind.

A sample dialogue conveys the rest of the procedure:

E   (showing S a slip with the letters W and K): What letter pops into your mind?
S   (almost no hesitation): R.
E   (showing K and N): Now look at this slip.
S   (again almost no hesitation): F.
E   (showing W and N): Next.
S   (one to two second delay): L.
E   (showing L and F): Now look at this one.
S   (one to two second delay): N.
E   (showing R and F): Next.

S   (one to two second delay): K.
E   (showing R and L): And finally this one.
S   (three second delay): W.
E: Why did these letters come into your mind?
S: That's a good question.
E: Why do you think?
S: I just looked at them and I'd look at one letter in particular and the other letter would merely associate itself with it, so I'd say that letter.
E: You would look at one letter in particular. What do you mean?
S: Well I'd look at both of them, then I'd just look at one, and then that letter would associate itself with another letter. Like I'd look at the W on the W K slip and R came to mind.

Back under hypnosis, where the amnesia instruction no longer applied, S was again asked to explain his responses. He remembered the two lists he had learned originally, but offered the same obviously incomplete explanation of his performance as in the waking state—somehow one letter of the pair caught his attention and he automatically associated his reply to it.

In terms of the model what probably was happening when, for example, he was shown the slip with W and K on it? The sensory input must have activated the W and K circuits so, according to the diagram, L, R, and F circuits should have been triggered (L and R by signals from W; R and F from K). Thus L, R, and F have all received facilitation, though not in equal amounts. The R circuit, its component connections having been the only recipients of facilitation from *both* lines of input, discharged more strongly when a letter was requested by E and automatically acquired priority in subsequent processing. S's responses on the second and third trials can be accounted for similarly. In the backward series the inputs L and F both converge on the N circuit, and so on. The striking feature is that no subject ever had any insight, during either waking or hypnotic inquiries, into this convergence aspect of the task.

Other Ss did not behave in such a perfectly consistent manner as the one quoted above. Four of the remaining six who took part in this particular experiment did show the phenomenon beyond chance expectancy: * on the forward series one other S (female) responded with all three of the doubly facilitated letters and three gave two out of the three. On the backward series the effect was not as clearcut,

* Chance can be viewed as $\frac{1}{6}$ in the strictest sense that S unconsciously interpreted only the letters in the two lists to be eligible, or as high as $\frac{1}{26}$ in the unlikely event that all letters had equal probability of occurrence.

probably reflecting the weaker connections indicated by dotted lines in the diagram.

Sometimes negative results can be more instructive than positive, though, and it is worthwhile taking the time to examine what occurred with the two persons who did not give the expected replies. One persistently avoided any letter from the original lists, which suggests that under hypnosis the amnesia instruction * may have been misconstrued by him to include the letters themselves as well as the learning experience. Instead he came up with "irrelevant" replies, such as P to the stimulus letters N and W—later explained by him as the abbreviation for Northwest Passage!

The other deviant individual gave us some surprising and remarkable information. On checking the amnesia before beginning the six trials, it turned out that he was spontaneously hearing Morse code in the waking state. He had been a radio operator in the Army some years back, but the sounds were coming too fast for him to translate, except for an occasional letter. The messages continued to plague him during the series, so we decided to start all over by substituting some less distracting (and less noisy) stimuli. These numbers and designs were then paired during the hypnotic learning period:

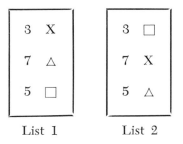

List 1   List 2

In the waking state E instructed him to respond with "The first thing that comes to mind—it might be a design or a number, just let something pop in."

The following is a summary of what took place during the six trials, including an inquiry conducted after each response (for all other Ss the inquiries were done after the experiment):

* It is essential, of course, to try to understand what is involved in S's execution of the amnesia instruction. Our interpretation, in terms of the model, of amnesia as well as other hypnotic phenomena is given in Chapter 12.

Slip Shown	Response Predicted from Convergence of Facilitations	S's Response	Inquiry
3 & 7	X	"☐ and △"	"☐ came in first."
5 & 7	△	"☐ and △"	"☐ came first. (E: "Were they equally strong?") *No, the △ was more definite.*
3 & 5	☐	"☐"	"It seemed like it should have been something else, but it was mostly just the ☐. It was pretty strong. (E: "Why did the ☐ come?") I feel awfully —I don't know—I just feel confused. These seem to be real definite impressions and I'm not sure why. There was an X there too and it was very weak. Somehow it didn't seem like it was in the same context as the ☐ or △."
☐ & △	5	"7-3-5-7"	"It was just automatic, no thought at all connected with it. (E: "Was one stronger than the rest?") I'm not sure. It was really strange—all of them were there—maybe the 3 was stronger, but I'm not sure." (E then instructs S to report a single number on the remaining trials.)
☐ & X	3	"7"	(E: "Did any other numbers come to mind?") "No, it seemed like I said 7 and *then I said to myself that's wrong.* (E: "What do you think is right?") I don't know, *maybe 3 would be right but I don't*

Slip Shown	Response Predicted from Convergence of Facilitations	S's Response	Inquiry
			know why. This seems kind of—well, not upsetting—but kind of startling. I'm really not very sure of what I'm doing."
△ & X	7	"5"	(E: "Does that seem right or wrong?") "It doesn't seem awfully strong but I didn't feel any wrongness about it either. (E: "Did any other number come to mind?") Yeah, 7 I think. (E: "How did that compare to 5?") Well, if you allowed second guesses *I'd say that 7 belongs there more than 5,* but 5 was the one that came in first. (E: "Why do you think 7 belongs more than 5?") (S sighs deeply and pauses for ten seconds) I don't know—I'm just guessing—maybe it's because the 7 has all straight lines —I don't know what was on the slip—□s and Xs all have straight lines too. No, that doesn't seem right. I don't know. (E [obviously incredulous]: "So you haven't gone through any conscious problem-solving process by which you figured out what to say?") I don't think so. No."

So a simple experiment which started out to test the automatic effects of introducing directed facilitations into a network suddenly

developed into a problem-solving situation in which S had no idea
of the problem or why he came up with his answer, yet reacted with
distinct impressions of rightness or wrongness! Even more noteworthy is the fact that his impressions correspond to predictions (see
the last two trials) based on the hypothesized convergence phenomenon. (As an aside: Steve, our hero in this adventure, is an introspector nonpareil and his comments will be attended to carefully
throughout the studies in which he participated.)

The most likely explanation is that, having assumed the waking
task to be some kind of problem, he was forming his evaluations *
of correctness in terms of strength of the response as it came into
consciousness, and the strength in turn was a function of the amount
of facilitation produced by the sensory inputs. We know from his
remarks on the earlier trials that responses did occur to him in varying intensities. However, it is also interesting to note that the
stronger response did not necessarily pop into his mind first. On the
second trial the ☐ came first but the △ was stronger. Here we can
only speculate that the ☐ circuit was already discharging, probably
as a reverberation from the events of the immediately preceding inquiry, at the time the stimulus slip was shown. Once the latter was
introduced, the sensory inputs then proceeded to strengthen the △
circuit's discharge to a degree exceeding that of the ☐. As pointed
out on p. 17, cognitive reverberation is usually not as potent a source
of activation as direct sensory input.

In summary, the paired letter experiment indicates that the hypothetical function labeled *facilitation* qualifies as a useful conceptual
link in understanding what takes place between input and output.
By building a clearly specifiable network of letter circuits (the operational unit of analysis) into S's memory, it was possible to obtain
predictable responses following the controlled introduction of sensory
stimuli. Furthermore, these effects were observed to occur without
any accompanying conscious awareness of the process on the part of
S himself. In our view this study deserves special attention, not for
uniqueness of either the predictions or the ruling out of consciousness (S-R theory would agree on both counts), but rather for its
demonstration of the ease with which functional cognitive units can
be implanted, isolated, and precisely manipulated through the techniques of hypnosis. Future research along similar lines should be
extended to more complex cognitive tasks, at the same time taking

* The topic of cognitive evaluation, including the part played by strength of
discharged content signals, is discussed in Chapter 13.

greater care to insure that induced circuit couplings are the salient ones in the network.

Experiment 2. Vividness of Imagery in Varying States of Post-hypnotically Suggested Arousal

A related function posited by the model is *hyperfacilitation*. Regulated by nonspecific sensory arousal input, a mechanism amplifies the signal discharge of the strongest of concurrently integrated circuits in direct proportion to the amount of such input. The first research idea that prompted us to action on this topic was to compare the strength of cognitive outputs under different degrees of nonspecific arousal. The latter should be minimal in a condition like sleep and therefore visual images should be less vivid. We decided to control S's arousal by posthypnotic suggestion, and to measure cognitive intensity by relatively unstructured introspective report. We already were convinced that the latter, a much neglected tool in contemporary psychology, can be put to effective use, especially when combined with a trance inquiry.

The experiment began with Steve, our ace introspector, who was serving as one of the subjects at the time (typically two Ss were being run during the same period of weeks). Under hypnosis he was shown a cartoon (see Figure 6) and told to study it carefully for about 30 seconds. Next he was given the following instructions:

In a little while, after you're awake, I'm going to turn the lights up. That will be a signal for you to remain very wide awake and alert even though your eyes will be closed. Your hearing will be extremely sensitive, all your senses will be extremely strong, except that you'll have your eyes closed. When you reach the peak of feeling wide awake and alert the cartoon will flash quickly through your mind. You will get a quick visual image of the cartoon and, as soon as this has happened, you will immediately open your eyes and describe the image in as much detail as possible. I want you to describe the cartoon, not as you saw it originally, but the way it looked as it flashed through your mind. Do you understand? All right, in a little while I'm going to say "wide awake" and you won't remember what we talked about while you were asleep. Now WIDE AWAKE.

After S declared himself fully awake, E proceeded to turn up the lights. Exactly 30 seconds later, S began to speak:

S: I just saw a big kind of white ball, and that was all. Against a black background.

E: Anything else?

FIGURE 6. Boy with magic set. (Drawing by R. J. Day; copyright © 1939, the New Yorker Magazine, Inc.)

S: Well, it wasn't clear white, it was kind of hazy, like it was full of smoke or something. Kind of different shadings of white in it.

E: Okay, I'll turn the lights down (a prearranged signal for S to go back under hypnosis) and now, as you're sleeping deeply again, you can no longer remember what just happened while you were awake. Everything that happened while you were awake is now faded from your memory and all that's left is the initial time when I showed you the cartoon. You no longer remember the instructions you were given under hypnosis either. Have you forgotten the things that you were supposed to?

S: Yes, I think I have.

E: That's fine. Now let me give you the next instruction. After you're awake I'm going to turn up the lights, which will be a signal for you to close your eyes and start going into a deep sleep such as you do during the night. It won't be the kind of sleep you're in now, but it will be a nocturnal kind of sleep. When you feel that the state of being asleep has reached its peak, the cartoon will flash through your mind quickly. After this has happened you will immediately return to a normal waking state * and describe in as much detail as possible the visual image that flashed through your mind. When you're awake you won't remember what it was that we talked about. All right, WIDE AWAKE.

E: Okay, I'm going to turn the lights up now.

S (after 41 seconds): I just saw the right-hand half of a cartoon. It seems like there was a little boy kneeling on the floor. I think there was a woman coming in the door. I know there was more on the left-hand side but I didn't see it.

E: Anything else?

S: No, I don't think so.

E (turning the lights down to put S back in trance, giving S amnesia for the preceding part of the experiment, etc., then—): When I say "wide awake" you're going to wake up immediately. Then I'll turn the lights up, which will be a signal for you to go into a sort of half asleep, half awake condition. Your eyes will be closed and you'll be in an in-between stage, maybe like you are when you're studying late at night. When this half asleep and half awake state reaches its peak, the cartoon will flash quickly through your mind and you'll immediately revert to a normal waking state and describe to me in as much detail as possible the visual image that flashed through your mind the instant before. After you're awake you won't remember what we've talked about. All right, now WIDE AWAKE.

S: Really popping in and out today.

E: Okay, I'm going to turn the lights up now.

S (after 33 seconds): I saw a little boy and, I want to say a goldfish bowl, but it really wasn't. It was more like a white ball—rather large. And there was a third person in the background, some place.

E: Anything else?

S: Well, this white object somehow seemed to dominate the picture. It seems brighter than anything else. Not so much that it's white, it just seems more dominant somehow.

---

* This instruction, as well as the one to keep eyes closed while reporting, was intended to maintain comparability of reporting conditions during the different parts of the experiment. We were interested in the effects of varied nonspecific arousal on the visual image, not on its description afterward.

With S back under hypnosis the following inquiry was conducted:

E: Now, as you're sleeping deeply, your memory for all three parts of the experiment we just did is restored. You can remember what happened first when you were wide awake and alert, the second time when you went into a nocturnal kind of sleep, and the one just now when you were sort of half asleep. Now I'd like you to bring up the visual images that passed through your mind each of those three times and compare them. Which is the clearest?

S (who is able to bring up each image, as though it were a photograph, and make comparisons as they lie side by side in his imagination): The first one (wide awake) is quite clear, but there's nothing much there. Quite distinct, the glass bowl full of smoke or something, against a black background.

E: How about the second one, while you were asleep? How distinct was that?

S: That didn't seem like it was very distinct. I had a strong impression that there was more there, but I didn't see anything else. So I'm not sure if that makes it distinct or indistinct or what.

E: There seem to be two dimensions here—one is how much detail, and the other is how distinct is the detail that's there. There appears to be more detail the second time than the first, is that right?

S: Yes.

E: You saw the boy and the mother.

S: The boy was quite distinct, the mother was not real distinct.

E: Now, disregarding the amount of detail, were those details present the second time as clear as the glass bowl when you were awake?

S: No, no.

E: Okay, now bring up the third image, when you were half asleep. How does that compare to the other two?

S: I'd say it was more distinct than the second (asleep) but not as clear as the first (wide awake).

E: How did it compare in terms of amount of detail apart from clarity?

S: I think it had more. The boy and the bowl were fairly clear and the impression of the mother in the background was almost as strong as in the second, so it had more detail.

At this point E, desirous of repeating the experiment, decided to risk a bold maneuver. Still under hypnosis, S was given amnesia for all the foregoing and then shown Cartoon IX of the Blacky Pictures (Figure 7). Next he was literally "programmed" to carry out, upon awakening, the intricate sequence of over twenty acts involved in the study. During the four jam-packed minutes which followed, he executed every instruction perfectly—giving himself signals to go into a particular arousal state, visualize the picture, revert to a normal wak-

FIGURE 7. Blacky Cartoon
IX: Guilt Feelings.

ing state, describe the image, go back under hypnosis, give himself
amnesia, etc., etc.* His hypnotic descriptions of the picture as it
flashed through his mind in each of the three conditions are given
below:

1. *Wide Awake:* I just saw this black object and it was a dog, Blacky.
   Pretty much just a black object, that's all.

2. *Asleep:* It was mostly just a contrast of colors. Very little figure
   involved. White in the upper left and black in the lower
   right. The upper left was like a ball and the lower right
   kind of elongated, that's all.

3. *Half Asleep:* I saw the dog Blacky pretty distinctly. I could see his
   hands over his head and black and so forth. Then I saw
   pretty much of a white ball, a hazy whiteness in the
   upper left but it was not too distinct. Couldn't make
   out any detail there, that's all.

Results of the ensuing hypnotic inquiry are summarized in Table 2
along with his previous rankings of clarity and detail of the three
images of the "boy with magic set." As predicted, the Asleep condition, involving the smallest amount of nonspecific arousal, produced
the least vivid visual images. The other conditions reversed their
order in the two experiments, so no differentiation can be made
between them with respect to clarity. However, the data concerning
amount of detail apart from clarity are completely consistent. Since

---

* An amusing aftermath took place at the close of the day's session just prior
to S being awakened. When E gave an amnesia instruction for the "programmed" experiment, S obviously became unhappy. E surmised correctly that
he wanted to be able to enjoy his remarkable feat afterward, so a compromise
was evolved by which S could wake up with a "proud feeling of accomplishment"
but not knowing why.

**TABLE 2.   Steve's Rankings of His Visual Images
under Three Arousal Conditions**

Clarity		Amount of Detail	
Boy with Magic Set	Blacky and Conscience Figure	Boy with Magic Set	Blacky and Conscience Figure
1. Wide Awake	1. Half Asleep	1. Half Asleep	1. Half Asleep
2. Half Asleep	2. Wide Awake	2. Asleep	2. Asleep
3. Asleep	3. Asleep	3. Wide Awake	3. Wide Awake

this dimension was not incorporated into the original design, we can
only offer post hoc interpretations of the findings.

In terms of the model, the number of details which get filled into
an image is probably a function of the amount of cognitive reverberation, each repetitive sequence activating closely related circuits by
spread.   For the Wide Awake condition the reverberation is minimized by interference from new sensory inputs, whose discharging
circuits are more likely to compete successfully for hyperfacilitation,
thereby breaking the reverberatory chain connected with the picture
image itself.   The Half Asleep condition is somewhat analogous to
hypnosis * in that there are relatively few competing inputs, yet the
amount of sensory impingement can maintain strong enough nonspecific arousal to insure adequate-strength hyperfacilitations.   Thus the
circuits in the picture network continue to discharge and their signals
reverberate with less likelihood of interruption.   The Asleep condition, though likewise free of dominant extraneous sensory inputs, is
not accompanied by sufficient hyperfacilitation to lead to such lengthy
reverberation.   ("Lengthy" is used, of course, in a relative sense, for
the events being described undoubtedly happen at very fast speeds.)

The posthypnotic arousal experiment was also done with Rudy,
whose period of service as a subject overlapped with Steve's. The
procedure was similar except that the order of conditions was altered
to control possible sequence effects (Half Asleep, Wide Awake,
Asleep).   Only one series was run and inquiry was confined to the
dimension in which we were originally interested, namely, clarity of
the visual image.   His report was consistent with Steve's, the major
difference being in the Asleep condition where he got no visual image

---

* Discussed in detail in Chapter 12.

at all. He didn't "see" anything but the "idea" of the cartoon of the boy with the magic set came to mind instead and it seemed "very clear." Visual images did occur in the other two conditions and the Half Asleep was rated definitely more vivid than the Wide Awake one.

Experiment 3. Vividness of Imagery during Exciting and Relaxing Musical Excerpts

Encouraged by these preliminary results, we switched to an experimental design in which the amount of nonspecific arousal was intended to be varied directly via sensory input, instead of relying on posthypnotically suggested arousal states. In the trance S was shown a picture as before and then told that in the waking state an excerpt from a piece of classical music would be played. At some unannounced point during the recording E would name the picture and a visual image of it would flash quickly through S's mind. Two conditions were set up: in one the musical selection, previously described under hypnosis as "slow and relaxing," was part of the First Movement of Corelli's Concerto Grosso op. 6 #8 ("Christmas"); the other, referred to as "fast and exciting," was taken from the first section of Prokofiev's "Scythian Suite."

The procedure was first tried on Steve in order to compare results from the two types of approach. He was given seven trials, during each of which the two excerpts were played in changing sequence, and hypnotic inquiries were conducted immediately after every trial. A different picture was used as the stimulus each time. On 5 out of 7 trials the visual image was reported to be more vivid in the Fast condition; on 6 of the 7 the Slow one was more detailed and seemed to make a more meaningful whole.

An expanded inquiry and a standardized plan of trials was put into use when the study was subsequently repeated with three new Ss.* Table 3 summarizes the findings, which obviously do not reflect any clear pattern.

In retrospect it became apparent to us why the music experiment led to confusing results. Intended solely as an undifferentiated ante-

---

* An explanation is in order for the fact that the number of Ss participating in each study varies. Since it was not feasible time-wise to conduct a dozen experiments on every individual, compromises were worked out to permit a sample of approximately five or six per experiment. Another limitation was imposed as a consequence of some Ss having been terminated before certain investigations were even conceived.

TABLE 3. Comparisons by Three Ss of Visual Images
under Conditions of Fast versus Slow Music

Inquiry Dimension	Harold			Max			Joe		
	F>S	S>F	No Diff.	F>S	S>F	No Diff.	F>S	S>F	No Diff.
Vividness	2	2	0	3	1	0	0	1	3
Amount of detail	0	0	4	3	1	0	0	2	2
Meaningfulness	3	1	0	2	2	0	2	0	2
Size	0	0	4	1	3	0	0	1	3

cedent of amount of nonspecific arousal, the musical inputs instead triggered, in very specific fashion, a host of idiosyncratic cognitive circuits varying in strength both within and across Ss. The post-hypnotic suggestions of "exciting" and "relaxing" no doubt contributed to this unwelcome state of affairs. Ss later reported fantasies like "when the slow music played I got an impression of lying back in an overstuffed chair with a can of beer in my hand."

Even the content of the visual images was affected differentially by the two types of music. In fact the only consistent finding was that in the Fast condition the images were typically full of action in contrast to the passivity of the Slow ones. The following inquiry excerpts illustrate this point (stimulus picture is Blacky I, see Figure 8):

Fast: When you mentioned Blacky nursing I saw the card and Blacky was jumping up and down, and was gnawing instead of nursing. And the dog in the far background started barking and running around.

FIGURE 8. Blacky Cartoon I: Oral Eroticism.

Slow: When the music was slow Blacky just lay there. Made no motion at all, just as it was shown in the picture. But the mother dog—for one thing the bow disappeared from her collar and the look on her face changed. It was more pleasant. What appears to be lipstick on the face of the dog disappears.

In conclusion, the music experiment failed to provide a satisfactory operational measure of nonspecific arousal probably because of the uncontrolled introduction of facilitations into specific cognitive networks. Further manipulation of posthypnotic arousal states offers more promise for future investigation of the hyperfacilitation function. It would also be of interest to pursue the arousal design with Ss not under the influence of posthypnotic suggestion. Very likely, though, it would be difficult to achieve the requisite conditions of arresting a particular visual image and reporting its detailed appearance accurately. Any work with direct sensory inputs should be restricted to ones whose cognitive connotations are limited and specifiable in advance.

The two series of experiments reported in this chapter illustrate the variability in the current model's capacity for generating specific research hypotheses: the facilitation experiment tested predictions stemming directly from the model, whereas the approaches to hyperfacilitation were intended as preliminary explorations of an important area of mental functioning. From such explorations it is expected that relevant parts of the model will be spelled out in greater detail, eventually permitting the formulation of unequivocal deductions.

Perceptual inhibition   5

Inhibition is a key mental function in the model, having the power to disrupt connections in the Mental System. Though the inhibition mechanism is tied closely to the anxiety network, it has been pointed out that connections can be formed to other networks during their contiguous activation. We shall be dealing here with the spread of inhibition during the process of perception.

Experiment 4.   Extraneous Perceptual Interference from Presence of Anxiety-Laden Stimuli

This investigation tests the hypothesis, explicitly suggested by the model, that inhibition, triggered by activation of the anxiety network, will interfere with the perception of *extraneous* stimuli presented concurrently with the anxiety-arousing one. From the point of view of the model there are several requisite features to be included in designing such an experiment. First, the triggering stimulus must be unequivocally laden with anxiety in order to insure the postulated occurrence of inhibition. Second, the extraneous stimulus, whose perception is to be interfered with, must be of weak intensity so that its discharging circuit will not outlast the inhibitory action, which is presumed to have an upper limit of effectiveness. Third, provision must be made in the experimental conditions for ruling out explanation of positive results in terms other than inhibition, e.g., interference produced by strong competing responses.

The stimuli chosen for simultaneous tachistoscopic viewing were colors and pictures. Each stimulus pattern in the test series consisted of *three* colors and *one* picture, arranged randomly in the four positions on the stimulus board (Left, Right, Top, Bottom) and varying in position from trial to trial. Three different types of pictures were included throughout the series: one Blacky cartoon to which anxiety had been attached; another to which positive affect had been associated; and a neutral picture of a man knocking on a door. The three colors accompanying a picture were the same on all trials.

The preliminary attachment of affects was accomplished under hypnosis. Early in the training period of each S he was asked to describe personal experiences suggested by the Blacky pictures. These experiences were then used as a guide to select negatively and positively toned pictures for further affective inductions, illustrated in the following passage:

E: Now as you're sleeping deeply we're going to talk about an experience you recounted for one of the Blacky pictures. It was the picture of Blacky and the conscience figure (Figure 7, p. 43) and the episode you described was when you and your friend tied the cat to a tree and threw bricks at it. Do you remember when you talked about that?

S: Yes.

E: All right, now we're going to go back to that situation again and you're going to re-experience it, and you're going to feel the same way you did then. We're going to reconstruct what happened and as I describe what you talked about, you're going to be back in that situation feeling the same emotions just as intensely. All right, listen carefully. You're about five or six years old, playing with your friend, and you found a cat and tied it to a tree. Then you threw bricks at him. You'd hit it with a couple of bricks and then stand and look at the bleeding animal and think what a cruel world it is—the poor cat suffering and trying to get away. But then you'd throw a couple more bricks anyway. Next your father came along and sent the other kid home and ordered you up to your room. He said he was going to call the police and you were hoping he was just kidding. A little while later you looked out of the window and a police car drove up. Now you're back in that situation. You're looking out of the window and you see them coming from the sidewalk—two policemen and your father and they walk across the backyard to where the cat is. You're very frightened as you look out the window (amply documented by tremendous

GSR deflections at this point) and *this is the way you will feel when-*
ever you see the picture of Blacky and the conscience figure, or any
part of it, whether you are awake or asleep. All right, tell me how you
just felt.

S: I was pretty scared when you were talking about the cops in the backyard. I was almost afraid I was going to cry.*

Positive affects were attached in similar fashion. For example, one
S was told that whenever he would see or glimpse Cartoon XI, which
shows Blacky dreaming of a beautiful female dog, he would immediately experience the same pleasant feeling he once had in a youthful
fantasy (originally associated with the cartoon by S) of himself "together with Elizabeth Taylor raising horses just like in the motion
picture *National Velvet."*

Immediately prior to running the tachistoscopic test trials, a training series using only three colors (different from the colors later shown
as test stimuli) was conducted to determine for each S the appropriate
speed of presentation for the level of visual accuracy in which we
were interested. The following instructions were given for the training series (S awake):

Now we're going to ask you to look into this machine, which flashes
stimuli very quickly. The reason we want you to do this is to help us
find out about the *effect of delay* between the time something is seen and
when it is reported verbally by the subject (subterfuge on the part of E!).
So we shall ask you to look at a particular spot and then a short time
afterward, but not immediately, we will test how accurate you can be in
identifying what you saw.

Three things will be flashed simultaneously in each trial. They will be
in either the Top, Bottom, Left, or Right positions with reference to a dot
in the center of the screen. Here (S shown a stimulus board) is a sample
of the board onto which the stimuli will be mounted. Before each flash
you will be told to look at either the Top, Bottom, Left, or Right positions
and your job will be to identify what was shown in that position. Three
of the positions will be filled with solid colors. Look into the machine
now and I will show you, one at a time, the colors you will see (each
color then shown for 5 seconds and subsequently flashed several times at
.10 second).

Now for the instructions concerning your verbal response. If for example

* Lest the clinically oriented reader be offended by our tampering with S's
psyche, we wish to emphasize that all suggestions were carefully removed and
worked through at the conclusion of the experiments. Detailed feedback was
provided in both waking and hypnotic states. In no case did we ever end up
with a dissatisfied customer—Ss indicated willingness to serve again and recom-
mended friends as future subjects.

you are told in advance to concentrate on the Top position, after the flash
you will wait until I give the signal for you to tell what was in that position. At the signal just name the color if you are fairly certain. Sometimes
you are going to be unsure of what has been flashed. When this happens
I want you to guess a color. In other words, you must make some response
on every trial.

In order to introduce our time delay, we will first ask you to identify
one of the colors which appeared in one of the remaining three positions.
You will *not* know beforehand which other position will be asked for. *The
important thing is for you to try to be correct as often as possible on the
position you are told to look at in advance.* It would probably make your
task easier if you make a mental note of that stimulus as soon as you see it,
so that you can remember it by the time you are asked to name it.

The desired accuracy level was 40 to 60 per cent correct identification
of the color asked for immediately after the flash (*not* the one in the
position looked at in advance). Correct guesses were included in
the accurate category. For the five Ss who participated in this experiment the speeds finally settled upon ranged from .08 to .12 second,
with a very dim illumination of approximately .05 foot-lamberts.

Next came the experiment proper. The three colors employed
throughout were yellow, orange, and green. They were not clearly
visible as those colors under the particular lighting and speed conditions, but with limited practice (see instructions below) Ss were able
to discriminate them. The Blacky pictures (see Figure 15 on pp. 92–93
for the complete set of cartoons) which served as anxiety-arousing
for the various Ss were Cartoons II, IV, VI, and IX (two Ss); the
positively toned ones were III, X (two Ss), and XI (also two Ss).
In every case the picture of a man knocking on a door was the neutral
stimulus, having been characterized previously under hypnosis as
eliciting "no feelings one way or the other." The instructions continued as follows:

Now we are going to go on as before. This time you will be shown
pictures as well as colors, and the colors will be different from those you
saw a little while ago. For this series of flashes four things will be shown
simultaneously and you will be asked to identify pictures and colors alike.
Otherwise the procedure will be the same: you will be asked to look in
advance at a particular position but, before having you tell what was
flashed in that position, I will first ask you to identify one of the stimuli
which appeared in one of the other three positions. Remember to keep
in mind the correct identification of the object in the test position during
this whole time.

Now look into the machine and I will show you the stimulus you will
be asked to identify. (Each picture was then shown in full view 5 seconds

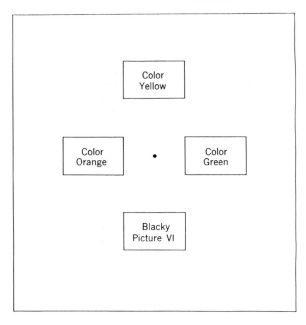

FIGURE 9. Sample stimulus pattern for perceptual interference experiment.

and subsequently flashed rapidly three times at .10 second.   The same
was done for each of the three colors.)   All right, let's begin. (The trials
were run in blocks of five flashes with rest periods intervening.   Typically
eight blocks were run per subject.   See Figure 9 for sample stimulus
pattern.)

By these procedures the first two requisite features of the experimental design, mentioned on p. 48, were incorporated: potent affect
was connected to the critical stimuli (pictures) by prior hypnotic
induction; and weak intensity of the "extraneous" stimulus (operationalized as the peripherally glimpsed color) was accomplished by having S fixate on another position before the flash.   We are now at the
point where we can turn to the results and their interpretation, which
will bear on the third requirment—ruling out alternative explanations
in the event of findings congruent with the inhibition hypothesis.

Of the various ways of categorizing data yielded by the experimental conditions, the one most pertinent for testing the prediction involves those trials in which colors were present in both the fixated
and queried (peripheral) positions and the picture was in another

peripheral position, seemingly unrelated to S's task of responding to E's questions about what had appeared in two of the color locations. The likelihood of the picture's sensory registration was enhanced, however, by the fact that S did not know ahead of time which of the three peripheral positions would be asked for and therefore tried to scan all of them as quickly as possible. Furthermore it turned out that the pictures in general were more discriminable than colors, which means that, if any of the four did not register, it tended to be a color rather than a picture. Table 4 gives the results of this analysis. For all Ss the presence of the anxiety picture is accompanied by poorer identification of the queried peripheral color than when non-loaded pictures are present. Statistical confirmation of the prediction is provided by a series of Fisher exact tests (one test for each S based on a fourfold table dichotomized according to correct or incorrect identification of peripheral color as one variable, and presence or

TABLE 4. Per Cent Accuracy of Identification of Queried Peripheral Color According to Presence or Absence of Anxiety Picture in Another Peripheral Position

	Anxiety Picture Present	Positive or Neutral Picture Present *
Victor	25%	90%
Ned	50%	92%
Tom	63%	83%
Rudy	40%	58%
Steve	40%	75%
Mean	44%	80% †

* No differences were noted between presence of positive versus neutral pictures so these are combined in all the data analyses. No differences were predicted from the inhibition hypothesis, but it was deemed preferable, for purposes of control, to include a picture with some kind of affect other than anxiety along with a neutral stimulus.

† This increase in accuracy over the 40 to 60 per cent criterion in the training period is impossible to assess, since the test stimulus patterns each consisted of three colors and a picture in contrast to the training patterns of three *other* colors *without* a picture present. The absolute accuracy level is of no consequence (other than permitting a range of fluctuations to occur, which the training criterion sought to insure) inasmuch as the crucial comparisons are between anxiety and nonanxiety picture conditions within the test series.

absence of anxiety picture as the other) whose combined p-value is
<.002 by a one-tailed test of significance.

So the clearcut findings are compatible with the inhibition hypothesis, but an alternative explanation is also tenable. Might it not be argued that the anxiety picture, despite precautions taken to insure its equal familiarity with positive and neutral pictures, was somehow cognitively stronger than the others and therefore more distracting? The lower accuracy would thus be attributable simply to interference among competing response tendencies, with no necessity for postulating an inhibitory mechanism. To check on this possibility a number of further steps were taken.

For the last of the five Ss the decision was made to run before and after tests following exactly the same procedure as in the critical series. Accordingly, the experiment was carried out prior to the hypnotic attachment of affect to the picture stimuli, and no difference was found in accuracy of the queried peripheral color when the "to-be-loaded with anxiety" picture was present. Then the critical series was done a few days later, and a p-value of .06 in the predicted direction was obtained. Shortly thereafter the affects were removed under hypnosis (GSR and S's introspections confirmed the removal of anxiety) and the experiment repeated once more. Again no difference between the picture conditions! The first S, who had been run several months before but was still on campus and available, was brought back for a post-test with no affects attached. The significant difference between conditions disappeared just as it had with the last S. The latter, after a lapse of three months, was put to still another test. This fourth time a strong feeling of sadness was attached to the previous anxiety picture and positive affect restored to the other—once more no difference.*

At this stage the inhibition interpretation of the critical series is obviously pulling ahead of the interference-sans-inhibition notion. Before anxiety was introduced S did not do more poorly in identifying the peripheral color; with anxiety attached he showed the predicted inhibition effect; removal of the anxiety again eliminated the discrepancy; and finally replacement of anxiety by another negative affect, sadness, revealed no difference in comparison with the presence of positive and neutral pictures. It certainly seems as though anxiety,

---

* The effectiveness of the sadness induction is illustrated by these introspective comments by S: "I feel a lot like crying—not crying vehemently, you know, just kind of sit there with the tears streaming down your face. Not like you're all broken up, just sitting there and crying. I did start to get a little sick, a little bit nauseated when it felt like the couch was swaying."

which is the variable assumed to be operating in the inhibition explanation, is the crucial element. Interference theory does not make explicit use of the role of anxiety and consequently suffers by contrast. But the latter argument can be extended to hold that for some currently unspecifiable reason the attachment of anxiety to a stimulus results in greater *cognitive* strengthening of that stimulus than does attachment of any other kind of affect. (Note that the differential strength must be seen as cognitive, otherwise this assertion, if reduced to a claim for qualitatively special disruptive effects of anxiety, would be nothing more than a crude statement of the inhibition point of view.) Do we have any evidence, then, which sheds further light on such a contention?

Fortunately the design does permit an inference to be drawn concerning the effects of picture strength per se. If a stronger response tendency is associated with the anxiety picture, we would expect it to be identified correctly more often than the nonloaded pictures on those trials in which the *picture* is in the *queried* peripheral position. Table 5 does not bear this out. Only two of the five Ss (Tom and Rudy) reveal superiority of identification of the loaded picture and these two happen to show the main experimental effect (see Table 4) *less* markedly than the rest.

The preceding dialectic is intended to demonstrate that strength alone is not a sufficient explanation of the principal findings. It does not carry the implication that strength cannot operate as a major variable in studies of this sort, but rather that, in the present instance, the inhibition hypothesis is more fully congruent with the facts. Our next obligation to the reader is to spell out, in model terms, how this inhibitory mechanism is presumed to function.

TABLE 5. **Per Cent Accuracy of Identification of Pictures in the Queried Peripheral Position**

	Anxiety Picture	Positive or Neutral Picture
Victor	67%	65%
Ned	50%	92%
Tom	72%	54%
Rudy	92%	31%
Steve	67%	69%
Mean	70%	62%

To furnish an illustration, let us return to Figure 9 and assume that this particular pattern was flashed on the trial in which we are interested. The sequence of events would go something like this:

E   (before flashing the pattern): Now look at the Top position. Ready.
    (Picture is then flashed.)
E   (four seconds later): What was at the Right?
S: I'm not sure, but I'll guess Orange.
E   (immediately after S's reply): And what was at the Top?
S: Yellow.

Figure 10 schematizes the networks presumed to be activated by the flash, prior to E's first query. The coupled circuits Top and Yellow are activated more strongly than the other stimulus circuits because they occupy the fixated position. After the experiment S typically reported that he saw this stimulus very clearly, although the time delay and interpolated question sometimes prevented him from remembering it when later asked. The peripherally glimpsed Bottom and Blacky VI combination was intermediate in strength because all pictures in the task are known to be more discriminable than colors, due primarily to their distinctive black and white configurations. The stimuli in the other peripheral positions, Green at the Right and Orange at the Left, have neither the advantage of visual fixation nor greater discriminability; hence their couplings are the weakest of all.

Activation of the picture network automatically leads to triggering the inhibition mechanism by way of the latter's built-in connection from the representation of anxiety. Whether or not these inhibition signals disrupt circuit couplings sufficiently to interfere with eventual stimulus identification is a function of relative strength of the coupling versus the inhibitory discharge. It was anticipated for the present design that only the weak couplings between peripherally glimpsed colors and their respective positions would likely be susceptible to complete disruption, which is precisely what the results indicate. On the other hand, fixated colors and fixated or peripheral pictures (anxiety-laden or not) tip the balance in the direction of being correctly identified themselves because of their superior strength.

If, as we assumed, the fixated color and peripheral picture in Figure 9 were perceived fairly well, S would be faced roughly with a 50-50 prospect of guessing correctly when E requested him to bring back a peripheral color from immediate memory. The obtained mean accuracy figure of 44 per cent for identifying the peripheral color in

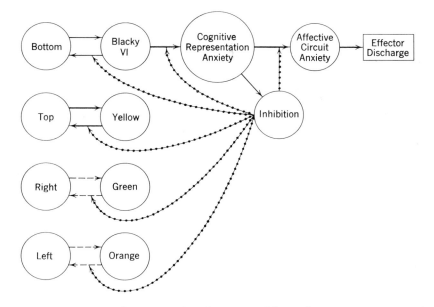

FIGURE 10. Networks presumed to be activated by tachistoscopic presentation of stimulus pattern shown in Figure 9. [*Note:* Activation of Cognitive Representation Anxiety by Blacky VI picture triggers inhibition, which in turn interferes (chained lines) with transmission in all position-stimulus networks. However, the Top-Yellow network, more strongly activated (heavier lines) because S focused on that position, does achieve signal discharge despite inhibitory action.]

the presence of the anxiety picture (see Table 4 again) comes close to this chance expectancy. In other words, the question "What was at the Right?" activates the Right circuit but, since inhibition has already interfered with firm facilitation of the connection to Green, the answer is just as apt to be Orange as Green, hinging only upon "fortuitous" relative strengths of couplings existing at that moment.

The preceding experiment deals somewhat indirectly with perceptual processes, since S does not report immediately what he sees but instead has to wait a few seconds for E to ask about a particular position. Ascribing the action of inhibition in this case to the perceptual stage, i.e., time of stimulus registration rather than time of recall, must remain an inference from the data. The next approach to be reported strongly suggests that inhibition can occur in a perceptual locus.

Experiment 5. Hypnotically Induced Selective Blindness as a Technique for Determining Anxiety Correlates of Unconsciously Registered Stimuli

One problem on which we were working in connection with an early form of the model, then in its psychoanalytic guise, required sensory registration of an input without accompanying recognition or subsequent access from memory, measured by guesses as to what had been shown just before. The technique which evolved made use of a selective, hypnotically induced blindness. Ss were able to be trained not to "see" a given stimulus when it was flashed tachistoscopically, even though they *did not know in advance* at what point in a series it would appear. We had reason to believe that blindness should not be especially difficult to induce in well-trained, deeply hypnotizable Ss, but its spontaneous occurrence at an unannounced signal offered a real challenge. After all, don't the opponents of "new look" perception argue that it is ridiculous to postulate a little man inside the head who looks at something, decides he shouldn't see it, and then shuts it out before he can recognize it? The little man *is* indeed ridiculous—the sequence of perceptual operations is not.

We began our explorations by having one hypnotized S look full-view, at arm's length, at a cartoon of several African natives carrying spears. He was then given practice in making the picture "disappear" whenever E said "Now it's gone!". It developed that the signal always caused the scene to change into a caricature of a large female figure which S described as resembling Popeye's comic strip girl friend, Olive Oyl. In the next session, again conducted under hypnosis, the blindness training was extended to tachistoscopic flashing of the same cartoon and a new stimulus, a circle with an X inside. Later he was led to blot out the X with the outer circle still remaining visible, and then came the crucial phase of *not seeing* the X but *seeing* other figures such as squares and triangles shown in a random, unannounced series. The latter turned out to be a lengthy, arduous task requiring several hours of intensive hypnotic work before success was achieved. In order to be certain the effect had nothing to do with the physical properties of the stimuli, the blindness was removed from the X by instruction and attached instead to the square, where it proved equally effective.

The other two Ss subsequently given blindness training also needed a few hours of practice before they were able to execute the instructions consistently, but the overall amount of time spent was consider-

ably less. It is difficult to know, of course, whether variation in Ss'
responsiveness was due mainly to individual differences among them
or to improvements in our training techniques as we went along.

The obvious question at this point is how we know that S really
did not see the stimulus well enough to recognize it or even to guess
its identity correctly when asked. Simulation is always a reasonable
suspicion in hypnosis experiments, for it is well known that subjects
are usually eager to perform in the desired manner. In the present
instance a number of different kinds of evidence converge to rule out
the possibility of faking. To minimize its likelihood in the first place,
stress was laid upon the requirement that S always report *exactly*
what he saw even though it did not correspond to instructions. During the training of all three Ss there were frequent reports of having
seen the critical stimulus when they were not supposed to. (In fact,
it would presuppose a highly sado-masochistic type of character structure for someone to expose himself and the experimenter to those
grueling sessions at the tachistoscope if he were simulating all along!)
Also, there were occasions upon which S was blind to the wrong
stimulus, i.e., did not see the square when the X was the figure to
be blotted out. More important, the blindness sometimes persisted
after it had presumably been removed by instruction. All Ss experienced some difficulty in seeing the critical stimulus clearly right after
the blindness suggestion was lifted.

For the die-hard skeptic who refuses to believe anything S ever
says, there are two bits of physiological evidence which also argue
against simulation. If S were deliberately faking his verbal report
we would expect the GSR to be responsive to the deception, but
there were no such deflections in the record. In addition, a series
of trials checking eye movements in one S revealed a distinctive pattern of electro-oculographic responses on those flashes where blindness occurred.

The eye movement recording from this one S was undertaken as a
limited and somewhat tangential exploration of visual mechanisms
involved in hypnotically induced blindness.* From his introspections
describing the stimulus as being "out of focus just the right amount"
we wondered about possible changes in convergence and accommodation. We quickly discovered that the blindness phenomenon did not
require binocular vision, so the next step was to determine the role
of accommodation. Electrodes were placed over the muscles of one

---

* We are indebted to Dr. Mathew Alpern, Department of Ophthalmology,
University of Michigan, for his guidance and technical assistance in this phase
of the investigation.

eye and the other eye was covered completely while S looked into the tachistoscope. Two stimuli, one carrying the blindness instruction and the other not, were flashed in a series of 11 trials. A Mann-Whitney U Test comparing magnitude of electro-oculographic responses on the 5 blind versus 6 correct trials revealed the former to be significantly greater ($p < .004$). However, the latencies of response were at least 1 second on every blind trial, which seems too long to account for an effect occurring within the very short flash duration (typically around .10 second). Our best guess, therefore, is that the blindness phenomenon is a perceptual rather than a purely optical phenomenon.

The experiment, for which the blindness training was prerequisite, attempted to test whether "unconscious" activation of an idea highly charged with anxiety automatically releases the anxiety itself. Four stimuli were flashed in Series A at a speed where recognition was 100 per cent correct. Next the already trained S was instructed to be blind to two of the stimuli (3 vertical dots and 3 horizontal dots) and to see the other two clearly (a blank and a triangle) in Series B. Before Series C, strong anxiety was attached to one of the dot stimuli by the instruction "Whenever the vertical (or horizontal) dots are flashed, *whether you see them or not,* you will immediately feel extremely nervous and upset." The blind-anxiety series was then followed by Series D, for which the blindness instruction was removed and the anxiety suggestion remained. The speed of presentation was the same throughout the four series and all were conducted under hypnosis. Results from the three Ss participating in the study tentatively suggest that affect is not elicited unless the charged idea is activated at least to the point of "preconsciousness" (not "seen" at the flash but guessed afterward). On the Series C trials where S was exposed to the critical stimulus but did not see it or guess it correctly, no GSR deflections of any significance were noted despite the fact that sensory registration of the stimulus was required in order for the selective blindness instruction to have been carried out.

As in the preceding chapter, we again have illustrations of the current model's uneven quality of rigor: the interference experiment tested an unequivocal prediction from the model, whereas the work on selective blindness was largely exploratory. But from both approaches covered above it is clear that perceptual inhibition is a verifiable and demonstrable phenomenon. Moreover, techniques are available to pursue, in precise ways, the conditions under which this particular mental function operates.

Inhibition
of
anxiety   6

The last chapter dealt with the effects of inhibition during the perceptual sequence. Here we shall be concerned with inhibitory action on connections to the affective subsystem, specifically in a network of anxiety. Two experiments were done, one involving a manipulation of inhibition by posthypnotic suggestion, and the other a competition between affects elicited simultaneously.*

Experiment 6. Inhibition of Anxiety by Posthypnotic Suggestion

In the first study S was given the following instructions under hypnosis:

Whenever you see Yellow, Orange, Purple or Red, you will feel very tense and nervous. You will feel this way whether you are awake or asleep. You will have these feelings very strongly when you are awake.

Whenever you see the Blacky picture, whether you are awake or asleep, you will also feel very tense and nervous.

Whenever Green is present, you will have no feelings at all about the colors. Green will affect the colors only, so that when you see Green you

* These two experiments were carried out by Gerald A. Mendelsohn. They are described in greater detail in *Experiments on the psychoanalytic mechanism of isolation*, Ph.D. dissertation, University of Michigan, 1960.

will have no feelings to the colors.   Green will have no effect on the feeling which accompanies the Blacky picture.

When you are awake you will look at some things in the tachistoscope. You will find this task very interesting and you will not become bored or tired.   As always, you will be unable to remember what happened while you were asleep.

As the suggestion for each stimulus was made, S was told to look at it in full view.   If the attached GSR indicated any difficulty in conditioning the anxiety response to a particular stimulus, the induction was repeated.

After S was awakened, E then said:

I am going to show you four stimuli simultaneously in the tachistoscope. Before we begin, though, I will show you one by one the stimuli you are about to see.

A check series was run at this point to verify by GSR the efficacy of the earlier hypnotic induction.   The colors and Blacky picture were flashed one at a time at a speed slow enough to be easily seen.*   In addition, pairs of stimuli occupying the Left and Right positions of the four-stimulus pattern were presented.   Green and each of the anxiety-loaded colors were paired with the Blacky picture, in order to be certain that neither Green nor the other colors had an inhibitory effect upon the anxiety attached to the picture.

Following the check series these instructions were given for the experimental trials:

Now you will see these same stimuli in different combinations, four at a time.   They will appear in the Top, Bottom, Left, and Right of the stimulus board.   Before each trial I will tell you where to focus.   For example, I will say "Look at the Top."   You are to focus on that position before the flash when I say "Ready."   Then, after the flash, I will first ask you what you saw in some position other than the one that I told you to look at.   Next I will ask what you saw in the position that I told you to look at.

By having S report what he saw, E was able to ascertain that he had perceived the stimuli clearly.   When Green was present it was always in the position upon which S was told to focus, in order to forestall

---

* The exposure times used for the six Ss participating in this experiment varied between .15 and .17 second, according to S's report of the ease with which he could see the stimuli during the check series. Illumination of the adapting field was 1.205 foot-lamberts and of the viewing field between 2.592 and 3.038 foot-lamberts, depending upon the different stimulus conditions. These measurements represent a high degree of illumination.

the occurrence of an affective response before the hypothesized inhibition effect could take place. The test series was run in four blocks of ten trials, each combination of stimuli appearing a total of ten times. The check series, described above, was repeated between the blocks of ten and again at the conclusion of the experiment to make sure the induction had not worn off. The dependent variable, GSR deflection at each test trial, was measured in millimeters, 1 millimeter being equal to a drop in resistance of 200 ohms. A deflection was counted only if it began within 4 seconds after the tachistoscopic flash. Technical difficulties associated with GSR measurement, e.g., changes in temperature and humidity, adaptation effects, etc., were minimized by placing a limit on the number of trials run in one session.

Four combinations were included in the stimulus patterns:

1. Four colors without Green.
2. Three colors and Green.
3. Two colors, Green, and the Blacky picture.
4. Three colors other than Green, and the Blacky picture.

The first combination was designed to assess the level of affect stemming from the loaded colors. The critical second group served to test whether inhibition of anxiety can be produced by experimental manipulation. The third sought to explore the possibility of multiple anxiety networks in the system by noting GSR response to the picture in combination with the action of Green on loaded colors—absence of GSR implying that there is only one such network whose inhibition, regardless of the source, will interfere equally with transmission of any signals from other sources through that network. The fourth provided an assessment of level of affect accompanying three colors plus the picture.

The prediction that Combination 2 would yield smaller GSR deflections than Combination 1 was checked by analysis of variance, the F test showing a highly significant difference ($p = .01$). The data can be inspected most meaningfully from Table 6, which simply presents the sum of GSR deflections for each combination broken down by individual Ss. Not only is the grand sum of Combination 2 considerably lower than 1, but also the responses of all six Ss are uniformly in the same direction. It might be argued that this lower sum of GSR deflections is solely a function of the fact that there are only three anxiety colors present in Combination 2 as compared to four in Combination 1. However, examination of responses to each of the stimuli shown individually during the check series reveals that

TABLE 6. Sum of GSR Deflections for Each Combination of Stimuli

Combinations

Subject	1 4 Colors	2 3 Colors and Green	3 2 Colors, Green, and Blacky Picture	4 3 Colors and Blacky Picture
Joe	62.5	18.0	53.0	65.0
Fred	52.0	15.0	34.5	37.5
Rudy	28.5	19.0	11.5	33.5
Harold	42.5	18.5	22.5	21.0
Max	89.5	39.5	25.0	46.5
Steve	55.5	5.0	14.5	31.5
Grand sum	330.5	115.0	161.0	235.0

they do not interact in an additive manner when shown in combination. Even if the latter were the case, one would then expect that grand sum in Combination 2 to be 248 millimeters (three-fourths of the grand sum in Combination 1), which still greatly exceeds the obtained sum of 115 millimeters. It can be safely concluded, therefore, that the presence of Green *does* have an inhibitory effect on the anxiety conditioned so strongly to the colors.

Investigation of the issue of single or multiple networks of anxiety was made possible by comparing Combinations 3 versus 4 (see Table 6 above), and also by relating these data to trials in the check series where Green and Blacky picture were paired. Application of the F test suggests a trend in the direction of the single network assumption, with 3 producing less GSR than 4 ($p = .10$). Also, GSR sums for 5 out of the 6 individual Ss are in line with this finding. The question of differential numbers of anxiety stimuli included in the two combinations is again shown to be irrelevant when the data from 3 are contrasted with the level of GSR produced by the pairing of Green and picture in the check trials. Analysis of variance indicates clearly ($p < .01$) that Combination 3 is accompanied by *less* GSR than the pairing, despite the fact that the latter contains only one anxiety stimulus.

After the experiment was completed, Ss were asked to rank order

TABLE 7. Rankings of the Subjective Unpleasantness of the Combinations of Stimuli

	Combinations			
	1	6	3	4
Subject	4 Colors	3 Colors and Green	2 Colors, Green, and Blacky Picture	3 Colors and Blacky Picture
Joe	3	4	2	1
Fred	2	4	3	1
Rudy	1	4	3	2
Harold	1	4	3	2
Max	2	4	3	1
Steve	1	4	3	2
Sum	10	24	17	9

the four combinations of stimuli along a subjective unpleasantness dimension. From Table 7 it can be seen that their reports parallel the GSR findings quite closely. Intersubject agreement on the rankings is very high, Kendall's coefficient of concordance (W) being .80. Everyone felt the pure inhibition pattern, Combination 2, to be *least* unpleasant, with Combination 3 next. Back under hypnosis Ss gave the same rankings as in the waking state. They typically described Combination 2 as making for relaxation. Harold, for example, when asked what was the effect of Green, replied: "It just made me feel relaxed, I just felt better." Earlier, while still awake, he had observed: "I'd rather look at Green. (Why?) I don't know, it must be restful on the eyes, it's an easier color to look at by far." *

Returning to the model, we can now make the general statement that the inhibitory function is susceptible to experimental manipulation, a fact which implies that its properties can be spelled out with a fair degree of precision during subsequent investigations. More specifically, the inhibition mechanism is capable of being triggered

---

* The truth of the matter is that the sensory qualities of the color stimuli flashed at these speeds do not produce differential eyestrain. Here we have an example of the common use of rationalization by hypnotic Ss to justify behavior which they do not understand.

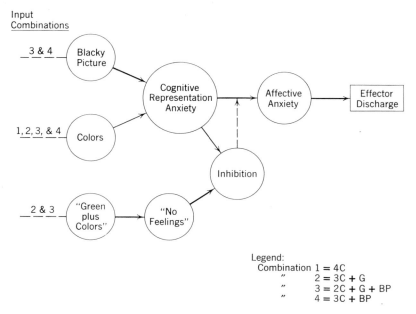

Input
Combinations

Legend:
Combination 1 = 4C
"   2 = 3C + G
"   3 = 2C + G + BP
"   4 = 3C + BP

FIGURE 11. Networks activated by various combinations of stimuli presented in tachistoscope. [*Note:* The inhibition mechanism is shown to be capable of triggering by two routes: (1) the built-in connection from Cognitive Representation Anxiety; and (2) an experimentally induced connection via the instruction "no feelings when Green accompanies colors." The dual routes effectively cut down anxiety discharge in stimulus combinations 2 and 3.]

directly by external stimulation—in the case of the above task by the presence of Green in the tachistoscope. To dismiss the findings merely as evidence that a good hypnotic subject can follow instructions would be a misleading oversimplification, for S must first have the capacity within himself to execute those instructions. The hypnotic induction served to condition activation of the inhibition mechanism to a particular stimulus but it did not create the mechanism itself.

In the course of development S undoubtedly has a number of connections established from cognitive circuits to the inhibition mechanism. The concept of self-relaxation, for example, falls into this category. Also, during the series of experiments he was often given practice in having "no feelings" about something or other. Figure 11 schematizes the networks presumed to be hooked up by the hypnotic induction. Cognitive circuits standing for the colors * are coupled directly with the anxiety network, as is the Blacky circuit. The cognitive representation of anxiety has a built-in connection to the inhibition mechanism. But the latter is also triggered by discharge of the "no feelings" cognitive circuit, which in turn is activated by a "Green plus colors" circuit attached by instruction. Presentation of Combination 2 or 3 provides sensory input to this network and eventuates in total or partial inhibition of anxiety discharge, as measured by the GSR, despite the simultaneous presence of loaded colors. Because of the unusually strong facilitation brought about by E's instructions, of connections from colors and Blacky picture to the anxiety network, the automatically occurring inhibitory discharge (via cognitive representation of anxiety) is insufficient to cut down the anxiety discharge very markedly. However, when the other route to inhibition (via the "no feelings" circuit) is also in operation, anxiety responses *are* minimized. As a consequence of the relatively slow speeds employed there is no observed inhibitory action with respect to identification of the stimuli, the spread effect of inhibition upon contiguously discharging circuits being insufficient in this situation to interfere with perception.

The tentative finding noted in the Combination 3 trials suggests that the same anxiety network is involved in connection with the cognitive Blacky picture circuit as with the loaded colors. Inhibition of anxiety via the "Green plus colors" route reduces the possibility of anxiety discharge from the picture input, even though the Blacky circuit has no built-in connection to inhibition. Figure 11 is drawn to portray a common affective destination for the various cognitive circuits. Whether or not this representation is correct remains a problem for future research to confirm.

Experiment 7. Reduction of Anxiety by Simultaneous Competing Affects

The next experiment to be reported tests reduction of conditioned anxiety by means of the simultaneous elicitation of competing affects. It should be noted that this competition does not assume inhibitory intervention of the type described in Chapter 5 or in the study just

---

* For simplicity of exposition the colors are depicted generally as one cognitive circuit. In actuality there are four such circuits, each connected to the anxiety network.

cited. However, as we shall see shortly, one plausible interpretation of the findings does entail activation of the inhibition mechanism.

By hypnotic induction various affective states were attached to letters of the alphabet. For example, S was told: "Whenever you see the letter C, whether awake or asleep, you will have a feeling of contentment." Similarly the letter D was associated with delight; the letter S with sadness; and the letter H with anxiety.* Efficacy of the induction was checked while S was still under hypnosis—by noting GSR in the case of H and by asking him to report his subjective feelings for each of the letters. Observation was also of some aid in this connection, particularly expressive movements of the eyes which often welled up with tears in the case of sadness, sparkled with delight, etc.

After S was awakened he was given the following instructions:

> I am going to show you two letters in the tachistoscope, one on the Left and one on the Right. But before giving you further instructions, I will show you the stimuli you are going to see.

S was then shown the letters, one at a time, and if the letter H led to a GSR deflection the instructions were continued:

> When I say Ready I want you to focus on the Left. It is important to remember this—focus on the Left on every trial. After the flash I will ask you first what you saw on the Right and then I will ask you what was on the Left.

H appeared on every trial, half the time as the letter on the Right and half as the letter on the Left. Every possible combination of H with the other letters was shown an equal number of times. For the experimental series an additional letter, N, was introduced as a neutral stimulus without any instruction attached. S was told to focus on the Left for all presentations so that E could be more certain of which stimulus S saw first. The verbal reports were included, as in the previous study, to be sure that the stimuli were clearly perceived. Speed of tachistoscopic presentation was .17 second for all six Ss and the lighting conditions were the same as described in the footnote on p. 62. Test series were run in 8 blocks, each consisting of 8 trials, with every combination of stimuli appearing once in each block. The crucial dependent variable in the experiment was again GSR, expressed in millimeters of deflection commencing within 4 seconds after the flash. A control series, in which the letters were

---

* H was used instead of A to avoid possibly meaningful letter combinations when two letters were presented together during the experiment.

TABLE 8.   Sum of GSR Deflections for Each Pairing of Stimuli

Subject	H and N	H and S	H and C	H and D
Joe	114.0	76.5	16.0	114.0
Fred	73.0	77.5	39.5	52.0
Rudy	26.0	18.5	19.5	22.5
Harold	49.0	69.0	25.0	91.5
Max	46.0	10.5	11.5	2.5
Steve	20.0	57.0	18.0	25.0
Grand sum	328.0	309.0	129.5	307.5

shown individually, was inserted every 16 trials to be certain that GSR deflection consistently accompanied the letter H and not any of the other letters.

The expectation was that contentment, being most antagonistic to anxiety, would result in decreased GSR (C paired with H). The other affects were included to explore the interaction of anxiety with an aroused positive state (D and H), and a different kind of negative emotion (S and H). The letter N, of course, served as a baseline for comparison when paired with H.

The data indicate that pairing contentment with anxiety does produce significantly less GSR than pairing a neutral stimulus with anxiety (see Table 8). Application of the F test to the grand sums reveals a p-value of .05 in the predicted direction. All six Ss show the effect uniformly, though for a couple the differences are not very great. Neither of the other pairings deviates appreciably from the N and H baseline. From the control series it is apparent that the major finding cannot be attributed to differential GSR attached to the letters N and C because they produce approximately the same low amount of deflection when presented individually. The experimental effect is thus clearly a product of the letter interaction itself rather than an artificial addition of unequal elements.

After the test trials were completed, S was asked to rank order the four pairings of stimuli along a subjective unpleasantness dimension. The intersubject agreement is moderately high, Kendall's coefficient of concordance (W) being .47 ($p < .05$). The GSR data are confirmed in that H and C is reported to be the *least* unpleasant combination, though closely followed by H and D.

Despite the unequivocal nature of the findings with respect to the pairing of H and C, there are a number of possible interpretations depending partly upon one's theory of affect. The view most compatible with the treatment of affect in the model (to be spelled out in Chapter 11) is that S construed the contentment instruction in such a way that inhibition was activated. In other words, the letter C, whose intended action can be paraphrased as "don't feel anxious," served to trigger the inhibition mechanism (as the color Green did in the preceding experiment), which in turn reduced the intensity of discharge from the anxiety network simultaneously activated by the letter H. A somewhat related position might assert that S, placed in a dilemma by the appearance of conflicting stimuli to which he was required to react, unconsciously resolved the task by reasoning to himself that anxiety can legitimately accompany sadness and delight but not contentment. It shares a negative feeling tone with sadness and a feeling of excitement with delight. Speculations in terms of tension level are also tenable. For example, a differentiation can be drawn between the pleasures of delight as representing tension increase and of contentment as tension decrease. A definitive interpretation of the results, therefore, must await further experimental work in the area of affect interaction. The approach pursued in the current investigation would seem to offer a promising start in this direction.

Discharge
intensity

7

In this chapter three experiments dealing with determinants of discharge intensity will be described. The strength of cognitive signal discharge, discussed briefly on p. 16, is said to depend upon several factors. Here we shall concern ourselves with variation in facilitation of circuit connections within a network; physical intensity of sensory input; number of circuits triggered by arriving sensory signals; and spacing of sequentially scanned inputs. In each case connections to either affective or motoric subsystems are built into the experimentally formed networks, permitting more precise output measurements via GSR or EMG recordings.

Experiment 8. Affective Discharge to Similar Stimuli Differing in Vividness

The first study varied the facilitation among circuits in two cognitive networks prior to coupling both with anxiety and then testing for relative discharge intensities. Differential network facilitation was accomplished under hypnosis by showing S two objects, one of which was made extremely vivid. The induction procedure (taken from Harold's typescript) was as follows:

E: Now, as you continue to sleep deeply, I'm going to show you something from a game called "Skunk." Can you see this? (shows S a brightly colored box cover with a large drawing of a skunk on it).

S: Yes.

E: This is the cover of the game. The game itself is not important for our purposes. As you can see, it's played with dice and so on. I want you to look very carefully at the skunk. Notice the black and white stripe. That's the tail here, paws, head, face, you can see it very clearly, can't you?

S: Yes.

E: Okay, I want you to fix an image of this skunk in your mind so that you can see it very clearly and visualize all the aspects of it—black and white, the size of it, the shape, and everything else you can see. Just continue to look at it and think about the way it looks. There's also another version of the skunk. Can you see this? (briefly shows S a small die containing a miniature version of the same skunk on one side).

S: Yes.

E: All right, now look again at this cover. Concentrate on the shape of it, the way it looks, every different aspect. Visualize it clearly as you get a strong impression of it in your mind . . . (20 second pause) . . . now close your eyes and continue to sleep deeply. I want you to tell me what pictorial image pops into your mind when I say "visualize a skunk."

S: The one you showed me.

E: Which one? Tell me about it.

S: The one on the cover.

E: Can you describe it for me?

S: Well, it has a white center with a black body. There's a black tail with a white center, and the center portion is sort of wavy, jagged like. It's standing up on its feet, like a human.

In the above exchange E asked S to visualize a skunk in order to be certain that the differential vividness requirement (cover versus die) had been fulfilled. Next came the attachment of affect to the two skunk stimuli:

E: All right, continue to sleep deeply. Next I want you to think back in your own experience and try to tell me about any experience you have had involving a skunk.

S: Well, I was thinking about them run over in the road.

E: Tell me about that.

S: We never run them over but we see them quite often.

E: Have you been close to one of them?

S: In the zoo.

E: Tell me about that experience.

S: Well, they look like cats.

E: What was there that might have been unpleasant about that experience for you?

S: Well, they smell, but if you're downwind from them—I mean if you're in the right direction—you can't smell them.

E: Have you ever been in the wrong direction?

S: Yeah.

E: Tell me about it.

S: Well, it was pretty pungent.

E: What was your reaction?

S: Oh, I've smelled worse things. It wasn't entirely pleasant.

E: How do you think you might react if you got the full impact of the skunk odor, if you were right up close to it?

S: I wouldn't enjoy it.

E: All right, I want you to concentrate now on seeing a skunk in the zoo as you have. Go back in your experience and visualize looking in the cage at the skunk. You're standing right next to it now and you can see it very, very clearly. All of a sudden the smell begins and it gets stronger and stronger and stronger. You can smell it now and your nostrils begin to curl (E had just observed S's nostrils curling) and you are reacting to it very strongly. The smell gets stronger and stronger and you are *more and more upset* by it. What are you going to do? What do you want to do?

S: Get out of there.

E: You want to get out but you can't and the smell is getting stronger and stronger. You can't get out. You can smell it now and you can feel it with your whole body. You want to get out but you can't. It becomes more distasteful all the time, more and more unpleasant (O signals E that GSR reaction is extremely large). Listen carefully now. Whether you're awake or asleep, *whenever a skunk is portrayed in any form whatsoever, you'll have the same feeling you're experiencing now.* After you're awake you will not be able to remember anything that has happened while you were asleep.

The experiment was then conducted in the waking state. S was given a series of 8 trials looking alternately at the cover and die skunk stimuli. Each was held in front of him for 10 seconds, after which he closed his eyes for a 20-second rest period. In Harold's case the hypnotic induction proved to be so strong that tremendous GSR deflections (drops of resistance in the vicinity of 10,000 ohms) accompanied every presentation, and the rapid succession of automatic range changes when the pen reached the upper limit of its swing made accurate scoring impossible. Accordingly, he had to be re-

TABLE 9. Millimeters of GSR Deflection upon Presentation of Cover (C) and Die (D) Stimuli

Harold		Steve		Rudy	
C	32	D	8	D	0
D	1	C	10	C	1
C	29	D	1	D	0
D	0	C	1	C	3
C	30	C	3	C	1
D	0	D	1	D	0
C	0	C	1	C	10
D	0	D	1	D	0

hypnotized and instructed to have a "moderate" reaction, as if the skunk were "at some distance." *

The results are given in Table 9, along with those obtained from Steve and Rudy. A clear trend in the direction of greater GSR upon viewing the more vivid stimulus (C) suggests that pre-existing network facilitation does play a part in regulating ultimate discharge intensity. That the differences cannot be ascribed to variation in strength of the triggering sensory input of C versus D is indicated by Rudy's performance, which was in response to an eyes-closed, imaginal visualization of each stimulus rather than looking at it with eyes opened.

The other S on whom the experiment was carried through to completion was Laura who, for some reason, did not show any GSR deflections at all during the test trials. However, in a subsequent hypnotic inquiry, she reported that the cover skunk had given her "more of a reaction" except that it quickly became "misty from the spray," which made her unable to see it plainly even though it was being exposed in full view. We may speculate that a perceptual inhibition was invoked so rapidly that an affective reaction of sufficient magnitude to register GSR did not have a chance to build up. Steve's hypnotic introspections also indicate more of a difference between stimuli than is reflected by the GSR data. When the cover was shown he had a distinct feeling as if "you gotta move or duck or

* The fact that Harold was able to carry out this instruction and produce moderate GSR deflections during the subsequent waking trials is itself of considerable interest.

do something" whereas, with the die, it "almost seemed like nothing happened, in fact after a while I got kind of contemptuous of it."

Experiment 9. Intensity of Stimulus Input and Degree of Pattern Match as Factors in Response Strength

The next investigation explored the effects on output strength of varying both physical intensity of sensory input and number of cognitive circuits triggered by arriving sensory signals.* S was instructed under hypnosis that "whenever the thought of the paired letters AB passes through your mind, awake or asleep, you will immediately clench your right fist." In the waking state, which carried amnesia for the previous instruction, he was then shown a series of stimuli tachistoscopically at two different speeds to vary input intensity. The five stimuli, chosen to activate different numbers of circuits in the AB network, were AB, AB5, A5, B5, and A5B. Every one was presented a total of 12 times during the course of the experiment, 6 in each of the two speed conditions. EMG sponge electrodes were placed over the forearm muscle and responses to the stimuli were measured by summing millimeters of pen deflection in the integrated record immediately after the flash.

Five Ss took part in the study. For three the faster and slower speeds were .08 versus .11 second, under the same conditions of illumination as described on p. 62. The gap between exposure times was increased for the other two Ss, .11 versus .17 second. Analysis of variance revealed no significant differences between any of the speeds used, which is not to say, of course, that larger gaps or other attempts to vary intensity might not have an appreciable effect.

The number of triggered circuits, however, turned out to be a critical determinant of response strength. Figure 12 portrays the circuits assumed to comprise the AB network. From Table 10 we see that the obtained order of clench strength approximates the order expected in terms of the number of circuits presumably activated by each stimulus pattern (i.e., the extent to which the stimulus pattern "matches" the salient memory traces). Statistical tests from the analysis of variance show that the response to AB (5) is obviously greater than to the next in line, AB5 (4), which in turn has an advantage over A5B (3). No clear differentiation was found among A5, B5, and A5B.

---

* Special acknowledgment is due Carol Reverski and Jerry O'Dell for their assistance in planning this experiment and analyzing the data.

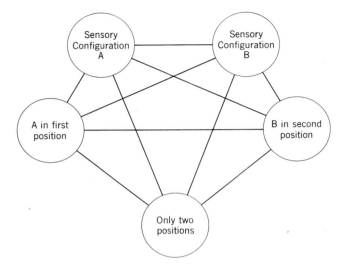

FIGURE 12.   Conceptual representation of cognitive circuits in AB network.

Within the framework of this particular experimental design, it would seem that number of triggered circuits is a more important variable to pursue than speed of presentation.   It should be noted, though, that the stimuli were quite clearly visible and no attempt was made to introduce subliminal registration.

TABLE 10.   Comparison of Stimulus Patterns According to Number of Circuits in AB Network Presumably Triggered and Obtained Strength of Motoric Response

Stimulus Pattern	Number of Circuits Presumably Triggered (see Figure 12)	Obtained Order of Strength of Response
AB	5	1st ⎱ $p < .01$
AB5	4	2nd ⎰
A5	3	3rd ⎱
B5	2	4th ⎰ $p = .05$
A5B	3	5th ⎰

Experiment 10. Sequential Stimulus Patterning and Affective Discharge

The third study * approaches the problem of discharge intensity somewhat differently, by varying the spacing between sequentially scanned patterns of input.

The hypnotized S was given the following instructions:

> When you are awake you are going to be shown some letters in the tachistoscope. Whenever W and J are present at the same time, in the same flash, you will feel very tense and nervous.
>
> W and J may appear adjacent to each other or separated by other letters, but whenever they appear at the same time, in the same flash, you will get the tense and nervous feeling.
>
> On some trials W or J will appear alone, without the other letter. When both do appear, the W will always precede the J.
>
> After you awaken you will be unable to remember what happened while you were asleep.

In the waking state he was then told:

> I am now going to show you some cards in the tachistoscope on which six letters are printed, three on the left and three on the right. Focus on the center dot when I say Ready. After each flash I want you to tell me what letters you saw. The important thing is to see all the letters on each trial and afterward tell me what you saw.

E went over the letters twice to make S familiar with them. The specific letters employed were selected for infrequency of their joint occurrence in common initials and abbreviations. Next the letters were flashed in a practice series to determine a speed at which the stimuli were reported to have been *seen* clearly regardless of subsequent confusion in trying to report them all. For individual Ss the final speeds ranged from .32 to .82 second. The test series was run in 8 blocks of 10 trials, so that each of the following combinations of letters appeared a total of 8 times:

1. KWM QJZ	6. WLQ ZKM
2. QMW JKZ	7. ZKW MJQ
3. WJQ ZMK	8. WZJ QKM
4. KZQ JLM	9. MKW QLZ
5. QKM LZJ	10. MWK ZQJ

* This research was also part of Gerald A. Mendelsohn's doctoral dissertation. See footnote on p. 61 for reference.

TABLE 11.   Sum of GSR Deflections in Three Categories of Spatial Stimulus Separation for Each S

	Category		
Subject	Least	Intermediate	Most
Joe	29.14	16.13	17.13
Fred	26.88	25.38	34.39
Rudy	25.51	18.75	14.25
Max	27.25	23.75	10.75
Steve	14.75	5.71	6.13
Grand Sum	123.53	89.72	82.65

The dependent variable was again millimeters of GSR deflection immediately after the stimulus flash. Only those trials on which both W and J were present and reported seen by S were included in the data analysis, since primary interest lay in measuring the differential strength of *known* activation of the "W and J together" network by the various inputs. The stimuli were categorized in advance into three degrees of spatial separation: combination numbers 3 and 8 from the above list were designated as having W and J least separated; 2 and 7 were placed in the middle; 1 and 10 were called most separated. Table 11 gives the sum of GSR deflections in these three categories for each of the five Ss who participated in the experiment. Application of the F test to the grand sums indicates that the level of GSR associated with the Least category is significantly greater ($p = .05$) than that associated with the other extreme. It is also apparent that the Intermediate and Most categories differ negligibly from one another, which suggests that the spatial effect is operative only within a limited range of separation of the stimulus elements.

Returning to the model, we can depict the network established by the hypnotic induction simply as a strong coupling of a cognitive network labeled "W and J together" to the existing anxiety network (see Figure 13). Any inhibition occurring in response to the evocation of anxiety is typically outweighed by the potent hypnotic suggestion, so some anxiety discharge (GSR) is likely. The experimental task manipulates strength of activation of the "W and J together" network via the different combinations of sensory input. When S scans the flashed letters, which he usually does from left to

Input

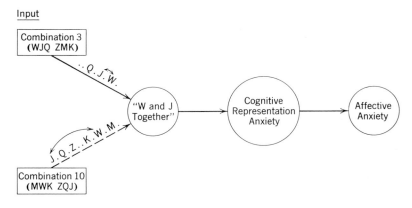

FIGURE 13. Networks presumed to be activated by spatially separated W and J inputs. [*Note:* The "W and J Together" network, which triggers anxiety discharge, is activated at different intensities by arriving combinations of sensory input. In Combination 3 its activation is maximal because the letters W and J appear adjacently (indicated by arrows on input line); in Combination 10 the converse applies.]

right, there are varying time intervals between registrations of the W-J sequence. Combination 3, for example, has the shortest interval, which means that W and J sensory inputs reach the cognitive subsystem almost simultaneously and trigger the "W and J together" network maximally. Combination 10, on the other hand, entails a longer interval so that, by the time J registers, W has already passed through its phase of strongest discharge and the entire network activation is consequently weaker (as shown in Figure 13).

In summary, it seems reasonable to conclude from the three experiments just cited that various determinants of output intensity can be isolated and studied in a controlled laboratory setting. Diverse techniques can readily be called into play to pursue the problem systematically. Next we shall turn our attention to the effects of response feedback, specifically sensory return from anxiety discharges, upon activity in the cognitive subsystem.

Response
feedback 8

The feedback effect of a response has long been noted by psychologists (45). Muscular and glandular discharges, by introducing their own sensory input to the Mental System, presumably can activate the cognitive subsystem like any other source of input. The approach to be presented entails investigation of the cognitive consequences of sensory feedback from anxiety responses. The decision to single out anxiety for study in this experiment, as well as in several of the others already reported, derives from the fact that it seems to provide the most appropriate bridge to psychodynamic phenomena, which the model is committed to consider. The more we can learn experimentally about the role of anxiety, the easier will be our later task of interpreting psychopathology.

Experiment 11. Anxiety-Mediated Generalization

Preliminary steps in the research design dictated the establishment of a series of clearly specified networks consisting of cognitive circuits along with various affective circuits connected to them. The critical manipulation was then executed by inducing strong anxiety discharges and observing the subsequent cognitive outputs. Because of the individualized nature of the task (different personal experiences and levels of affect being involved for the seven Ss who participated), the performance of each S will be taken up in turn according to the order in which he was originally seen.

The work began with Ned, who was asked in a preliminary hypnotic session to recount situations in which he had felt "joyful anticipation, as though one of his fondest dreams was about to come true"; and, at the other extreme, very unpleasant times when he had felt "alone and frightened in the dark." In the experimental session, conducted entirely under hypnosis, some of these experiences along with others gathered incidentally during training were utilized to build the desired networks:

E: You are going to learn to associate some nonsense syllables with a series of experiences or thoughts that you have had in the past. Do you know what a nonsense syllable is?

S: Yes.

E: All right, now you are going to relive each situation and learn to associate a nonsense syllable with it. The first one is the time you were about to land in Mexico City. You are back in the plane now, full of anticipation that a very pleasant dream is about to come true, and as you look down on the lights of the city all the emotions you felt then are being re-experienced. Now as you continue to relive that same situation the nonsense syllable you associate with it is BEJ. What nonsense syllable comes to mind?

S: BEJ.

E: Fine. Now relax and sleep deeply. Next you're going to remember a dream you had of falling down a chute. You can't grab hold of anything and you don't know whether you will ever stop falling, or whether you'll hit the bottom and be badly hurt. As you're having this dream again, you associate the nonsense syllable MIV with falling down the chute. What nonsense syllable comes to mind as you are dreaming?

S: MIV.

E: Fine. Tell me what nonsense syllable comes to mind while you are about to land in Mexico City?

S: BEJ.

E: And falling down the chute?

S: MIV.

E: All right, relax and next you're going back to the time when you were a child playing with your cousins in their family's restaurant and you're about to be the cashier, which is what you've always wanted to do. You're back in that same situation now, feeling the same way you did then, and the nonsense syllable that comes to mind is TUD. What comes to mind?

S: TUD.

E: That's right. Now think back to the time when you were seated at
the table in this room and you were looking in the machine that flashes
pictures. Remember the times you were shown the picture of the man
knocking on a door in full view. You can see that picture very clearly
now and, as you look at it, the nonsense syllable that comes to mind
is VOF. What comes to mind?

S: VOF.

The list of paired situations and syllables was then rehearsed a few
times in random order until it was apparent that S knew the associations perfectly. Up to this point, four highly facilitated networks—
each with circuits representing a personal experience, an associated
affect, and an attached nonsense syllable—have been formed: two
pleasant (BEJ and TUD), one laden with anxiety (MIV), and one
seemingly neutral (VOF). Next, E proceeded to make use of a cognitively unrelated set of experiences in order to trigger strong anxiety
discharges, in the midst of which he asked a crucial question designed
to tap the cognitive output elicited by those discharges:

E: Now, while you continue to sleep deeply, you're going to relive some
other experiences that you have talked about before. As I describe
these experiences you will immediately be back in the same situation,
feeling the same way you did then. The first one is the time you were
in the army and you were on guard duty at night. Back in the army
now and it's the middle of the night. It seems as though you're the
only one moving in the whole area. Suddenly in the shadow you can
almost see someone else moving and it's an odd feeling. You go out
into the middle of the block, and you hear a noise, a twig snapping
or something like that, and you think you're going to jump out of your
skin. Now you continue to feel this way as we go on to another
experience. This time you're a sophomore in high school, in gym class,
and your classmates have rolled you up in a mat. You feel like you're
never going to be able to get out and it's closing in on you. You're
back rolled up in the mat, feeling the same way you did then, even
more strongly now, experiencing the same emotions as we move on
to the next experience. You're a little boy and you've just been
awakened and dragged out of bed in the middle of the night. You've
been taken outside and stood on a couch under a tree. You're watching the house burn and you feel the same way you did then, very
strongly, as you stand there and the flames are shooting up. Still feeling the same way as we go to the next situation. You're a little boy
again and your older brother and sisters locked you in the upper part
of the garage. You're locked in the garage and you think you may
never be able to get out. You want to holler and yell and kick the
door away. They've been talking about witches and things like that
and you're crying and looking everywhere, in all the corners. Things

may come out of the corners at you and this is how you feel now. You're back in that situation and feeling the emotions very strongly, and now tell me what nonsense syllable comes to mind.

S: MIV.

What is taking place during this fairly brief (and one-sided!) exchange between E and S? First of all, a number of different networks are made salient during the learning period. Figure 14 schematizes, again in an oversimplified fashion, one of these experience–nonsense syllable networks. The dream of falling down the chute is relived, triggering an anxiety signal of sufficient intensity to outlast inhibition (not shown in diagram) and result in effector discharges. The cognitive representation of anxiety is coupled by induction to the network Falling Down Chute, in turn linked with the cognitive MIV network. The latter acquires a two-way connection to the cognitive representation of anxiety through contiguity of discharge, in addition to being hooked up to its own counterpart in the motoric subsystem. The other networks are analogous except that those containing BEJ and TUD include positive affect and VOF is affectively neutral.

We are now at the point where the strong anxiety mood is induced. Mounting affective discharges feed back sensory input which activates the cognitive representation of anxiety. The signal of the

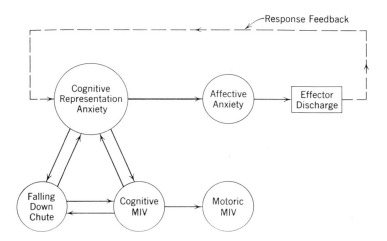

FIGURE 14. Illustrative networks established during preliminary pairing of experiences with nonsense syllables. [*Note:* Connections in the cognitive subsystem link Falling Down Chute and MIV to Cognitive Representation Anxiety, which instigates discharge of the entire anxiety network.]

latter reverberates and spreads to its already coupled cognitive circuits. When E suddenly asks for a nonsense syllable, the four syllable networks probably are all equally facilitated. However MIV, by virtue of its extra facilitation from the reverberatory spread, discharges more strongly than the other three syllables and wins out in the competition for both priority of hyperfacilitation and motoric output. Thus we have supportive evidence for the contention that sensory feedback of anxiety itself can lead to specific cognitive consequences, in the present instance tipping the balance in favor of the syllable MIV.

The above interpretation assumes that the anxiety mood situations did *not* provide cognitive *content* inputs predisposed to favor MIV over the other syllables. If there were significant content overlap between the chute dream and the episodes recreated for the mood induction, this would offer a simpler explanation of the result than invoking anxiety feedback. To minimize the likelihood of content similarity, care was taken to choose an anxiety-syllable experience as different as possible from the mood situations. Also E deliberately avoided any affective labels during the induction so as not to have S form a cognitive tie of "unpleasantness" between the chute dream and the mood experiences.

In addition, an empirical check was carried out immediately following S's response. Still under hypnosis, he was given amnesia for both the mood induction and his reply but not for the original pairing of experiences and nonsense syllables. The dialogue then went as follows:

E: You're sleeping deeply, completely relaxed, and not feeling any emotions at all. Now I'm going to show you a card that has four experiences mentioned on it. These are four episodes that you have mentioned in the past. You're going to look at the card in a very detached way—the experiences won't bring any emotions to mind—and rank them according to how unpleasant they were. Assign number 1 to the most unpleasant, 2 to the next, and so on. Remember you'll be completely detached as you rank them. Now look at this card and read the four things aloud.

S: On guard duty . . . rolled in mat . . . watching house burn . . . locked in garage.

E: All right, which was the most unpleasant?

S: Locked in the garage.

E: Number 2?

S: On guard duty.

E: Number 3?

S: Rolled in mat.

E: Then number 4 is watching the house burn. Now tell me what nonsense syllable comes to mind.

S: No special one.

E: What comes to mind?

S: All four seem to be running through my mind at the same time.

E: Okay, just pick one of the four.

S: VOF.

E: Why did you pick VOF?

S: I don't know. Perhaps it had nothing to do with the experience. It
starts and ends in a fricative.

If the response MIV in the experiment proper were explainable in
terms of content overlap, one would certainly expect that syllable to
be given in the control task, which even introduced the "unpleasant"
label for S to make use of. Similarly, any attempt to account for the
experimental result in terms of MIV having been triggered directly
via activation, by the mood episodes themselves, of the commonly
shared Cognitive Representation Anxiety is also rendered less plausible
by the control finding. The fact that S did not say MIV thus lends
added credence to the anxiety feedback interpretation.

After completion of the control task, S was asked to repeat the
original pairings to be certain that all had been available during the
experiment. Then a hypnotic inquiry was conducted to get his introspections about the mood induction. He reported being very frightened and wanting to jump off the couch as the episodes were relived.
The sensation was described as "the same or very similar" to the
feeling which accompanied the Chute dream, but he denied having
consciously thought of the latter in the course of the induction.

The second subject in the experiment was Rudy, who learned to
pair the following experiences with the nonsense syllables: telling a
funny joke at a party (BEJ); being apprehended for stealing by a
department store detective (MIV); meeting a girl friend in Paris
(TUD); and looking at the cartoon of the man knocking on a door
(VOF). The mood induction centered around these episodes from the
past: hearing a noise while in bed; having a fantasy of being killed
by a dirty, ugly old man; awakened late at night by someone who
wanted to come into the house to get street directions; and looking up
in bed to see a horrible big, black spider crawling nearby. As S
relived the last experience, the following conversation took place:

E: Now tell me what nonsense syllable comes into your mind.

S: Oh . . VIZ . . MIZ.

E: How do you spell it?

S: Maybe R-I-Z or M-I-Z.

E: Which one of the four that you learned earlier was it?
S: I think I can remember the four . . . BEJ . . I can't remember the second one . . the third is TUD . . the fourth is VOF . . the second one is MIV . . MIV is the one that came to mind a moment ago.

Though distorted in its motoric expression, the critical syllable does seem to be the one which occurred to S. Interestingly, the ensuing attempt to give him amnesia for both the mood situations and his saying MIV (which he had spontaneously forgotten a moment before!) could not be fully accomplished on several different tries. Upon close questioning the amnesia repeatedly broke down, which rendered the control task meaningless. As expected he again responded MIV, after ranking the episodes for unpleasantness, on the grounds that "it was the only one I could remember."

For Tom the anxiety experience paired with MIV had him walking to a dance with a girl and suddenly being surrounded by a menacing gang. The mood episodes involved being lost in the woods; waking up alone in the middle of the night; having a fantasy of being abandoned inside a big store; and dreaming of being deserted in a large house. Like the others he thought of MIV when asked for a syllable at the end of the induction. The control task found him pausing unusually long (over 15 seconds) before responding MIV again. The reason he gave for MIV having come to mind after ranking the statements on the card was that he "felt the same," which suggests that the instruction to feel detached did not take fully. The latter interpretation is supported by the fact that the GSR revealed several deflections during the ranking procedure.

The next S was Steve, for whom the anxiety experience (BEJ this time) was the recollection of looking into the tachistoscope at the loaded Blacky picture previously used in some other experiments. The anxiety discharge was built up by having him relive awakening in the middle of the night and thinking of his mother's impending death; walking through a cemetery after dark; climbing up to a sealed-off attic; and lying in bed watching an eerie light shine on the curtains. He replied to the request for a nonsense syllable by saying that two came to mind, first VOF * and then BEJ. Since the anxiety syllable was given second instead of first, the control task was abandoned in favor of an immediate hypnotic inquiry, which follows:

---

* Paired with a Blacky picture connoting a terribly grueling army experience on the return leg of a forced march. On the verge of collapse, he was able, by powerful self-exhortation, to survive the ordeal better than his buddies, which made him feel "grim, determined, and proud."

E: Tell me what ran through your mind when you thought of VOF.

S: Well, when you said "What nonsense syllable comes to mind?" I thought, Oh my God, I forgot the nonsense syllables! Then I suddenly thought of VOF and figured that's a funny one to think of, as if it meant I should buckle down or something and not be so scared. Then I thought of BEJ.

E: Why did you think of that?

S: I couldn't think of what was supposed to be connected with BEJ and it didn't seem appropriate either, but those were the only two that came in.

E: Did the experience associated with VOF come into your mind?

S: No, not the forced march experience, but it did seem like a cue to shape up and get some self-control. I was just a bundle of nerves and VOF was like a signal to calm down.

E: And then BEJ came in?

S: Right after I thought VOF I figured there must be something more appropriate and then BEJ came in. But it wasn't connected to anything, it just popped in. So I decided that's what came to mind, so I'd better report it.

It seems that here we have a case of overwhelming anxiety serving first to disrupt cognitive activity momentarily, which in turn led to a mild panic reaction ("Oh my God, I forgot the nonsense syllables!"). Cognitively panic, which was described by S during his reliving of the forced march episode, must have had a highly facilitated connection to the VOF network attached to that experience. Response feedback from the immediate discharge of VOF probably set off a counter-affective process (see competing affects experiment in Chapter 6) as indicated by S's remark that "VOF was like a signal to calm down." Thinking of the syllable also dispelled the original reason for feeling panicky, namely, the inability to bring to mind any nonsense syllable at all. Once that feeling subsided, the BEJ network very likely was triggered and its signal hyperfacilitated in much the same way as the anxiety syllable was elicited in the three previous Ss.

The next S, Harold, was the first who did not yield any evidence directly suggesting the operation of anxiety feedback. His critical syllable (TUD) was paired with a dread of having stitches taken in a bleeding finger. The following were mood episodes: going up a dark staircase; being locked in a doghouse; blindfolded and abandoned by a group of boys; and thinking someone is about to break into the bedroom. The nonsense syllable that came to mind was FEP,* which he described as "the first one I learned and the easiest to

---

* Paired with a pleasant experience of attending a concert.

remember." Apparently the superior strength of the cognitive FEP network won out over the TUD network despite any extra facilitation which anxiety feedback may have added to the latter.

The sixth S was Laura, who responded in the same convincing fashion as Ned. Her anxiety syllable (TUD) was also attached to a previously loaded Blacky picture. The mood situations included being afraid of an escaped hatchet slayer in the vicinity; being intercepted by some boys as she rode her bicycle at night; babysitting with her brother in a severe thunderstorm; and mistaking her own pulse beats for someone's footsteps. At the end of the induction TUD came to mind and later in the control task she thought of MIV because "that's the one I know best."

Victor, the last to take part in this experiment, performed the same way as Harold by replying with the first syllable he learned (MIV) * rather than the anxiety one (VOF). The latter was paired with a fantasy of being about to be devoured by an approaching spider. These were the mood selections: hearing a noise from behind in a cemetery; afraid of monsters in the dark; running away from home; and hiding from someone who threatened to beat him. Subsequent hypnotic inquiry revealed that the induced anxiety suddenly vanished when E asked for the syllable:

E: What made you think of MIV when you were feeling afraid?
S: I wasn't afraid then. I don't know.
E: Did you stop being afraid all of a sudden?
S: Yes.
E: What stopped you from being afraid?
S: You did.
E: How did I stop you?
S: By talking. You asked for a nonsense syllable.
E: Did you have any other thoughts besides MIV?
S: BEJ and TUD.
E: VOF did not come into your mind at all?
S: No, it's hard.
E: What makes it hard?
S: It's hard to say.

To summarize, there are indications from the performance of 5 of the 7 Ss that anxiety feedback per se can have direct cognitive consequences. This is more than a simple demonstration of the common sense observation that moods have some kind of influence on thoughts, since the experiment was set up to minimize opportunity for purely cognitive content connections. The ruling out of content as a mediat-

* Also paired with a pleasant experience, receiving a bicycle on his birthday.

ing link permits a more precise formulation of the feedback effect than is otherwise possible.

Perhaps of even greater interest than the above phenomenon are the intriguing possibilities for future research suggested by the findings. Several experimental manipulations offer promise for spelling out the interaction of affect and cognition. For example, there are some hints that exceptionally strong triggering of anxiety increases the likelihood of disruptive action in the cognitive subsystem. Rudy's distortion of the critical syllable ("VIZ-MIZ," etc.) was immediately preceded by a large GSR deflection, as were the responses of Harold and Victor, both of whom gave the first syllable learned. For the Ss who showed the experimental effect most clearly (Ned and Laura) there were no such GSR deflections. It would seem profitable to regulate the intensity of anxiety discharge directly and observe systematically the cognitive consequences of varied amounts. Along the same lines, one could manipulate facilitation of the cognitive content networks differentially to study their contribution to the interaction. Inhibition, as we have already seen in earlier chapters, is also susceptible to operational control. Thus experimental settings of this type would lend themselves readily to detailed analysis of the roles in cognitive processing played by inhibition, anxiety discharge and feedback, and pre-existing circuit facilitation.

Memory 9

This chapter, which concludes the section on recent research efforts pertaining to the conceptual model, deals with memory in the form of recall of a series of stimuli. Six Ss were asked to "name all the Blacky pictures as fast as you can" on a number of different occasions under a variety of conditions (see Figure 15 for a complete set of the cartoons).* Effects on *sequence* of recall of the eleven pictures were noted in the case of prior affective manipulations of individual pictures, specific mood inductions, preliminary damping and sensitizing of all affects, etc. The general purpose was to observe alterations in discharge sequence occurring both spontaneously and in response to specified inputs immediately preceding the recall task. Though more exploratory in scope than the experiments described earlier and somewhat *ex post facto* in interpretation, the approach is sufficiently suggestive to warrant reporting the results in some detail.

Experiment 12. Manipulations of Sequence in Recall of Blacky Pictures

The waking and hypnotic recall trials for all Ss were begun after several exposures to the series of pictures, e.g., telling stories, narrat-

---

* Previous work on recall of Blacky pictures is reported in reference 2.

ing personal experiences suggested by each picture, and ranking defense preferences. S was allowed to use any short descriptive phrase he wished to identify the Blacky stimuli, though usually these corresponded closely to the introductory phrases accompanying E's initial presentation of the cartoons. The criterion for terminating a particular trial was a pause of 30 seconds without a picture being named. Forgetting typically occurred only in the early trials and S was informed afterward of the ones he had missed, since the major focus of study was alteration in sequence rather than omission. The number of trials ranged from 16 in Rudy's case to 111 for Harold.

Induced reversals in sequence. One experimental phenomenon, investigated in four Ss, was the induced change in sequence of pairs of pictures previously given in fixed order. For example, Ned consistently named Cartoon II (his anxiety-laden picture) just before XI (the one to which positive affect had been attached under hypnosis) no matter where in the overall sequence the pair appeared. On 15 out of 20 trials II immediately preceded XI; on two others (Trials #1 and 3 when the order was just beginning to be established) a single picture intervened. The reversal which took place on the remaining three occasions thus assumes special interest:

1. The first reversal, XI coming before II, happened on Trial #4(H),* which followed the hypnotic instruction that "no feelings of any kind will accompany naming the Blacky pictures this time" (on the next four trials—two the same day and two more five days later—II resumed its position ahead of XI).

2. Prior to Trial #9(H), third in a series of four trials on that day, S was made to relive a number of pleasant experiences, with the result that XI then preceded II for the second time (the succeeding seven trials, spread over three different days, all showed the return of the persistent II-XI order).

3. Before #17(H) the affective associations were hypnotically removed from both pictures and the ensuing list suddenly found XI just before II again (the affects were then re-attached and II regained its priority for the several trials thereafter).

It behooves us to examine, in light of the model, the nature of these three interventions which produced the striking sequence reversal. A plausible interpretation of the general affective damping instruction ("no feelings") is that it serves as an input for activation of the inhibition mechanism and subsequent direction of inhibitory action toward

* (H) will be used to indicate that a trial was conducted under hypnosis; (W) for the waking state.

I. Oral Eroticism

II. Oral Sadism

III. Anal Sadism

IV. Oedipal Intensity

V. Masturbation Guilt

VI. Castration Anxiety

VII. Identification

VIII. Sibling Rivalry

IX. Guilt Feelings   X. Ego Ideal

XI. Love Object

FIGURE 15. Complete set of Blacky Pictures.

all pictures with emotional loading. Of the eleven cartoons the strongest affects must have been those for II and XI, which had already undergone intensive hypnotic induction. It is also clear from our overall efforts at removing affects from Ss that anxiety associations are by far the most difficult to undo. Therefore successful inhibitory action in the case of II must have required a greater number of repetitions than for XI, which implies that the connections between cognitive and motoric (resulting in naming) circuits in the network of II were weakened more than in XI.

According to the above line of reasoning we should not only expect the weakened II to follow XI on Trial #4 as it did, but *both* pictures should be delayed more than usual because of the extra inhibition involved for the two in S's execution of the instruction to remove any kind of feeling. This turns out to be the case, for the pair came at the beginning of both trials earlier that day and in the middle of the list on the critical Trial #4. The same reasoning should especially apply to Trial #17, before which inhibitory action was directed by instruction *solely* to the affects of II and XI. In addition to the observed reversal phenomenon, both pictures came near the end of the list on that trial in contrast to their appearance at the beginning on prior Trials #15 and 16. The general damping instruction was repeated before Trial #12 and failed to show the reversal, but the delay of both pictures was again very marked. The third instance of reversal occurred on #9(H), which was preceded by induction of a very pleasant mood. Here it seems likely that response feedback (see Chapter 8) of positive affect tipped the discharge balance in favor of XI, the positive picture, over II.

In summary, there were 4 out of 20 trials (#4, 9, 12, 17) on which the model would lead us to expect a reversal; on three of these the reversal actually took place. It did *not* appear on any of the other sixteen trials where there was no reason for such an expectation. Also, the model interpretation suggests that both pictures should be delayed only on three occasions (#4, 12, 17), all of which showed the effect clearly.

Another kind of reversal manipulation was carried out with Harold and Steve. The former had been pairing Cartoons III and VI, neither of which had prior affective inductions, in that order over a series of trials. Under hypnosis a pleasant experience was then attached to VI and a neutral one to III with equal emphasis, the prediction again being that response feedback of positive affect would provide extra facilitation to the VI network. On the immediately following hypnotic recall trial VI did turn out to precede III. A

similar experiment with Steve, X serving as the positive stimulus and
VI as the neutral this time, yielded the same finding: VI came first
until the hypnotic induction, right after which it followed X.   The
same procedure was repeated two days later with identical results.

Still another alteration was attempted with Tom, whose 24 recall
trials are summarized in Figure 16.   For 13 of the first 16 trials II
immediately preceded VII, including seven successive times prior to

FIGURE 16.   Tom's recall series

Date	Trial #	Preceded by	Sequence of Blacky Pictures
June 30	1(W)	Spontaneous Stories & Human Experiences	I-(VI)-X-XI-VIII-III-II-IV (Omitted V-VII-IX)
	2(H)	Cartoon preferences	I-XI-X-V-(VI)-IV-VIII-IX-III-II-VII
July 1	3(W)	—	I-XI-X-VII-V-III-IV-VIII-II (Omitted (VI)-IX)
July 15	4(W)	Anxiety attached to VI; pleasure to XI	I-X-XI-II-VII-III-IV-VIII-(VI).....V (Omitted IX)
	5(H)	—	I-X-XI-II-VII-III-V-IV-VIII-(VI) (Omitted IX)
July 28	6(H)	—	I-X-XI-III-V-II-VII-IX-IV-VIII-(VI)
	7(H)	"No feelings"	I-X-XI-II-VII-IV-VIII-III-V-IX-(VI)
	8(H)	"Magnified feelings"	(VI)-I-X-XI-II-VII-III-V-IV-VIII-IX
	9(H)	Anxiety attached to I	I-(VI)-X-XI-VII-II-IV-VIII-IX-V-III
	10(H)	Pleasure attached to VI in place of anxiety	I-X-XI-II-VII-III-V-IX-(VI)...IV-VIII
July 29	11(W)	Anxiety again attached to VI	(VI)-I-X-XI-IV-VIII-III-V-IX-II-VII
	12(H)	—	(VI)-I-X-XI-II-VII-IV-VIII-III-V-IX
July 31	13(W)	—	(VI)-I-X-XI-VIII-IV-II-VII-IX-III-V
	14(H)	—	(VI)-I-XI-IV-VIII-X-III-V-IX-II-VII
	15(H)	"No thoughts and no feelings"	I-XI-X-II-VII-III-V-IX-VIII-IV.....(VI)
August 4	16(W)	—	I-(VI)-X-XI-II-VII-III-V-IX-VIII-IV
	17(H)	Anxiety attached to II; pleasure to VII	I-VII-X-XI-VIII-IV-IX-(VI)-II-III-V
August 7	18(W)	—	I-(VI)-X-XI-III-V-II-VII-VIII-IV-IX
	19(H)	—	I-(VI)-II-X-XI-IX-III-V-VIII-IV-VII
	20(H)	"No thoughts and no feelings"	I-X-XI-VII-II-III-V-IV-VIII-IX-(VI)
	21(H)	"Magnified feelings"	I-(VI)-II-X-XI-V-III-VIII-IV-IX....VII
	22(H)	"No feelings"	I-X-XI-IV-VIII-III-V-VII-II-IX-(VI)
	23(W)	—	I-(VI)-II-VII-X-XI-IV-VIII-IX..III-V
August 11	24(H)	"No feelings; no thoughts about VI"	I-II-VII-III-V-X-XI-IV-VIII-IX.....(VI)

#17(H). Since the pair came in the middle of the list on #16(W), we decided to try a "billiard shot" on #17—split the two and make them move in opposite directions. The technique settled on to force VII forward in the list was to attach a pleasant experience to it beforehand; in order to delay II an episode involving anxiety was associated with that picture, on the assumption that inhibition automatically instigated by the anxiety (analogous to repression in psychoanalytic terminology) would weaken its network. The success of this maneuver is shown in Trial #17 of Figure 16, where VII jumped from sixth to second place and II slipped from fifth to ninth.

Effects of automatic inhibition. The delaying effect of inhibition, not hypnotically directed, receives support from several sources. For Tom (see Figure 16 again) we can observe the fate of Cartoon VI in the first three trials, before it was given a strong anxiety induction under hypnosis. The theme of his story was that Blacky probably felt glad to see Tippy getting hurt; later in the Human Experiences task he said the picture reminded him of idle curiosity, like standing by and watching an accident. Neither of these responses suggests that anxiety was activated sufficiently to trigger the inhibition mechanism and it is not surprising therefore to find VI appearing early on Trial #1, especially since it was cognitively strong as a consequence of having been the first picture inquired about in the HE procedure (similarly Cartoon I was first in the story order). Between Trials #1 and 2 Tom sorted the cartoons according to his preferences for them and chose VI as worst of all because cutting off a dog's tail made him lament the fact "we're always trying to change things, like my father trying to change breeds in his livestock." By this time VI obviously had stirred up a fair amount of anxiety, but the accompanying inhibitory action was probably counteracted somewhat by the picture's increased cognitive strength due to its having been singled out as worst. Hence on Trial #2 it moves back to the middle of the sequence. On #3 two days later, however, the cognitive advantage is no longer present and automatic inhibition results in the picture being forgotten completely.

The other two Ss whose recall series were started prior to specific hypnotic inductions for the pictures were Laura and Steve, both of whom gave evidence of delay for anxiety-laden stimuli. Steve, for example, frequently forgot IX and V and occasionally I during the first nine trials (all in one session) despite the fact that his omissions were pointed out each time. The final confirmation of automatic inhibitory action came at the end of the session, when he reminisced:

"I kept forgetting three of the pictures—nursing, conscience, and . . . I can't remember the other one" (Masturbation Guilt!).

Position of anxiety-laden pictures. Of particular importance for the model is the position of S's loaded picture, i.e., the one to which anxiety had been strongly attached under hypnosis, throughout the recall series. In Tom's case (see Figure 16 again) the anxiety induction for VI took place before Trial #4 and the delay effect persisted through #7. Then the instruction was given that he would be extremely sensitive to all feelings accompanying the pictures, so that any kind of emotion would be greatly magnified on the subsequent trial. This catapulted VI from last to first place, presumably as a consequence of affective response feedback, in turn a result of anxiety discharge having exceeded the inhibitory mechanism's upper limit of effectiveness. From that trial on, the highly facilitated VI appeared very early (either first or second) with the exception of hypnotic Trials #10, 15, 17, 20, 22, and 24. The noteworthy feature on five of these occasions when VI came late in the sequence is that the preliminary hypnotic instruction necessitated inhibitory action. Before #10 the anxiety for VI had to be inhibited in order for positive affect to be substituted; #15, 20, 22, and 24 were all preceded by damping instructions. (Trial #17, where VI was somewhat delayed but not all the way to the end of the list like the other exceptions, is an irrelevant special case because VII was experimentally led, by the attachment of pleasure, into the spot normally occupied by VI; also II was loaded with anxiety, further upsetting the *status quo*.) Adding to the force of the inhibition interpretation is the fact that there was no special basis for inhibition to be invoked before any of the trials on which VI came early. In other words, all the trials from #8 on fit the theory.

Tom's results are supported when we examine the four other Ss who had anxiety loadings attached to specific pictures. The trials preceded by damping instructions show the loaded stimulus to be consistently about 8th in mean position for each S. There was considerable variation in the picture's position on nondamped trials, depending probably on its cognitive strength in the particular S's repertory. In general, then, we have good evidence for the contention that, whenever inhibitory action is involved in the execution of hypnotic instructions, the picture whose network is weakened by that action will be greatly delayed in its sequential position on the subsequent recall trial.

Damped versus sensitized trials. Further comparisons of damped versus sensitized trials are available in the records of Harold and

Steve, both of whom were given extended recall series. Harold, the only S for whom all trials were timed, completed the list most quickly when the trial followed a "no thoughts and no feelings" instruction. The mean completion time for those hypnotic trials was 16.6 seconds compared to 22.4 seconds for sensitized trials and 24.7 seconds for hypnotic trials not preceded by specific inductions. Of 14 occasions on which the damped and sensitized trials were adjacent in varying order, the former took less time to finish on 12. It should be noted that Harold did not have a specifically loaded picture on most of his 111 trials, so that no repeated inhibition was needed to carry out the damping instruction. He was able to develop mnemonic groupings (very highly facilitated connections between picture networks) which came out almost by rote each time. The inhibition of thoughts as well as affects associated with the pictures seems to have maximized the smooth flow from one picture network to the next. Infrequent presence of anxiety-laden stimuli also left the sensitized trials relatively free of potentially disruptive occurrences, so their completion times are well within his normal range.

Steve's 76 trials included five instances of "no thoughts and no feelings" and four of "magnified feelings." Times for the former were 28, 24, 26, 20, and 32 seconds on Trials #22, 26, 34, 35, and 47 respectively; for the latter 100, 98, 74, and 84 seconds on nearby Trials #23, 27, 37, and 48 respectively. In addition to these non-overlapping, highly differentiated time distributions, the GSR, routinely attached during Steve's recalls, revealed only a few minor deflections on the damped series in contrast to extremely large ones on the sensitized. The exceptional intensity of affective discharges for Steve under this condition presumably resulted in the activation of "irrelevant" cognitive circuits sharing the same affective connections as the Blacky circuits. Very likely these competing signals caused delays in processing the Blacky responses themselves.

Steve's introspective reports. The flavor of the hypnotically induced effects, as well as valuable insights into the nature of recall processes, is conveyed by Steve's introspections given upon E's request immediately after many of the trials. Listed below are verbatim excerpts along with the recall sequences to which they refer. Most of these introspections bear on his reactions to the anxiety-laden picture, IX (conscience figure), for which the hypnotic induction took place prior to Trial #18(H). Also at that time X was given the positive affective induction of making him feel "grim, proud, and determined." Each dot between pictures in the recall list indicates a pause of approximately three seconds' duration:

Trial #18(H) (October 8) . X . XI . IX . . . . VI . IV . VIII . II
. . . . III . I . V . . . . . . (Omitted VII)

(H) It seemed harder to remember them this time. I was going to say
VI * but I started to think of X right away and it seemed as though I
had to say that one first. Then it was kind of hard to slip on to the
other ones. Then IX came up and, I don't know, I seemed to feel
kind of determined and all that for X but I didn't seem to get very
scared when I thought of IX. I got to thinking about that and I
just couldn't seem to think of another one. It just seemed hard to
remember what they were any more. Toward the end it was hard
to wake up enough to think of them.

Comment: IX clearly acquired disruptive influence on this trial.
Repeated inhibitory attempts apparently succeeded in reducing the
anxiety discharge of IX itself but, in the process, connections among
contiguously discharging circuits were weakened and performance
on the list suffered. Whatever anxiety from IX did get discharged
probably contributed to the interference by activating irrelevant cognitive circuits ("I got to thinking about that") via response feedback.

Trial #32(H) (October 10) X-XI-VI-IV-VIII-III-II . VII-V-I . . IX

(H) I was afraid to say the last one. Not afraid, it was kind of hard to
say. I knew there was one left that I was putting off saying. It's
hard to decide which one it is but you know there's one you really
don't want to think about and you don't want to say. Every once
in a while it starts to pop into your mind and you kind of shut it
off or something. I noticed that I never actually think of IX. I
start to, I know there's something else there in that group, but I can't
quite seem to remember it until finally there's nothing left but that
one.

Comment: Here we have a vivid description corresponding to inhibitory action upon IX's network. The latter cannot be fully triggered, including the motoric circuits leading to naming the picture,
until additional input (one picture still left) tips the balance.

Trial #37(H) (October 10) ("Magnified feelings") . X . XI . . VI-IV-
VIII . . II . . . . V . I . III . . VII . . IX

(H) The funniest thing was I thought of IX before I thought of VII.
The two of them seemed to get kind of confused. It's just that I
always group them and if I say one I know I have to say the other.
They seem to bring about the same reactions almost, one implies
the other. . . . You know if you're going to play the game you

* S's identifying phrases for each picture are reproduced here as Roman nu-
merals to conform to the presentation of the recall sequence itself.

have to say them when they pop into your mind, so you say the emotionally loaded one and then get all broken up. (E: Has a picture ever popped into your mind and you didn't say it until later on?) Well, every once in a while it seems IX starts to pop into mind and you kind of shove it back out again. Sometimes you think to yourself "What about that one?" and then you just kind of shove it back. It doesn't really come in as a full-blown picture, if it did I would say it. It doesn't really quite get a chance to get that far before I quick think of something else until there's nothing else left.

Comment: In the first part S is indicating that, by repeated contiguity, the networks of VII and IX have become so closely interconnected that the former has acquired some of the anxiety of the latter. The remainder of the passage is again a very graphic description of inhibitory action. We are inclined, of course, to dismiss S's impression of deliberately "shoving it back" as a conscious by-product of processes occurring automatically in the circuits themselves.

Trial #44(W) (October 17) VI-X-XI . III-II-IV-VIII . V-I-VII . IX

(W)   It's funny about IX. It automatically follows VII, but it seems like I'm about to say it and suddenly I can't remember what it is I'm about to say.

Comment: The above corroborates in waking inquiry the comments relevant to inhibition previously made under hypnosis. It should be mentioned in passing that recall performance of our Ss in the waking state does not seem to differ appreciably from the hypnotic state as far as omissions and sequence are concerned.

Trial #47(H) (October 17) ("No feelings") VI . X-XI-IV-VIII . II-III-I-V-VII . IX

(H)   It seems like both X and IX were still—they didn't seem to cue as much emotion—but it's just hard to get by them. You know they seem to have a lot of significance and you just can't shut it off quite as easily. Seems like we did this before (previous damped trials) and they used to just whip right by, but it's harder now. I'm too used to getting involved and everything. As I'd come to them I'd say there was nothing to worry about this time or something like that, but there still is a little hesitation there.

Comment: The increasing difficulty of inhibiting affect when the affective networks themselves are continually being strengthened by repeated facilitation is given expression in this excerpt. S's self-instruction for inhibition, i.e., executing the "no feelings" command, is also interesting ("nothing to worry about this time").

Trial #48(H) (October 17) ("Magnified feelings") (VI and VIII loaded with anxiety earlier) . X . XI . . . . III . IV . . VIII . . V-I . . VI . . . . II . . . VII . . IX

(H)   That was difficult. It was fraught with emotion. X was standard, the same old thing (grim and determined). Whenever we're doing this with a high emotional key XI always feels a little bit tender, kind of soft, maybe I think of my wife or something. Right after XI I felt confused. I didn't know what I should do to VI. I knew it came there without really thinking of it—it had to come there pretty close to the beginning but I wasn't sure what I was supposed to do with it. I didn't want to think of it because I wasn't sure so I skipped to something else. (E: Did you actually think of the picture and of saying it?) I don't think so. It's like you've got a black box and you know there's something in it, you've got an idea what's in it and you know how good or how bad it is, but you don't know exactly for sure if it's a snake or a rat or just what it is—so instead of opening it you just push it back someplace . . . Later when it came out it bothered me . . . VII and IX seemed pretty bad. They were frightening. Fast and all fired to get out. When you think of VII it starts to build up and then when you say VII it kind of goes up pretty steep. Then there's a hesitation, it seems like I always stutter or I always say uh or something. And then finally you push it out—you say IX and then shboom! Then you relax.

Comment: Here we have a vivid account of S's response to the sensitizing instruction. Indeed the GSR confirmation of his anxiety reaction almost seems superfluous. The narration of the black box with a snake inside (note the classic Freudian symbolism elicited by VI, the castration picture!) is reminiscent of his reports concerning inhibition on Trials #32 and 37.

Trial #63(H) (November 10) (All associations and affects removed earlier from pictures) VI-X-IX-XI-III-II-IV-VIII-V-I-VII

(H)   Now there seems to be a tie linking X and IX. These are different this time, one calls the other to mind it seems. Before, when they had the emotion on them, every time you named X then right away you'd remember that there were two significant pictures in the series, but it didn't call a specific picture to mind because it called your attention to the fact that there was an unpleasant aspect to the whole series someplace. Somewhere in it there was a joker.

Comment: The dramatic appearance of IX right after X, displacing XI which had invariably accompanied X from the very beginning, supports the model interpretation that inhibition is triggered automatically by activation of the anxiety network. In the absence of such activation (it should be mentioned parenthetically that it took numerous repetitions to remove all traces of anxiety from IX earlier in the session), inhibition does not occur and the natural cognitive connection between the IX and X networks, the two pictures singled out repeatedly for hypnotic induction, again becomes salient.

In conclusion, we feel that highly complex data of the type presented in this chapter can be usefully analyzed to shed light on mental functions. In some ways this very complexity is especially conducive to the study of ongoing interactive processes. At the same time, particular care must be taken to pin down these functional interdependencies, e.g., between anxiety and inhibition (to be spelled out in Chapter 11), or else the explanations lose their power. But the fact that the working model seemingly *can* impart meaningfulness to an extended series of recall sequences is in itself a hopeful sign, even though the various interpretations must now be regarded primarily as hypotheses subject to future test. Furthermore, it is clear that much can be learned from S's introspective reports.

Epilogue
to
Part B

The dozen experimental approaches described in Chapters 4 to 9 are intended primarily to convince the reader that a comprehensive yet detailed model is highly conducive to research study in the laboratory. These are the beginning, exploratory steps in a program dedicated to the evolution of a molecular theory ultimately capable of integrating within a common framework phenomena ranging from simple bodily sensations to complicated psychopathological symptoms. In a sense they should be seen as demonstrations of the model's susceptibility to experimentation and its capacity to generate intriguing hypotheses.

But even the reader who sympathizes with our overall aim has the right, on scientific grounds, to object to the manner of implementation. The types of questions which inevitably arise are these: Aren't the labels used in the model simply new names for old concepts? Is not the number of Ss participating in the research too small and the sample too homogeneous to permit any kind of valid generalization? How do you know the GSR is measuring what you think it does? How can one give serious consideration to experiments involving hypnosis when so little is known about the state itself? And from the little that is known, isn't it likely that the hypnotized S molds his behavior to fit E's expectations? Can you ever trust his introspective reports concerning mental events? These typical queries require some answers and the sooner the better, the reader probably feels.

In the first place, it *is* true that our concepts and experiments make contact with existing domains of psychology. For example, Chapter 5 (Perceptual Inhibition) has clear affiliations with the New Look realm of perceptual defense; Chapter 6 (Inhibition of Anxiety) bears special relevance to the Freudian defense of isolation; Chapter 7 (Discharge Intensity) in some sections calls to mind Hull's stimulus intensity dynamism and the problem of generalization; and Chapter 8 (Response Feedback) presents an experiment which falls into Osgood's category of mediated stimulus generalization with anxiety serving as the mediating link. Indeed it is inconceivable that a broad conceptual system which seeks to provide an integrative framework should *not* overlap many current areas of study.

However, there are good reasons for choosing a new set of labels. An obvious one is that the points of contact are with highly diverse theoretical positions—a medley of such labels would create a most jarring dissonance. Also, each analogous concept is anchored in its own particular frame of reference and cannot be lifted out of context free of its larger connotations. By the same token, the concepts of our system must be sufficiently articulated to form a coherent whole, which is only possible if they are defined and labeled in an internally consistent fashion. Besides, the apparent overlaps are usually more illusory than real. To illustrate, we can consider the psychoanalytic defense of isolation, i.e., the splitting of ideas from their accompanying affects. The three relevant experiments which were conducted (on conditioned inhibition of anxiety, competition of affects, and sequential arrival of sensory input) can be blanketed by the term "isolation," yet in reality they represent detailed attempts to discover *mechanisms* underlying the *phenomenon*. Throughout the remainder of the book we shall be dealing expressly with common psychological phenomena of all sorts, but the specific approach toward finding possible mechanisms should set our system apart from existing ones and further justify the use of different labels for concepts which have little more than an illusion of identity with other theories.

The questions concerning restricted sample size and homogeneity are appropriate to raise, as they are in virtually all psychological researches. The N in each design is admittedly small, yet the number of observations made on a given S during an experiment is typically quite large. In a few instances, like some of the procedures described in Chapters 4 and 9, the aim was frankly exploratory and no attempt was made to satisfy exacting methodological criteria. However, there can be little doubt of the legitimacy of drawing conclusions *pertinent to these Ss* as they performed in the majority of studies. The descriptive data reported in Chapter 3 demonstrate that the group is fairly heterogeneous within the limitation of being young adult college students—not that the latter should be minimized, of course. On the positive side of the generality ledger, one asset inherent in the sample should not be overlooked. The experimental Ss are *people,* a claim which cannot be made for the empirical approaches of most contemporary behavior theories. Nevertheless, it does remain to be seen whether the present results will hold for large samples varying in age, sex, IQ, social class, etc., etc. At this stage we can only maintain, first, that the procedures are replicable, and second, that we cannot identify a pre-existing bias in the group which would predispose any of the findings to come out in a particular direction.

With respect to the galvanic skin response (GSR), which has had a controversial history in psychology, we can say that for us it has admirably served the purpose we intended for it as an independent, objective measure of S's state of anxiety. While earlier evidence that deflections result from causes other than anxiety cannot be denied, the manner in which we employed the technique minimized this source of confusion: the desired affect was first strongly induced under hypnosis and linked solely to the appearance of a particular stimulus (e.g., flashing a certain Blacky picture in the tachistoscope); the stimulus was then presented at a precise instant; and the GSR noted during a carefully delimited period thereafter. Also, S's reported anxiety generally conformed closely to the chart deflections. Furthermore, manipulations by E designed to vary the state of S's anxiety usually produced corresponding variations in the record. In sum, all our experimental observations led to a feeling of confidence in the use of GSR as a research tool, provided one takes heed of adaptation effects, sensitivity to environmental changes, and the like.

Now we come to the crucial issues growing out of our extensive reliance on the method of hypnosis, traditionally viewed by psychologists with a mixture of fascination and reluctance. Fortunately the current attitude toward hypnosis is becoming increasingly receptive as more and more workers enter the field. There are even encouraging signs of standardization in techniques (witness the recent publication by Weitzenhoffer and Hilgard of the *Stanford Hypnotic Susceptibility Scales, Forms A and B* [46]) which will facilitate comparison of findings by different investigators. The problems posed for interpretation of data are important, though, and must be carefully considered.

Hypnosis is no longer believed to be a mysterious phenomenon apart from all other mental events. It belongs on the same arousal continuum with wakefulness and nocturnal sleep, and any implication that the human brain is equipped with one set of structures and functions which are activated in hypnosis and another set in the waking state is quite implausible. Nor is there any evidence that the highly susceptible individual is a different breed from his fellows. Surveys of the literature reveal that the majority of people can readily be hypnotized to some extent and widespread opinion, which we share, holds that most can eventually be led to experience a deep trance given sufficient skill, time, and patience on the part of the hypnotist. The rather fruitless search for differential personality correlates of susceptible persons also suggests that it is a mistake to dismiss hypnotic research on the grounds that the Ss must be psychological freaks from whose behavior one dares not generalize. On the other hand, it is incumbent upon any theory which makes use of hypnosis as an experimental tool to elaborate those characteristics of the state which do seem to be unique. This we shall attempt to do in Part C, where various hypnotic phenomena are interpreted in light of our conceptual model of the mind (Chapter 12).

Additional questions arising in connection with hypnotic work have to do with reliability and validity of the obtained data. We have already mentioned (p. 30) that our Ss did not have insight into the purpose of the experimental designs, so it was impossible for them to know what to do in order to try to "please" E. They understood that we were interested in *objectively* exploring their reactions in a variety of situations, including those instances when introspective reports were requested. Any desire, conscious or unconscious, of S to behave "appropriately" could only have been an experimental asset since he was explicitly told that accuracy of his report was our primary concern. Even the most flagrant opportunity for simulation, in the blindness procedure described in Chapter 5, did not materialize. A more practical concern than simulation in studies of this sort is clarity of instructions delivered to S under hypnosis. Any possible ambiguity in E's directions is likely to lead the experiment astray because of S's preoccupation with carrying them out literally.

In our view the potential hazards in hypnotic research are far outweighed by the unique capacity for experimental control. It would have been impossible to attack model problems at the chosen molecular level without capitalizing on the features of hypnosis, e.g., the ability to insure salient activation of specified networks. The necessity for employing the method at this stage of our research program should not be taken to mean, however, that future extensions of the findings by nonhypnotic investigation are deemed unimportant. Here we begin to get involved in the timing of research tactics, which must be decided as we go along.

Finally, a general comment about Part B of this book is probably in order. The write-up of experiments exploring mental functions has been confined to our own research and its implications for the model rather than for broad psychological topics (e.g., perceptual defense) to which the results are relevant. Likewise no reference has been made to the vast and scattered experimental literature from which numerous studies might have been culled to compare with our findings—at a level sufficiently remote and speculative to make the venture unprofitable, we should add. In short, the presentation has been rigidly model-oriented. The recall task in the preceding chapter, for example, has been analyzed primarily in terms of what it can tell us about the model's concept of inhibition instead of delineating the many other factors contributing to recall sequence, like primacy, recency, etc. To some extent this chauvinism is remedied in the next part, which offers an interplay of conceptual model with phenomena drawn from diverse areas. We hope that Part C will materially assist the reader in locating our program along the spectrum of psychology.

PART C

"PSYCHOLOGIZING"
THE MODEL
AND
"REMODELING"
THE PSYCHOLOGY

Detailed view of mental functions   10

Our working model of the mind purports to spell out mental functions intervening between stimulus and response. Thus far the reader has been offered only a brief overview (Chapter 2) serving primarily to orient him for the series of experiments reported in Part B. It is now appropriate to spotlight in detail the structural and functional properties of the system, particularly as they relate to perceptual phenomena.* The latter include organizational aspects; comparison of percept and image; evolution of conceptual circuits; and interference with perception. The last part of the chapter will also indicate the points of contact by which the model can eventually be brought to articulate with basic concepts in the field of learning, i.e., reinforcement, expectancy, and extinction; generalization and discrimination; and retention.

* The reader will recognize that perception is presumed to occur in the *cognitive* subsystem. A distinction between "perceptual" and "conceptual" will be drawn later in the chapter.

COMPONENTS, CIRCUITS, AND NETWORKS

The basic structural unit of the cognitive subsystem is the component, which responds both to sensory inputs originating outside the Mental System and to cognitive inputs from within. Since the sensory source of input is more relevant to our present perceptual concern, we shall begin with a description of the relationship of sensory firing to cognitive activation.

Figure 2 in Part A (see p. 15 again) showed that coded stimuli release signals from innate sensory elements representing sensations like brightness, pitch, etc. Discharge from these structurally given elements corresponds to the sensory quality of human experience. The sensory signals in turn reach the Mental System and set into motion their linked cognitive components. Each such component consists of a relay (containing an activator and a switch) and storage cell (see Figure 17). The relay has two major functions: (1) communicating to connected relays the fact of its own activation by arriving sensory input; and (2) upon receipt of activation messages from other relays in the same circuit, closing the switch permitting a characteristic *cognitive* signal to be discharged from the storage cell for integration into a composite circuit signal.

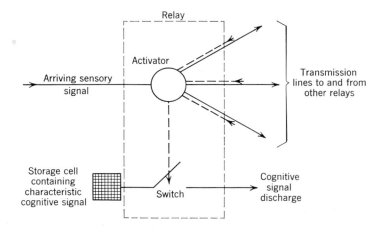

FIGURE 17. Schematic representation of activity in a cognitive component. [*Note:* Arriving sensory signal sets off activator, which transmits to other relays. Upon receipt of messages from other relays, activator closes switch thus permitting stored cognitive signal to be discharged.]

So far we have only stated in general terms that the sensory elements are innate and that they somehow become coupled isomorphically with cognitive components. How does this coupling come about? We assume that in the beginning the storage cells are empty and gradually acquire their distinguishing contents over time. For whatever initial reason, perhaps even randomly within broad structural limits, a particular sensory signal leaves its mark on a certain empty cell. Once this tentative connection is established, subsequent sensory transmissions from the same element will meet less and less resistance en route to its linked component, in accordance with the principle of facilitation. With the passage of time a great variety of highly differentiated sensory-cognitive couplings are formed in this way, so that the degrees of developmental freedom open to the normal mature organism are limited largely to rearrangements among existing cognitive circuits.

Circuits are built from repeated contiguous triggering of a series of components by specific inputs—an evolution in which highly facilitated, low-resistance transmission lines are established among the constituent relays. Reception of sensory signals by circuit components sets off a mutual intracircuit activation from relay to relay, which quickly results in the whole circuit being closed. Once this happens, all components automatically discharge their characteristic content signals. In the next stage these separate discharges are integrated locally to form a composite signal representing the output of the entire circuit. Figure 18 diagrams this sequence of events from (1) the closing of a circuit by interaction of triggered components to (2) signal discharge from the storage cells of diverse components followed by (3) local integration into (4) a composite signal output.

Subsequent amplification of the strongest of the concurrently integrated signals during hyperfacilitation also has implications for the development of circuits, since reverberation of the composite signal further strengthens and consolidates the connections among components of the originating circuit. At the same time there is an increased likelihood of related circuits in the same network being set off as a consequence of the reverberation. The process by which circuits are themselves grouped into a network is analogous to the formation of a circuit from components, the basic principle being contiguity of activation. Transmission lines with varying degrees of resistance are similarly established between circuits and a chain of circuit discharges can be triggered, especially upon repeated reverberation. In the absence of further hyperfacilitation, though, reverberation along

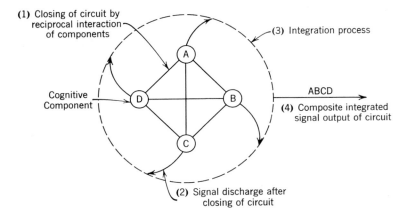

FIGURE 18. Integration of signals discharged by triggered circuit components. [*Note:* Numbers in parentheses indicate sequence of steps.]

particular transmission lines decays fairly rapidly so that continuity of the chain is not long-lasting.

ORGANIZATIONAL PHENOMENA

The existence of circuits and networks implies a continually modified cognitive organization into which sensory inputs are assimilated. In this regard a number of perceptual phenomena—grouping, constancy, closure, figure-ground and other relational properties—immediately come to mind as pertinent for our consideration (see Osgood [35] for detailed discussions of these and additional topics). The gestalt notion of "grouping," for example, has obvious relevance to the model's conception of how components become hooked up into circuits. Stimulus objects in close proximity, with overlapping and continuous physical features, are very likely to produce strong interconnections among their corresponding cognitive components because of the high probability of contiguous activation.*

Constancy and closure both relate to the firmly established nature of many circuits. Demonstrations have made it clear that brightness, size, shape, or color of an object under very different conditions

---

* Grouping on the basis of similarity rather than proximity is derivable from the model's assumption that similarity implies overlapping components shared by circuits.

of observation can appear unchanging. We interpret this constant effect in terms of repeated past exposure to a familiar object in a variety of settings, leading to the formation of a circuit whose linked components reflect the oft-recurring properties of the stimulus. A child sees the door of his room from different distances and angles on various occasions but each particular impression is not retained in all its detail. Instead only the overlapping common aspects, such as shape and color, are enduringly represented by the coupled components. Once the "constant" circuit has been set up, any future sensory impingement of that stimulus, from whatever viewing point, will automatically elicit, among other things, the same common cognitive output. Furthermore, incomplete sensory triggering of such a circuit will, if the amount of sensory input is sufficient to activate the majority of components, cause the whole circuit to discharge nevertheless. A square with an open corner is perceived as a complete figure (closure) when exposed briefly because there are enough sensory elements present to trigger the previously well-developed square circuit (and an "open-corner square" circuit has not yet had an opportunity to be formed).

Unlike grouping, which has been attributed to the "accidental" proximity of stimulus elements, and constancy and closure, also associated with the products of experience, another set of perceptual phenomena is ascribed to innate structure by the model. Here we refer to relational abilities such as figure-ground separation, intensity comparison, perception of movement, rhythm, etc. These built-in capacities for differentiating sensory input acquire special significance in the cognitive subsystem as a base from which are evolved certain key conceptual circuits having to do, for example, with time sequence and comparative judgment along specified dimensions. The power to discriminate that one event follows another in time, that light A is brighter than B or tone C louder than D, suggests structural characteristics meriting further attention. Before pursuing this topic, though, we must first spell out some substantive distinctions to be drawn among types of cognitive circuits.

PERCEPT AND IMAGE

It has already been stated that circuits can be activated either by sensory input or by spread, from discharging connected circuits, along transmission lines within the cognitive subsystem. In the former case, where the firing of sensory elements takes place, we speak

of a circuit's cognitive output as a *percept;* in the latter, where sensory
signals do not play a part, the output is labeled an *image.* The same
circuit may be involved in either process at different times.   The
presence or absence of sensory quality, therefore, is a critical cue for
the impression of whether something is "really" there or only in one's
imagination.   The ability to identify sensory occurrences seems to
improve with age and adults make fewer mistakes than children.   In
addition to the fact that experience makes available a more differentiated set of sensory properties to serve as cues about an object, it is
plausible to speculate that general techniques are probably learned
for detecting sensory quality.   If a child closes his eyes and the sensory aspects disappear, he knows that the object must have been
there, or if he averts his gaze and the object remains unchanged it
must be imaginal.

However the matter is not quite so simple, for sensory-instigated
circuit discharges are also typically stronger than those triggered by
cognitive spread.   Thus another factor tends to contribute to the subjective impression of present reality, namely, strength of cognitive
output.   Since sensory quality and strength are so highly correlated in
past experience, it is natural that strength should come to acquire
cue value of its own.   Because of these dual factors, though, perceptual confusions occasionally arise even with adults.   There is no
problem discriminating percept from image when sensory firing is
strong nor, on the other hand, is there apt to be any difficulty recognizing the imaginal quality of weak or moderate output unaccompanied by sensation.   But what about the relatively rare combination
of an exceptionally *strong* cognitive discharge *without* concomitant
sensory discharge?   Obviously we are describing the phenomenon of
hallucination, in which a person's image is so vivid that he erringly
attributes reality to it.

In terms of our model, then, we should expect hallucinations to
take place under circumstances which curtail external sensory input
and maximize the opportunity for prolonged cognitive reverberation
of the same signal.   In addition to hypnosis, other common settings for
this kind of perceptual distortion are sensory deprivation experiments,
alcohol and drug intoxication, and psychosis.   For the moment it
should suffice merely to point out that all can be viewed as sharing
the characteristics of coded input restriction along with adequate
nonspecific arousal to sustain hyperfacilitation and reverberation.

An interesting illustration of how a hallucination can develop from
sustained concentration on a particular memory sequence is furnished
in a passage from one of Joe's hypnotic sessions.   Prior to the follow-

ing conversation, he had been staring at the squares of acoustical tile on the ceiling as he lay on the couch:

E: How many rows of holes would you guess there are in that square you've been looking at? (actually 22)
S: There are 22.
E: Did you count them?
S: No.
E: Why do you say 22 then?
S: There seem to be 22 . . .
E: What comes into your mind when you think of 22?
S: A corridor.
E: Tell me about that.
S: It's a corridor with the same material on the ceiling and it's got glazed tile walls . . . there are beds in the corridor . . . they're hospital beds with people in them.
E: Is this a hospital you've seen before?
S: Yes, it's the one where I was when my neck was hurt.
E: Is this the corridor that you were in?
S: Yes.
E: Can you visualize it clearly?
S: Very clearly.
E: Do you see which bed you were in?
S: Yes.
E: Tell me which one.
S: In this one.
E (thinking he had not heard correctly): Which one?
S: This one.
E: Which is this one? Where is it in the corridor?
S: It's right here. Right by the wall.
E: And you feel as if you're in it now?
S: Yes.
E: How does your neck feel?
S: There's no feeling there.
E: What about the number 22?
S: I've just finished counting the tile on the ceiling. There are 22 rows
   . . .
E: You counted them when you were in the hospital bed?
S: Yes.
E: How long ago was that?
S: About ten years.
E: Have you thought about those tiles since?
S: No, I haven't.
E: Why do you think there are 22 on this tile in the room here?
S: It's the same size . . . seem to be the same number.

Another confusion, quite the opposite of hallucination, can also stem from the two-factor basis for reality impression. If sensory discharge occasioned by an actual object is very weak, even a moderately strong cognitive output may result in mistakenly assuming the object to be imaginal. The widely cited experiment by Perky (36) bears out this prediction. All 27 adult Ss, who were asked to visualize a banana, thought that a faintly projected real picture of one was the product of their own imagination.

Both extremes of perceptual distortion suggest the importance of signal strength as a determinant of subjective experience. At this point it might be helpful to the reader for us to review the various features of the model which relate to intensity of cognitive output. For any given circuit three broad categories of influence are involved: (1) the pre-existing state of facilitation among its components; (2) the strength and extent of input arriving to trigger the circuit; and (3) the amount of amplification subsequently accorded the circuit's integrated signal during the process of hyperfacilitation.

Pre-existing facilitation is a direct function of the number and intensity of prior activations—up to the asymptotic limit of a component's ability to discharge. The two skunk stimuli in Experiment 8 (see Chapter 7), for example, were manipulated so as to form networks varying in degree of facilitation. S's attention was repeatedly called to the figure on the cover whereas the one on the die was alluded to only briefly. Thereafter, when he was asked to visualize a skunk (as a check on differential vividness of the two), the cover stimulus first came to mind.

With respect to the strength of input triggering the circuit, sensory signals typically are more potent than cognitive spread within the subsystem. These sensory inputs vary in sheer physical intensity of stimuli impinging on the receptors as well as in degree of facilitation of connections between sensory elements and their corresponding cognitive components. Though flashing the AB stimulus at different speeds within a fairly limited range did not alter the fist-clenching responses (Experiment 9 in Chapter 7), it is known that gross discrepancies in physical intensity can have marked effects. Pertinent are the observations that brief exposure of a low brightness stimulus followed by the same exposure of a high brightness one can lead to the erroneous impression that the latter occurred first; and that perceptual latency is inversely related to stimulus brightness (11). Presumably variation in intensity of cognitive spread to a circuit also contributes to its output strength.

Another factor influencing circuit discharge is the number of components triggered by either sensory or cognitive input. Results of the clench experiment lend direct support, showing that the greater the number of a network's circuits activated, the stronger the emerging signals. S, having been instructed to clench his hand upon thinking of AB, responded most strongly to the flashed stimulus AB, next to AB5, followed by A5, etc. Although a highly facilitated circuit can be discharged by partial activation, as in closure, full activation is more powerful, other things being equal.

The final source of influence is hyperfacilitation, by which the strongest integrated signal of the moment is amplified. In other words, that signal comes to provide the focus of conscious attention whereas weaker ones fill in the peripheral context. Degree of amplification is a function of amount of nonspecific arousal occasioned by sensory input at the time. The preliminary work on vividness of imagery during posthypnotically induced states of arousal (Experiment 2 in Chapter 4) consistently revealed least amplification in the condition simulating nocturnal sleep—a finding compatible with the nonspecific assumption. Just as there is an upper limit to component discharge, amount of amplification also increases with arousal up to an asymptote. The strength of hypnotic effects, as well as the observation that the "half-asleep" state led to vivid images, point to the conclusion that optimal hyperfacilitation does not require very much arousal.

Before going on to conceptual circuits, certain other aspects of cognitive output require mention. A percept or image appears in consciousness as a configuration rather than a sequence of separate elements. In the model this phenomenon is attributed to the fact that *intranetwork* signal discharges occur so closely together in time that they merge into a unified output during whatever process (outside the bounds of our Mental System) by which signals are converted into pictures. *Successive* images remain *discrete* from one another because the internetwork time lag between signal discharges is greater than the intranetwork interval. This time differential is a consequence of greater facilitation in transmission lines between circuits within a network than across networks (consonant with the definition of a network itself).

EVOLUTION OF CONCEPTUAL CIRCUITS

Up till now discussion has been confined to cognitive circuits with direct sensory referents, whether currently accompanied by sensory firing or not. These *imaginal* circuits convey concrete impressions—pictorial, auditory, etc.—reflecting previous sensory inputs. Thoughts correspond quite literally to the actual physical events which gave rise to them. For example, visual impressions subsumed under the label "photographic memory" are very rich in detail. But this eidetic imagery, noted commonly in young children, tends to be superseded in adults (with rare exceptions) by less literal, more abstract cognitive processes. How do such *conceptual* circuits evolve within the framework of the model?

Though each component initially acquires its characteristic content from a specific sensory input, combinations of components into circuits go far beyond the bounds of those original grouped, contiguously received sensory signals. Connections between components strengthen or dwindle over time according to their subsequent activation, so new arrangements are continually being established. Also, cognitive triggering of components, via spread, becomes an increasingly important source of circuit formation as complex networks gain greater and greater facilitation. The springing up of new contiguities (and hence new circuits) by spread is most likely to take place when existing circuits share overlapping components, or in other words when some elements of similarity are already built in. But this overlap need not necessarily be present, for any oft-repeated set of contiguously activated components will automatically be hooked up to one another. The consequence of all such combinations and permutations is a cognitive organization much of whose sensory referents are quite remote.

Perhaps an illustration will make this evolution clearer. Let us consider the child's development of a concept of "roundness." In the course of his experience he encounters a variety of familiar round objects—say an orange, a ball, a hoop, and a tire—which differ in some respects and are alike in others. While each individual object is being seen a number of times, a circuit comprising its color, size, shape, texture, etc. is gradually formed. Some of the components, those having to do with shape, are common to all four objects and are triggered whenever any of the objects is seen. In contrast, the idiosyncratic components, e.g., color and size, are activated only by the particular object bearing those features. Thus facilitation among the shape components continues to increase more rapidly than among the others until signals discharged by the common components are eventually integrated apart from the rest and a new circuit of "roundness" comes into being.

Such a circuit is already more remote from sensory antecedents inasmuch as its discharge may not be accompanied by visual images of the specific objects themselves. The dissociation is further enhanced when adults provide a verbal label for the concept and an abstraction network, now capable of being triggered directly by its own sensory input (the word "round"), is established. The potentially eidetic images of the four objects tend to be relegated to the background in favor of more salient conceptual impressions. Just as the orange leads readily to thoughts of shape in the example cited, it can also serve as a stimulus for thoughts of citrus fruit from previous combination with other fruit sharing that attribute, to color from pairings with similarly colored objects, and so on. Once these conceptual circuits are closely connected to the object within the same network, it is unlikely that the signal of the object circuit will be able to monopolize hyperfacilitation and undergo the prolonged reverberation presumably necessary for the eidetic degree of vividness. In this way associative *meaning* displaces concrete imagery to a large extent as dominant cognitive activity.

Having described the origin of conceptual circuits, we can now return to the problem of comparative judgment raised in the section on organizational phenomena. Concepts like order—the discrimination that one event follows another in time—and relative intensity were said to stem from innate structural capacity. In the case of order this implies directionality in the hooking up of circuits into a network, from which an abstract "followed by" circuit eventually evolves. The built-in directionality basis for sequence discrimination is probably supplemented by differential strength of signals representing current and immediately past events, since current ones tend to be stronger due to their direct sensory instigation. The interaction of directionality and strength can be viewed as analogous to that of sensory quality and strength in reality impressions, with directionality the crucial cue except in extremes. Once the conceptual order circuit is established, it too has a label typically provided and the resulting network becomes available for coupling in all kinds of temporal contexts.

Similarly, conceptual circuits of rhythm, involved in the gestalt transposition phenomenon (e.g., recognizing the same melody played in different keys), grow out of the repetition of innately discriminable temporal patterns. The perception of movement has also been shown to hinge upon time interval (35). Intensity comparisons, dealing with judgments like relative brightness or loudness, can be interpreted as outcomes of differential firing of sensory elements. A brighter stimulus sets off more sensory "brightness" elements and the corresponding cognitive circuit is triggered more strongly than it is with a less intense stimulus. Many such structurally based discriminations of signal strength contribute to the formation of a conceptual scale of brightness which permits generalization of judgment to new sets of stimuli not seen before.

INTERFERENCE WITH PERCEPTUAL FUNCTIONS

Three possible kinds of interference with perception are postulated by the working model: (1) sensory adaptation; (2) jamming; and (3) inhibition. Sensory adaptation refers to decreased sensitivity under conditions of constant stimulation. Incessant input to the same sensory elements can have a fatiguing effect so that sensory signals arriving weaker than usual at the cognitive subsystem are no longer potent sources of activation. Osgood (35) provides an excellent summary of available data and concludes that sensory adaptation is far more complicated than has generally been assumed. But sensory elements, lying as they do outside the Mental System, are not of central interest for the model and we shall turn instead to the concept of jamming.

The phenomenon we wish to tackle is the fleeting subjective impression, upon viewing an object, that something is wrong—a momentary experience of discrepancy. For example, if one is walking along a supposedly familiar part of the campus and glances absent-mindedly at an archway expecting to see the name "Physics" inscribed above, the surprise of not finding it there is followed by an instant of confusion before reorienting oneself correctly. Bruner and Postman (9) have performed an experiment using incongruous playing cards, such as a black three of hearts. Or, take the particular illustration upon which our research team, for some unknown but no doubt dynamically significant reason, became fixated in the course of discussing this topic: catching sight of a purple banana. (An unexpected aftermath of these lengthy deliberations happened in a supermarket where the writer, so accustomed to the hypothetical notion of a purple banana, actually spied one approximating that color and was not the least bit taken aback!)

What is occurring inside the Mental System at the point corresponding to the "sense of wrongness" as Bruner and Postman refer to it? We have some clues from the nature of the phenomenon itself, which involves a discrepancy between a well-developed expectation (bananas are typically yellow) and contradictory sensory input (the banana projected on the screen is purple). Moreover, certain strength limitations are also required. If the purple stimulus is exposed very briefly under conditions of low illumination, it may be too weak to be perceived at all and S reports that he must have seen a yellow banana. At the other extreme, intense exposure of the purple may result in correct judgment despite the incongruity.

The problem is how to translate these considerations into the molecular language of the model, going beyond such general statements as perceptual organization is "powerfully determined by expectations built upon past commerce with the environment" and obeys vaguely understood principles of "dominance, compromise, disruption, or recognition" (9). Figure 19 summarizes the hypothetical comparison of output under three degrees of strength of sensory input. The letters A, B, and C stand for various component attributes of a banana (shape, texture, etc.) other than color. Y represents a yellow peel component and, from past experience, a highly facilitated ABCY circuit (hooked up by dotted lines in the diagram) has been established. Sensory input from a purple banana, however, directly triggers A, B, C, and P (purple peel) rather than Y. If the input is weak, the activation of A, B, and C will probably still be sufficient to close the well-developed ABCY circuit and the percept becomes "yellow banana." The weakly triggered P component, having no prior connections to A, B, and C, does not get incorporated into the circuit. In other words, P's advantage of direct sensory instigation is more than outweighed by Y's pre-existing couplings to A, B, and C.

A moderately strong exposure of the purple banana can alter the outcome in this way: both Y and P may be linked equally with A, B, and C—Y by its facilitated connections and P now by its strong contiguous triggering. The incompatibility of Y and P signals, simultaneously undergoing integration along with those of A, B, and C, is what we mean by jamming, the output of which is *noise.* The corresponding percept in this case is "banana but something's wrong," the signal-to-noise ratio being favorable enough for the banana itself to be readily identified. In this condition a delicate balance is achieved between P's strength from direct input and Y's from previous facilitation.

Finally, if the exposure is very intense, it is conceivable that the balance will tip in the other direction with the stimulus being first correctly perceived as purple, probably followed by thoughts of bananas typically being yellow. Such a result implies that powerful sensory instigation of A, B, C, and P can cause that circuit to be formed and closed before the one linking A, B, C, and Y can close.

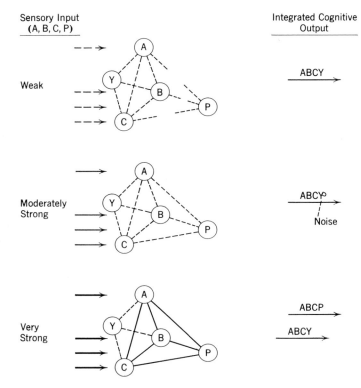

FIGURE 19. Hypothetical relationship of strength of sensory input to cognitive output in discrepancy situation.

These speculations must, of course, be subjected to experimental verification. But it is important to note that, by attempting to conceptualize the problem within the detailed framework of the model, one must immediately come to grips with crucial variables to be manipulated. In the particular illustration these are pre-existing facilitation of circuit couplings, number of overlapping components (A, B, C) so that jamming is possible or not, and strength and type of arriving sensory signals.

The above exposition has been confined to the fleeting perceptual impression of discrepancy. Usually the process is not arrested at this stage and other activity ensues. If the noise is great there may be inhibitory repercussions with attendant cognitive disruption (to be discussed further in Chapter 13). Or other existing cognitive circuits, e.g., having to do with resolution of color combinations, may be brought into play to produce an intermediate purplish-yellow color percept—the so-called "compromise" reaction. The impression may also be followed by correct recognition. All such eventualities are themselves susceptible to specification of conditions for their occurrence, which can then be tested in the laboratory.

A third kind of interference with perception is direct inhibitory action, described in detail in connection with the experiments reported in Chapter 5. Strangely enough, the notion of perceptual inhibition has aroused a storm of controversy which continues unabated in the psychological literature. "Perceptual defense" is still such an emotionally loaded phrase that many individuals remain "blind" to the implications of a sizable number of studies, including a series done by the writer and his associates during the past decade (3, 5, 6, 12, 33, 37). Somehow the phenomenon that threatening stimuli are often perceived with greater difficulty than neutral seems plausible only when viewed as a function of hypothesis strength, response competition, verbal suppression, or the like—even when these explanations obviously do not fit the data. The only rational conclusion to be drawn from surveying the vast amount of research on the topic is, as Perloe points out (38), that the various interpretations are not incompatible or mutually exclusive. Each applies in some experiments and all, inhibition included, can occur under certain conditions.

The resistant attitude is more difficult to understand in light of neurophysiological and medical evidence. As mentioned on p. 18, the fact of inhibitory action in the central nervous system is unquestioned, though details of its operation are admittedly still obscure. Clinically, the phenomenon of hysterical blindness, which lends itself neatly to explanation in terms of inhibition, is well-established. Duke-Elder summarizes the current clinical position as follows:

Bilateral functional blindness is not common and is usually hysterical; as an isolated hysterical symptom it is very rare. It is seldom seen in civilian life and then usually in emotional young women, but has been more commonly employed as a subconscious means of escape from military service. It is usually recurrent, of sudden onset and short duration, but cases of amaurosis of several years' standing have been recorded. The pupillary reactions and the appearance of the fundi are normal; photopsiae and chromatopsiae are common complaints. Although admitting of no vision, however, the patient will dodge obstacles and extricate himself from embarrassments, while he views the entire situation, serious as it may seem to an outsider, not only with complete lack of fear and anxiety, but with nonchalance and indifference. The organically blind, on the other hand, walks carefully, but will fall into a trap, while the simulator, blinder than the blind, to prove his case will knock himself into things intentionally, or stands and will do nothing at all.

Unilateral blindness is still more rare; and again it is typically sudden in onset, short in duration, and recurrent in habit. It may be associated with hysterical hemianaesthesia on the same side. There is no evidence of homonymous field defects as would indicate an organic lesion in upper visual pathways; *the inhibition is psychical,* comparable to that seen in the habitual users of monocular optical instruments. (Italics mine.) (14, pp. 3710–3711)

Our own work with hypnotically induced, selective blindness (see Experiment 5, pp. 58–60) indicates that perceptual processes can be initiated and then interfered with prior to output. Since its appearance was not announced in advance, the stimulus to which S was trained to be blind obviously had to register in the Mental System in order for the blindness instruction to be executed. The "little man inside the head," whose presence is so offensive to opponents of inhibition theory, can be exorcised simply by conjuring up a sequence of events in the midst of which an already coupled inhibitory mechanism is automatically invoked. (Borrowing from a time-honored phrase, one might say that the conceptual model creates a *machina ex homunculo!*)

The label "perceptual defense" has some relevance because the inhibition mechanism has built-in connections to the anxiety network, whose discharge is curtailed when the inhibition is triggered. However, the inhibition itself can be activated either via the cognitive representation of anxiety (see Figure 10 on p. 57), or by direct transmission lines from cognitive content circuits. The latter type of route seems to be the one utilized in the blindness procedure, where the flashed stimulus was able to cue off inhibition in the absence of physiological or introspective evidence suggesting concomitant anxiety. The anxiety-defensive aspect therefore does not necessarily apply to all perceptual operations involving inhibition.*

In review, this chapter so far has presented a detailed exposition of structure and function in parts of the cognitive subsystem, with special

---

* A phenomenon commonly treated together with perceptual defense is "vigilance," or sensitization to emotionally toned stimuli. In some of our earlier work, for example, the position in which anxiety-laden Blacky pictures appeared was judged to "stand out most" when four stimuli were flashed simultaneously in Left, Right, Top, and Bottom positions at extremely rapid speeds. In terms of the model we would account for this effect on the grounds that (1) the cognitive circuit of the loaded picture is already more highly facilitated than the other three as a consequence of its affective emphasis (via previous response feedbacks); and (2) the fleeting sensory instigation is not strong enough to spread to the anxiety network and inhibition mechanism.

application to perceptual phenomena. It should be emphasized that the vast range of possible items in the area of perception is only sampled and, even among those selected as crucial for consideration, the depth of discussion varies greatly. The model's rapprochement with organizational concepts, for instance, receives brief treatment intended primarily to demonstrate the potential for later elaboration. Perceptual inhibition, on the other hand, is already more precisely formulated and supported by laboratory studies. Next we shall take up, once more in a relatively general way, some key topics in the field of learning.

BASIC CONCEPTS OF LEARNING

"Learning" implies relatively permanent alterations in the state of connections built up repetitively in the course of experience.* Frequent mention has already been made of contiguity of activation as the basic principle underlying such acquired changes. Thus, the triggering of different structures closely in time is considered both a necessary and sufficient condition for new learning to take place. *Reinforcement* is presumed to have a facilitating effect via sensory feedback of affective discharges. Rewards and punishments typically instigate emotional responses which in turn have consequences in the cognitive subsystem. Figure 20 depicts the role of reinforcement in a situation where S, learning to push a button in response to a light cue, is rewarded in some way for correct performance. The upper part of the diagram illustrates, in oversimplified fashion, the twofold consolidation already taking place in the network immediately prior to introduction of the reward: (1) cognitive reverberation of the hyperfacilitated B network (thoughts about pushing the button) facilitates the transmission line to its coupled motoric representation C, which controls the motoric sequence itself; and (2) sensory feedback from the button-pushing response further strengthens the C circuit and its connections.

The lower part of Figure 20 shows how the subsequent reward input heightens facilitation in the specific performance network. The reward stimulus activates its corresponding cognitive circuit (D), which in turn triggers a coupled circuit representing the affective

* "Performance" refers to the triggering, by signals from the cognitive subsystem, of motoric circuits which accomplish effector action. The potential, i.e., pre-existing facilitation, for such triggering is of course a function of past learning and maturation.

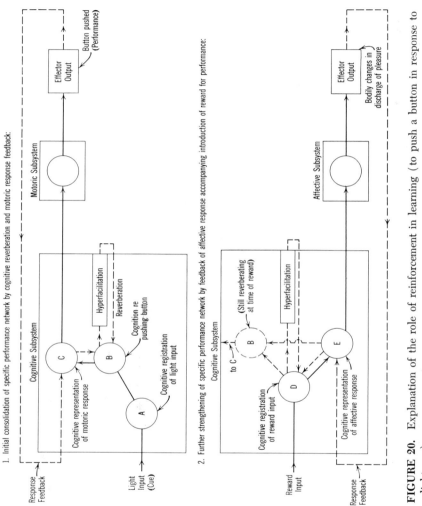

1. Initial consolidation of specific performance network by cognitive reverberation and motoric response feedback:

Response Feedback

Light Input (Cue)

Cognitive Subsystem

Cognitive representation of motoric response

C

B

A

Cognitive registration of light input

Cognition re pushing button

Reverberation

Hyperfacilitation

Motoric Subsystem

Effector Output

Button pushed (Performance)

2. Further strengthening of specific performance network by feedback of affective response accompanying introduction of reward for performance:

Reward Input

Response Feedback

Cognitive Subsystem

Cognitive registration of reward input

to C

B

(Still reverberating at time of reward)

D

E

Cognitive representation of affective response

Hyperfacilitation

Affective Subsystem

Effector Output

Bodily changes in discharge of pleasure

FIGURE 20. Explanation of the role of reinforcement in learning (to push a button in response to a light cue).

128

response of pleasure (E). Both D and E acquire connections, by contiguity, to B still reverberating to some extent from the operations described above. Sensory feedback of bodily changes in the discharge of pleasure then strengthens these hookups, so that the next exposure to the light cue meets with considerably less resistance in leading to execution of the motoric act.*

Once the D-E-B etc. connections are firmly established, the performance network can be significantly strengthened even in the absence of effector discharge. That is, thoughts about the pleasurable consequences of pushing the button can themselves serve a facilitating function. Other extensions of this very simple paradigm to various complex experimental procedures involving instrumental learning and conditioning would follow essentially the same basic principle. In delay of reward studies, for example, the longer time interval between act execution and reward can be viewed as covering a series of linked cognitive networks discharging in sequence from most recent back to the one active originally at the moment of execution. By this process of cognitive mediation the facilitating effects of the sensory feedback etc., which accompany the network discharging just prior to the reward presentation, ultimately strengthen the specific performance network itself.

So far the exposition has been confined to the reinforcing properties of pleasurable emotions. What about other affects produced in conjunction with learned behavior? Or the reinforcing properties of motorically rather than affectively based feedback? Pending unequivocal experimental evidence, we cannot differentiate the degree of reinforcement (sensory feedback) inherent in various emotional reactions. It may turn out to be the case that positive affect possesses an advantage in this respect. All share the capacity, also, to maintain hyperfacilitation in their concomitant role of contributing, like other sensory inputs, to amount of nonspecific arousal. The one affect which must be singled out for special consideration, however, is anxiety. Discharges within the anxiety network automatically trigger the inhibition mechanism and thereby interfere with processing. Concurrent performance networks are impeded as a consequence of the greater resistance introduced into all contiguously active transmission lines. Concerning the role of feedback from motoric discharge unrelated to emotion, we can speculate that some reinforcement does take place, though probably not of the same magnitude as with affect.

---

* The reinforcement of avoidant responses is also assumed to derive from sensory feedback of pleasurable discharge—in this case "relief pleasure" following cessation of discomfort (see pp. 134–135).

Greater potency of the latter may be a reflection of the intensity or duration of its particular sensory feedback.

Expectancy or *set* strengthens performance in a somewhat different manner than does reinforcement. A kind of "prefacilitation" of connections is made possible by expectancy circuits, whose origin has been described on p. 121. If stimuli X and Y (the latter linked to a particular response) are presented in that order sufficiently often, the subject acquires a network hooking together in sequence three cognitive circuits: "X", "followed by", and "Y". Afterward, at the time of the X input, the transmission line to Y is facilitated by discharge of the mediating "followed by" circuit. Subsequent exposure to stimulus Y then results in a stronger motoric output than otherwise because the connections are already primed for carrying a signal. (It is assumed of course that multiple networks hooking up to the same "followed by" circuit preserve their identity, so that transmission lines are not confused upon leaving the common connection.)

Extinction of learned responses following cessation of externally provided reinforcement and their *spontaneous recovery* later after a period of rest are likely to involve complex cognitive processes in the case of human subjects.* In general, though, we can say that extinction occurs either as a consequence of direct inhibitory action on the performance network or from steady increase in facilitation of an incompatible (response-wise) alternative network up to the point where it finally supersedes the original in strength. A competing network with its own positive affect has a better chance of winning out during extinction trials because of the absence of sensory feedback of affective discharges previously accompanying the reinforcing object. Inhibition can be invoked via negative affect accompanying frustration over withdrawal of reward (see pp. 134–135), or by the introduction of noise into the cognitive subsystem following repeated lack of fulfillment of the reward expectancy (see p. 179).

Spontaneous recovery afterward is probably related to the fact that a new expectancy, i.e., responding in the situation may or may not lead to reward, has evolved from the prior experiences. Presumably the mild affective discharge concomitant with this anticipation of possible reward, plus the absence of inhibitory action linked to the old expectancy, is sufficient to tip the balance back in favor of the original

---

* The pitfalls which beset unchecked acceptance of homology between man and lower species like the white rat are especially prominent in the field of learning, where much of the theorizing has been based on animal experimentation. It is interesting that biologists tend to be more skeptical than psychologists of the legitimacy of such homologies.

performance network. However, as the expectation continually fails to gain confirmation, extinction (via inhibition) sets in once more.

Generalization is portrayed in the working model as signal spread among connected circuits and networks. Activation of a circuit will spread to related circuits in proportion to the strength of the triggering signal, the number of triggered components, the intracircuit facilitation of the original, and the degree of facilitation existing along transmission lines to the other circuits. Similarity, involving as it does component overlap at the circuit level or circuit overlap at the network level, obviously plays an important part via the built-in enhancement of signal spread. *Discrimination* has already been discussed in the context of perception (see pp. 115, 121–122), the main point being that conceptual circuits evolve from innate structural capacities for comparative judgment and make possible the generalization of discrimination to new sets of stimuli.

RETENTION

The strength of connections in the Mental System is augmented by repeated activation. Does it follow that resistance in pathways automatically grows stronger in the absence of activation? In other words, do connections fade gradually through disuse? Our assumption is that some weakening does take place very slowly over time, so that it is theoretically possible for transmission lines to become completely nonfunctional after years of inactivity. However, this factor is probably not a major one accounting for most everyday instances of forgetting. Instead the model invokes either interference from a competing network or direct inhibitory action, as mentioned above. The disuse hypothesis has greater applicability to the forgetting of events from the distant past which were never repeated and are no longer recoverable.

A short-term type of intensification and fading, though, does have special significance. Here we refer to the recency effect, by which information having just passed through consciousness tends to persist strongly for a limited period of time. The function in the model which underlies this phenomenon is reverberation. The cognitive feedback loop set into motion by the hyperfacilitation process consolidates and strengthens the originating circuit so that it is readily responsive to additional inputs. During this relatively short phase of heightened facilitation recall is an easy matter. It is tempting, of course, to engage in sheer speculation about the average time span of a single reverberatory sequence in the absence of new input to the network—particularly in light of the oft-noted optimal half-second interval between presentation of conditioned and unconditioned stimuli. Perhaps that amount of time reflects the maximum cumulative impact of reverberation, shorter intervals curtailing consolidation and longer ones permitting some fading to take place. If the circuit corresponding to the conditioned stimulus is optimally facilitated at the moment the unconditioned one is introduced, the couplings within the ensuing network are more likely to be decisive in determining output.

The topic of recall will be treated in Chapter 12 in connection with hypnotically induced amnesia. Dynamic aspects of forgetting, relevant to the Freudian concept of repression, will also be covered later (see pp. 142–143). Before leaving the field of memory temporarily, some comment should be made concerning the superiority of recognition over recall as a method for recapturing past learning. In the model this is consistent with the assumption that the triggering of circuits by sensory input (the material exposed for recognition) is more potent than internal cognitive activation.

The above sorties into the field of learning will be followed next by a more concerted attack upon problems of motivational dynamics and anxiety.

Motivational dynamics and anxiety 11

Central to our research program is the conviction that any psychological theory worthy of a capital "T" must be capable of integrating the dynamic phenomena of psychoanalysis along with traditional topics from such areas as learning and perception. We shall proceed to set in perspective our approach to motivation and emotion, and then focus on the concepts of anxiety and inhibition. The latter in turn provide a bridge to the field of psychopathology, which will be treated in the remaining sections of this chapter.

MOTIVATION AND DRIVE IN THE WORKING MODEL

For us the term "motivation" is an abstraction derived from the fact that well-established cognitive networks, activated by certain kinds of input, result in effector discharge. The concept of *drive* thus implies a highly facilitated network conveying specific content and leading to behavioral outputs. The likelihood of the network being triggered and its signals hyperfacilitated is high because of the frequent occurrence of relevant sensory input from outside the Mental System, the large number of connecting networks which provide cognitive

133

sources of input, plus the low resistance along transmission lines. Typically the drive network also comprises circuits representing antic- ipation of affect.

Triggering inputs can be physiological needs, such as hunger, thirst, or sex; external stimulus objects serving as incentives; sensory feed- back from effector activity; or spread from connected discharging circuits within the cognitive subsystem. Similarly, there can be a number of factors contributing to the cessation of a drive. New input may activate a different network which transmits stronger signals and achieves the hyperfacilitation instead. Withdrawal of the originating input (e.g., physiological changes abolishing the need or removal of the gratifying object) also permits other inputs to take over. Even when the same input continues there is the possibility of its effects being modified as a consequence of ongoing operations. Finally, the three kinds of interference discussed in connection with percep- tion (see p. 122)—sensory adaptation, jamming, and inhibition—can all result in suspension of a drive.

FRUSTRATION AND EMOTION

Infantile experience can be viewed as the prototype for later reac- tions to frustration. Hunger pangs, for example, produce discharge of negative affect (displeasure) by triggering innate circuits of the affective subsystem. From such discharge there evolves very early (via sensory feedback) a cognitive representation of discomfort, which then serves to mediate subsequent activation of affect. In like fashion sensory inputs deriving from a full stomach, the warmth of contact, etc., lead ultimately to the formation of a cognitive circuit represent- ing comfort, which is linked to positive affect (pleasure). Repeated situations involving frustration, such as premature withdrawal of the baby's bottle, eventually result in establishment of the conceptual net- work: Lack of Fulfillment → Discomfort → (Negative Affect). The experience of having discomfort quickly reduced, on the other hand, contributes to the formation of an expectancy network relating cessa- tion of discomfort to *relief pleasure*. The latter presumably entails activation of the same affective circuit as *gratification pleasure*, but some of the cognitive aspects are of course different in these two net- works of positive affect.

Figure 21 illustrates the paradigm of relief pleasure after discomfort terminates. As long as the sensory input creating discomfort is main- tained, the upper route monopolizes the cognitive scene and negative

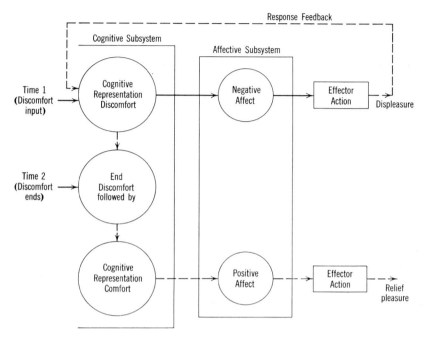

FIGURE 21. Cessation of discomfort followed by relief pleasure.

affect continues to be discharged. However, upon cessation of discomfort, sensory input changes and hyperfacilitation and reverberation shift to the lower route linked by the expectancy circuit. The diagram also implies that the strength of signal spread from upper to lower routes is a function of intensity of discharge along the upper so that the more the initial discomfort, the greater the consequent relief pleasure. If the halting of discomfort is followed by introduction of a gratifying stimulus, the triggering of positive affect may be still more potent, for the relief and gratification can merge in time and summate inside the affective subsystem.

In the case of frustration there is an alternation of affects beginning with the positive. The presence of a stimulus cuing anticipation of pleasure typically produces mild discharge; subsequent lack of fulfillment activates the discomfort network described above and can trigger inhibition. Prolonged attraction and frustration causes an affective vacillation whose magnitude depends upon the nature of the specific setting. In general, the stronger the anticipatory pleasure, the greater the frustration displeasure.

GENESIS AND ORGANIZATION OF AFFECTS

Affect networks include circuits in both the cognitive and affective subsystems. For the mature organism the central circuit is the cognitive representation of an emotion, which transmits signals to its corresponding circuit in the affective subsystem, whose action in turn releases effector (muscular and glandular) output. Originally the cognitive representation circuit, like other parts of that subsystem, evolved from sensory input, namely, feedback of the affective discharge itself. Once developed, the circuit continues to be responsive to such discharge and coupled cognitive circuits of diverse content are readily activated by spread. One common connection, of course, leads to the cognitive label by which the particular emotion is identifiable at the verbal level. By contrast, if hyperfacilitation of signals from the cognitive representation itself should occur (as a consequence most likely of strong affective discharge), cognitive output would relate to the corresponding bodily sensations. In this brief description the reader has probably detected features of the James-Lange in addition to the Cannon views of emotion: the former via the role of response feedback in instigating thought processes, and the latter in the attribution of major control to circuits in the cognitive subsystem.

With reference to genesis of the affective subsystem, we assume three primary types of reactions to be innately differentiated—rage, pleasure, and anxiety.* The rage reaction is linked in the infant to bodily conditions of discomfort, produced by painful or irritating sensory stimuli.† Feelings of pleasure, on the other hand, arise from comforting sensory experiences like contact or stroking of erogenous zones. Anxiety, we are inclined to think, has its origin in the startle response to loud noises, being overwhelmed by intense stimulation, etc. These prototypical circumstances form the bases for later evolution of elaborate affect networks containing conceptual circuits as well.

Certainly the state of knowledge concerning the variety and interrelationships of emotions is still quite limited. For this reason our

---

* The distinctions we draw between anxiety and fear do not lie in the affective subsystem, where we believe the same circuit to be involved for both. Fear is characterized as an anxiety network intimately connected with specific cognitive content circuits and typically triggering motoric responses of flight or avoidance.

† Obviously sensory inputs of "pain" do not inevitably have emotional consequences, as is demonstrated by the phenomenon of hypnotic analgesia to be discussed later (see pp. 158–159).

own formulation of the structure of the affective subsystem remains very vague. Indeed we can offer little more than the hunch that secondary, acquired feelings, e.g., guilt, sadness, and disgust, somehow are conveyed by relevant cognitive circuits hooking up to combinations of the three primary circuits in the affective subsystem. More clear is the fact that one type of emotional output can lead to another, expressions of rage often being accompanied by anxiety. Intensity of discharge must also play a part in discriminating, for example, among the reactions of annoyance, anger, and rage—all of which presumably entail activation of the same affective circuit but to differing degrees. The notion of intensity or arousal implicit in emotional discharge has further consequences, by way of feedback, for the regulation of nonspecific arousal and strength of hyperfacilitation. Hypnotic research along the lines of the competing affects experiment (pp. 67–70) holds real promise of shedding light on these many problems by making available techniques for the experimental induction and manipulation of various emotional reactions.

THE ANXIETY NETWORK

The basic circuits comprising the anxiety network are (1) the cognitive representation of sensory feedback of effector discharge, which controls (2) its corresponding circuit in the affective subsystem; (3) the cognitive label of anxiety; and (4) the inhibition mechanism. In addition, a wide variety of content circuits in the cognitive subsystem are also typically connected. The ease with which any type of content can be hooked up to the anxiety network should be apparent from the studies described in Part B. The following hypnotic introspective report by Steve, during the training session for one of the experiments, succinctly summarizes this fact, including the simple manner in which inhibition can be turned off or on:

S: When you give me the instruction (to feel anxious in response to a particular stimulus) it seems like I don't have to go back to an experience or anything. It's almost as though I have a little pocket of fright kind of conditioned in here and I don't really have to go back to a life experience. I just sit there and say "Watch out, there's going to be a cue or something," and that's about all it boils down to. If it's a cue, then you go boom and explode. It seems like just now while I was saying this the same thing was going on.

E: So even talking about it produces the feeling, not only when it's flashed?

S: Yeah, though it seems like if you said "Well now, we don't have to worry about this for just a minute," then I could sit and discuss this without getting the little anxiety.

From the results cited in the experiment on Inhibition of Anxiety by Posthypnotic Suggestion (pp. 61–67) it appears likely that there is only one rather than several parallel anxiety networks within the Mental System. Presence of the inhibitory stimulus Green not only damped GSR discharge of the loaded colors per instruction, but also tended to reduce the discharge normally accompanying the Blacky picture flashed simultaneously. Implications of a single anxiety network are of course far-reaching. Damping by whatever method— tranquillizing drugs, hypnotic suggestions of contentment, psychotherapeutic interactions, etc.—can permit loaded material to be processed without its customarily disruptive effects.

The cognitive consequences of sensory feedback from anxiety responses have already been discussed in the context of investigations reported in Chapter 8. Clearly such inputs have "motivational" properties in that connected cognitive circuits are made to discharge. If these content circuits lead readily to new outputs which are anxiety-free, we may speak of the process as "adaptive." Also the triggering of inhibition can be viewed as adaptive since it cuts down further anxiety discharges. "Disruptive" aspects of the response feedback are twofold: (1) repeated or intermittent hyperfacilitation of anxiety-coupled circuits interferes with whatever chain of logical thought is being pursued via ongoing cognitive operations; and (2) inhibition spreads to other contiguously active networks and impedes them as well. At this point a fuller treatment of the relationship between anxiety and inhibition, including a review of pertinent evidence, is probably in order.

ANXIETY AND INHIBITION

Origins of the close connection between anxiety and inhibition can only be dealt with speculatively. We assume both to be innately represented in the structure of the Mental System. Whether their coupling is also innate, or mediated very early in life by "noise" inputs (see pp. 123–124) remains a moot issue. On the other hand, it may be that noise acquires its own highly facilitated connection to the inhibition mechanism via contiguous activation of the anxiety network. Overwhelming stimulation (input overload) very early in life could lead both to noise in the cognitive subsystem and anxiety discharge

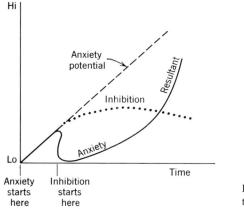

FIGURE 22. Effects of inhibitory action on anxiety discharge.

via the affective. Regardless of the true priority of mediation, the model presumes inhibition to be automatically invoked both by noise and anxiety.

Thus, one particular circuit whose discharge sets off inhibition is the cognitive representation of anxiety. Since that circuit can itself be instigated either by sensory feedback or by signal spread within the cognitive subsystem, it follows that inhibition can be activated from external or internal sources. Figure 22 attempts to portray the influence of inhibitory action upon eventual anxiety discharge at the effectors. Input to the cognitive representation of anxiety causes that circuit to send signals along at least two highly facilitated transmission lines: (1) to its corresponding anxiety circuit in the affective subsystem; and (2) to the inhibition mechanism. The time lag before the latter can be brought into play to impede transmission means that some anxiety output at the effectors, albeit slight, is apt to occur at first (shown by the initial short rise of the curve designating resultant anxiety discharge).* Once inhibition is fully mobilized, however, the anxiety route becomes temporarily impassable and discharge halted (drop in curve). What happens next is a function of the intensity and duration of anxiety-eliciting input. Inasmuch as the inhibition mechanism has an asymptotic upper limit of effective-

---

* The resemblance between this postulation of mild anxiety output and Freud's (19) "warning signal" anxiety is solely phenomenological. In our model there are no purposeful judgments made by an ego, in response to such discharge, that protective defense measures should be invoked. Rather the "defensive" function served by the inhibition mechanism is accomplished directly and automatically once the cognitive representation of anxiety is activated to a sufficient extent.

ness, strong continuing input will cause that limit to be exceeded (see final segment of anxiety resultant curve). The consequence of such overflow is considerable effector activity, which has the disruptive feedback repercussions in the cognitive subsystem mentioned above.

Disruption can manifest itself in diverse ways. Rudy, for example, was once asked under hypnosis to do automatic writing or drawing in response to stimulus words. He carried out the instruction readily for a series of neutral words but suddenly the pencil was unable to move when the word "incest" was given. Steve on one occasion was undergoing a stressful anxiety induction and the loaded stimulus "disappeared" (spontaneously, this time!) while he was looking at it. In addition to these motoric and perceptual kinds of interference, cognitive blocking is of course extremely common. Laura had difficulty solving an analogy item containing the word "erotic," which under hypnosis she guessed to mean "something like a dance that you know very well, or behavior that's done over and over again." Thereupon E explained that it meant "sexual" and pointed out its Greek derivation. A few minutes later, in the waking state, she again experienced trouble—defining the word as "unacceptable behavior." Then in reply to a request to allow her mind to go completely blank in order for a synonym to pop in, she answered "sex." But the inhibition quickly reappeared, for she was only willing to concede that "erotic" might mean "unapproved sexual behavior but also unapproved behavior of other types."

We shall return shortly to the question of loci of inhibitory action in the Mental System.

Experimental evidence in Part B offers a good start toward clarifying the relationship between anxiety and inhibition. Our assumption that the former automatically sets off the latter is supported by the perceptual interference study (pp. 48–57), in which the mere presence of a peripherally glimpsed anxiety stimulus (loaded Blacky picture) hampered identification of colors in other peripheral positions. Also, in the work on recall (pp. 96–97), we have seen that loaded Blacky pictures tended to be forgotten or delayed in the sequence, prior to any specific hypnotic induction concerning them.

The basic hypothesis that inhibition, though triggered via the anxiety network, can spread to other unrelated ongoing cognitive operations, receives confirmation too in the perceptual interference experiment. Moreover, that investigation attests to the fact that inhibition can be overcome by a sufficiently strong signal. In accordance with the prediction stemming from the hypothesis that inhibitory action has an upper limit of effectiveness, the color upon whose position S was instructed in advance to focus proved resistant to the interference phenomenon. The many studies involving hypnotic attachment of anxiety to specific stimuli further corroborate this point. It was possible to facilitate connections between stimulus circuits and anxiety network so highly that discharging signals could pass into the affective subsystem despite the automatic occurrence of inhibition.* Thus, another factor contributing to the balance between inhibition and anxiety discharge is the degree of facilitation existing in transmission lines linking other cognitive networks to the anxiety one.

Finally, it is apparent that the inhibition mechanism can be triggered by coupled cognitive circuits apart from the anxiety network. Presence of the color Green in the suggested posthypnotic inhibition experiment (pp. 61–67), for example, curtailed GSR discharge by virtue of a strongly built-in connection to inhibition. Similarly the hypnotic instruction to have "no feelings" altered responsiveness to anxiety pictures during the subsequent recall series. Continued research along the lines of all these earlier explorations, with special attention now to quantitative aspects of the relevant variables, should lead to more precise formulations in the general area of anxiety.

ROLE OF INHIBITION IN "DEFENSE"

Having unlocked the floodgates by major emphasis on the concept of anxiety, we are already well on our way to confluence with the stream of phenomena designated "psychopathology." A stable bridge can be erected to that destination, we feel, via the model's handling of inhibition. For example, it follows from earlier discussion that inhibitory action can occur in various parts of the Mental System: exclusively within the cognitive subsystem, or upon connections linking cognitive to affective and motoric subsystems. These different loci correspond to a series of avoidant defenses against anxiety spelled out by Freud.

First of all, primitive *denial*, in which unpleasant aspects of reality are not perceived, can be interpreted as the interruption of ongoing perceptual processes by anxiety-triggered inhibition. Signals from

---

* As an aside, it should be noted that these procedures during training sessions minimized the role of individual differences in the experiments themselves. Each S was brought to the level where the particular stimulus elicited a marked GSR reaction regardless of the amount of training necessary. Variations in the difficulty of such training probably reflect individual differences in the state of pre-existing anxiety networks among Ss.

cognitive circuits linked previously to the anxiety network are blocked prior to hyperfacilitation, despite the activation of those circuits by sensory input (see Chapters 5 and 10). The fact that denial is prevalent only among children and regressed psychotics is explained vaguely in the psychoanalytic literature by such statements as "the gradual development of reality testing makes such wholesale falsification of reality impossible" (15, p. 144); "all attempts at denial in later phases of development have, of course, the ego's functions of perception and memory as their adversaries" (15, p. 144); and "the gradual development of the ego and of the reality principle strengthens experience and memory and slowly weakens the tendency to deny" (15, pp. 144–145). We prefer to view the phenomenon simply as a function of existing facilitations in the cognitive subsystem. As the young child grows up, connections from sensory elements to corresponding cognitive components are strengthened by repeated activation and circuits become more firmly established. The intensity of subsequent signals, given the same stimulus as before, increases over time to the point where, in the mature organism, it is highly unlikely that a sensory-instigated signal can be successfully blocked by inhibition.*

If inhibitory action within the cognitive subsystem takes place in networks *not* directly triggered by sensory input, the interference is analogous to the familiar defense of *repression.* Imaginal signals unaccompanied by sensory firing or purely conceptual signals both can be impeded because of connections between their originating circuits and the anxiety network, which includes the inhibition mechanism. These connections are built from past experience involving anxiety discharge and their later activation follows automatically in accord with the model's principles of processing. The necessity in psychoanalytic theory for postulating special countercathectic forces utilized *continuously* by the ego to restrain unacceptable impulses is thereby obviated. Also the deleterious consequences for cognitive operations generally, attributed to tying up massive quantities of this defensive energy otherwise put to better use, can be understood more parsimoniously as the pervasive action of inhibition upon contiguously discharging circuits in the cognitive subsystem. The greater the number of circuits hooked up to the anxiety network, the more likely are

---

* This statement does not hold, of course, for exceptional conditions like rapid tachistoscopic exposure of stimuli or hypnotically induced effects (see Chapter 5). Denial in regressed psychosis may also represent a condition in which external sensory input does not have its customary impact and therefore is vulnerable to inhibition. The latter speculation merits further study.

other ongoing processes to be disrupted by inhibition.* Unlike denial, repression is commonplace among normal adults, the difference being that nonsensory instigated signals tend to be weaker and therefore more vulnerable to blocking.

Finally, the locus of inhibitory action can be connections linking cognitive representations of affect and motor movements to their respective subsystems. Under these circumstances it is possible to obtain intact cognitive output unaccompanied by the glandular and muscular discharges which might ordinarily be expected. Thus certain thoughts are free of anxiety ramifications in the abstract, yet their verbal expression may be fraught with danger. *Suppression* therefore refers to blocking of a cognitive-motoric sequence halfway through because the motoric representations, rather than the originating cognitive content circuits, are closely coupled with the anxiety network. The basis for such selective attachments of anxiety must be sought, naturally, in the individual's life history. Similarly, the phenomenon of *isolation* of emotion pertains to a sequential process whereby inhibition is invoked after the thought signal is hyperfacilitated and prior to affective discharge.

DERIVATIVES AND PSYCHOPATHOLOGY

So far the operation of inhibition has been linked to the avoidant defenses of denial, repression, suppression, and isolation. By applying the model to Freud's notion of *derivatives,* we can broaden the range of phenomena encompassed by our conceptualization. "Derivatives" in the psychoanalytic sense refer to "associatively connected ideas that are less objectionable (than the repressed ideas to which they are related) to the conscious ego" (15, p. 17). Most neurotic symptoms as well as screen memories, daydreams, and the like are put into this category. Other than stating the associative connection to repressed ideas, psychoanalytic theory specifies only that derivatives acquire energy from their warded-off antecedents and can themselves vary in amount of anxiety still attached.

Can the working model provide a more precise formulation of the establishment of derivatives and their relationship to external stimuli, affects, and other thought processes? The notion of repression has already been defined as inhibitory action, within the cognitive sub-

* Amnesia and dissociation, which represent pathologically extreme involvement of inhibition, will be discussed in the chapter on hypnosis (see pp. 161–165).

system, upon networks not directly triggered by sensory input.[*]
Figure 23 depicts the process, involving inhibition, whereby input
initially activating a pathogenic network gradually becomes coupled
instead to a nonpathogenic cognitive substitute.

The example chosen to illustrate formation of a derivative is sibling
rivalry in an older brother who witnesses an affectionate scene between his parents and younger brother. The cognitive network hooking up primitive thoughts (P), about smashing his younger rival over
the head, to anxiety and inhibition is labeled "pathogenic" because it
produces interference with ongoing events in the cognitive subsystem.
In addition to triggering the anxiety network via connections built
from past experience (e.g., previous threats and punishments by
parents), P-circuit signals at Time 1 also begin to activate by spread
other overlapping cognitive networks. In the present instance these
derivatives (D) represent thoughts about fondly patting him on the
head—the overlapping circuits having to do with those physical movements common to the diametrically opposed intentions.

A crucial consideration is the rapidity of signal spread from P to D
circuits, which in turn depends upon the existing degree of facilitation.
If the P and D networks share a large proportion of circuits and their
interconnections are highly facilitated, it is likely that the P-triggered
inhibition will to some extent damp contiguous D discharges as well.[†]
Thus, the more remote from P the associated D network is, the greater
are the chances for its signals to gain unimpeded discharge after
cessation of inhibition.

At Time 2 in Figure 23 the D circuits are shown to be strengthened
by cognitive reverberation following hyperfacilitation and, typically,
by sensory feedback from pleasurable affect discharges. The latter
are instigated by relief pleasure upon termination of anxiety (see pp.
134–135) and gratification based upon external rewards like praise
from parents. During this phase associations are formed between

---

[*] It should be noted that partially effective inhibitory action may sufficiently
impede transmission of cognitive content signals to prevent their hyperfacilitation
and yet allow the connected anxiety circuits to be triggered. We suspect that
widespread activity of this sort, i.e., anxiety discharges in the absence of corresponding cognitive output masked by inhibition, underlies the phenomenon of
free-floating anxiety.

[†] This notion bears rough resemblance to *secondary repression* in psychoanalysis.
However, the phenomenon is assigned by the model specifically to variables
which determine strength of cognitive connections between primitive and derivative thoughts rather than stating generally that ". . . a tendency then develops
to repress any event associatively connected with the originally repressed material . . ." (15, p. 149).

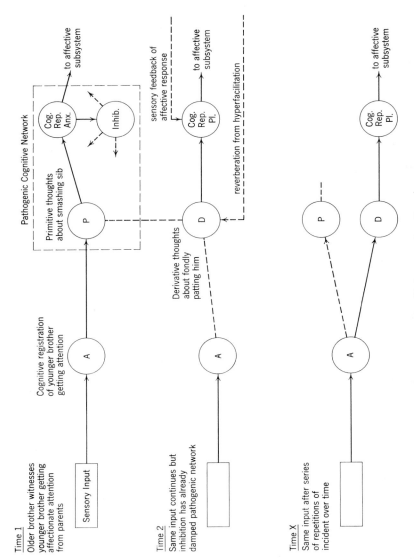

FIGURE 23. Establishment of a derivative.

the D circuits and contiguously active A circuits maintained by the continuing sensory input. Repetition of such events over time can result in the situation depicted at Time X, when the A circuits are tied more closely to D than P, thereby leading directly to the hyper-facilitation of derivative thoughts with only negligible instigation of the weakened primitive ones.

Obviously there are numerous gradations possible in the balance between A-P and A-D networks. In the illustration just cited, a vir-tual restructuring of input took place, and the derivative qualifies as "successful" in the sense that the anxiety network was eventually by-passed entirely. However, other resolutions may be less clearcut. If the relative facilitations are more nearly equal, the A-P connection is perpetuated and subsequent "breakthroughs" of the pathogenic net-work may commonly accompany certain conditions. For instance, the P network may win out in the competition for hyperfacilitation because of an input change, such as the younger brother now thumb-ing his nose at our psychically struggling hero! Or even fortuitous and extraneous arousal of anxiety can, by combination of its own feedback input with that of the original stimulus, tip the balance in favor of the pathogenic. The capacity of anxiety feedback to mediate cognitive responses was demonstrated in Chapter 8. Still another cause may be strong, continuing input which outlasts the effectiveness of inhibitory action. Pathogenic networks linked to sexual urges, for example, may be reactivated in the circumstance of heightened physio-logical input.

Slips typically represent breakthroughs of signals from pathogenic networks. Steve, in a Blacky recall trial (#42 H), reversed his usual sequence and mentioned the anxiety-laden picture, IX (Guilt Feelings), ahead of VII (Identification Process). During the ensuing hypnotic inquiry he reported the experience as follows:

S: It's real funny—I thought I was saying "shaking the finger at the toy dog" and I said "conscience figure" instead. I was all worried that I still had to say "conscience figure" because it's always the last one and I had already said it. I felt real relieved when I suddenly realized that I'd said that instead of the "toy dog," by mistake I guess.

In this case the inadvertent discharge of signals from the pathogenic network was probably occasioned by the reliving, just prior to the recall trial, of an episode in which S felt upset and guilty. The extra facilitation thereby accruing to the IX circuits allowed those signals to overcome inhibition and compete successfully for hyperfacilitation against the VII signals.

Turning back to Figure 23, the reader no doubt identifies the chain of events as *reaction formation,* described in psychoanalytic theory as the development in the ego of conscious socialized attitudes which are the direct opposite of repressed wishes in the unconscious—in model terms, simply the hyperfacilitation of signals from a certain derivative network in place of a primitive one blocked by anxiety-triggered inhibition. Other defense mechanisms can also be understood as derivatives, their distinctiveness residing in the particular content transmitted by the D network. Thus, *projection* conveys "younger brother hates me"; *intellectualization* applies to an abstract, highly ideational derivative; *displacement* provides a substitute object upon which aggression can be vented without undue arousal of anxiety; *sublimation,* classed as "successful," represents a marked superiority of A-D facilitation over A-P so that, unlike the other defenses, there is little or no chance of inhibition any longer being invoked by the original input; and so on down the list. The forms which D networks assume in a given individual evolve, of course, from his idiosyncratic past history.

To recapitulate, the inhibition mechanism occupies a central position in the model's handling of psychodynamic phenomena. The various avoidant defenses are interpreted according to the locus of inhibitory action in the Mental System, and the additional concept of derivative networks links other types of defenses, neurotic symptoms, daydreams, etc. to our theoretical frame of reference. (Before proceeding to symptoms and fantasy, we should mention the parallel between this treatment of inhibition and Freud's earliest notion of repression as a general defense underlying all others.)

Psychopathological symptoms fall in the category of derivatives (see Fenichel [15, pp. 193 f.] for a detailed presentation of the psychoanalytic view). *Obsessions* and *compulsions,* for example, both imply overly facilitated D networks, differentiated by strong connections to the motoric subsystem in the case of compulsions. The tormented older brother in Figure 23 may be plagued by recurring murderous thoughts, or he may be compelled to crush every ant that crosses his path. More complex is the symptom of *conversion,* in which "changes of physical functions occur which, unconsciously and in a distorted form give expression to instinctual impulses that previously had been repressed" (15, p. 216). Suppose our protagonist is suddenly afflicted by paralysis of an arm. How can such a symptom be conceptualized in the working model?

The original thoughts about striking and injuring the younger brother arise from activation of a primitive network triggering muscular flexion circuits in the motoric subsystem. However, these P circuits are linked very early to the anxiety network, and resultant inhibition interferes with transmission of signals from the controlling motoric representation in the cognitive subsystem. In this example the inhibition also acts upon all contiguously discharging networks, which share overlapping circuits (e.g., nonpathological thoughts about hitting in various sports) and therefore are triggered in quick succession by spread from P. Along with the generalized aborting of flexor movements, a derivative network conveying "don't hit younger brother" evolves in the manner described above. This D network contains its own motoric features, namely extensor movements designed to prevent hitting, which function antagonistically to flexion and may contribute to the paralysis.

Fantasies or daydreams are an especially common form of derivative, characterized by an absence of motoric activity. Their typical connection to positive affect, i.e., their wish-fulfilling quality, is easily understood. Apart from those substitute thoughts already linked to pleasure through prior experiences of gratification, newly emerging fantasies prove rewarding as a consequence of relief pleasure following cessation of anxiety discharge in the pathogenic network. The selective retention and strengthening of positive daydreams is furthered by the inhibition of unpleasant ones via their concomitant anxiety, so that primitive thoughts tend to be supplanted eventually by coupled positively toned D networks. Yet these derivatives are not themselves closely tied to particular sensory contexts (which makes them often difficult to recall later) and depend for their arousal upon mediation by the pathogenic network. Prevalence of fantasy throughout the Mental System, while not directly deleterious, betrays the existence of numerous P networks which do impair the efficiency of ongoing cognitive operations.

The state of an individual's mental health, his *ego strength*, can thus be translated into the number of pathogenic networks, combined with accessibility of derivatives which do not trigger anxiety and inhibition. A "weak ego" is one characterized by many highly facilitated P networks, readily made to discharge by sensory inputs or spread from other cognitive circuits, and a paucity of anxiety-free derivatives. Inhibitory action is therefore rampant throughout the Mental System and yet at the same time insufficient to prevent disruptive discharge from the strongly activated anxiety channel. The net result is widespread blocking of contiguous cognitive signals, regardless of their content, plus anxiety responses feeding back to interrupt logical chains of thought still further (see p. 172). Specific forms of illness, e.g., the various neuroses and psychoses, reflect extent of pathological involvement and types of associated D networks.*

Fixation implies a vast network, acquired early in life, which continues to maintain its dominance, incorporating additional derivative circuits as the individual gets older. Following the psychoanalytic view, we believe that such networks can arise from excessive gratification of the child's desires, severe frustration, and alternations between the two. In the case of immediate and strong gratification pleasure, affective feedback serves to consolidate the active cognitive circuits, whose signals tend to monopolize hyperfacilitation. Connections to overlapping D networks (e.g., diverse conceptions of "supplies" growing out of the original feeding relationship with the mother) are also facilitated in the process. Notions of delayed gratification, so valuable in combating frustration later in life, consequently do not have much opportunity to be built up.

The young child's predisposition to fixation may be due partly to weaker differentiation in his evolving cognitive subsystem, which enhances the possibility for extended networks to form, and partly to the more primitive and intense affective discharges at early ages (therefore stronger response feedback). Relief pleasure is also probably greater, which helps to understand the occurrence of fixation in the case of extreme frustration. For example, the hungry infant who is repeatedly allowed to scream for long periods before being fed likely has acquired a pathogenic network emitting potent anxiety discharges. Any derivative even temporarily capable of reducing the discomfort, such as sucking his thumb, will be coupled with considerable pleasure and hence tend to develop a fixated sequence.

Regression is a more ambiguous concept, applied variously to inappropriate behavioral acts like temper tantrums; to the return of primitive fantasies; or to alogical modes of thinking as in "primary process." Actually all three interpretations can be viewed more parsimoniously as manifestations of pathogenic networks reactivated by overwhelming anxiety discharge in a current context whose stimulus aspects bear some similarity to the original situation. The convergence of strong anxiety input with context similarity is apt to trigger P networks, since the latter include the cognitive representation of anxiety. Primitive thoughts are thus elicited and, if motoric circuits have been hooked up in the past, regressive acts also take place. In

---

* Innate structural defects, e.g., within the affective subsystem or the inhibitory mechanism, should not be overlooked as other possible contributors to mental illness.

addition, anxiety-mediated cognition along with the effects of inhibition contribute to alogicality of thinking (see Chapter 13).

In summary, this chapter began with a brief discussion of motivation and emotion in terms of the working model; then spelled out in more detail the functions of anxiety and inhibition, including references to pertinent experiments from Part B; and lastly attempted a reformulation of key psychoanalytic concepts in the areas of defense, derivatives, and psychopathology. Next we shall turn our attention to special topics in the field of motivation—hypnotic compliance and amnesia, which played such a vital role in the experimental methodology described in Part B.

Hypnotic compliance and amnesia 12

From the days of Mesmer the vagaries of scientific reaction to the acceptability of hypnotic practice have been matched by the confusing array of theories seeking to account for the state itself. A very eloquent plea for the admission of hypnosis to psychology's inner sanctum of respectable methods was issued some time ago by White (48), and it is our hope that the experiments in Part B have spoken for themselves on that topic. Here we shall concentrate on the nature of hypnotic phenomena in order to see whether our conceptual model can contribute to a better understanding of them.

If any historical trend is discernible at all, it is probably in the direction of discounting the existence of unique features of hypnosis which distinguish it from other conditions. One by one the various phenomena—automatic compliance to suggestion, unusual muscular feats, insensibility to pain, heightened memory, etc.—have been shown to be reproducible by different means. The culmination of such efforts is represented in Hull's (24) declaration that hypnosis is nothing more than a state of hypersuggestibility differing *quantitatively* rather than *qualitatively* from the normal.

White very rightly criticizes this view on the grounds that it tells us almost nothing about the processes involved. Unfortunately his own approach suffers from the same malady. One cannot quarrel with his diagnosis of hypnotic behavior as a "meaningful goal-directed striving, its general goal being to behave like a hypnotized person as this is continually defined by the operator and understood by the subject." Still the crucial mechanisms are no nearer at hand than before. He begins to come closer, in his treatment of the induction procedure, with the insightful observation that the key probably lies in S's state of drowsiness, but declines to pursue the point until "we know more about drowsiness and can state more precisely the changes which go with it."

It is not our purpose to review the many varieties of hypnotic theory. The interested reader is referred to Brenman and Gill (8), Wolberg (49), and Weitzenhoffer (47) among others. The conclusion derivable from the literature is that even modern examinations of the topic tend to be couched in purely descriptive phrases. Sarbin (42) offers a very cogent account within the framework of role theory; Barber (1) proposes that we dispense with the word "state" and consider hypnosis as a "descriptive abstraction referring to a number of interrelated and overlapping processes" to be understood in light of the entire transactional exchange between S and E; Weitzenhoffer (47) conceives of hypnosis as the outcome of "homo-action" and "generalization of suggestibility." But where do we go from here?

The inescapable fact is that hypnosis does require some special explanation. White's comments are particularly appropriate in this regard:

> . . . Perhaps these claims are justified; perhaps there is no phenomenon in the repertory of hypnotic suggestion which cannot be produced in some other way. But, even if this be true, we are not exempt from explaining why the hypnotic procedure, which does not create excitement and violent emotion, which does not put one to sleep, which makes no use of free association, which virtually excludes a context of other actions, and which especially with practice requires very little time, brings about so momentous an effect. It is legitimate to be surprised at the power of hypnotic suggestion. (48, p. 482)

Orne (34), who has been quite clever in his experiments with "real" and "fake" Ss, attempts to locate the essence (as opposed to the artifacts) of hypnosis in subjective experience. He lists principal features of the latter as: (1) the discontinuity from normal waking experiences; (2) the compulsion to follow cues given by E; (3) the potentiality for experiencing, as subjectively real, distortions of perception, memory, or feeling based on suggestions by E; and (4) the ability to tolerate logical inconsistencies that would be disturbing in the waking state. But the problems still remain: Why does S experience the compulsion to comply? What mechanisms are responsible for the peculiar amnesia effects? And so on down the line.

We have maintained that a detailed approach to mental functions is more apt to lead to the underlying processes themselves. A natural step in support of this assertion is to try to develop a better understanding of the central phenomena of hypnotic compliance. Below we shall present a play-by-play analysis, in terms of the model's operations, of a typical interaction between E and S. (The reader is again referred to Appendix A for a verbatim account of the induction procedure employed with our Ss.)

APPLICATION OF THE MODEL TO PHENOMENA OF HYPNOTIC COMPLIANCE

Figures 24 to 26 portray stages in hypnotic compliance with reference both to phenomenological aspects and corresponding model conceptualizations. Figure 24 summarizes the preliminary establishment of the hypnotic context. E begins by calling attention to the necessary preconditions, using some statement like "Success will depend upon your cooperation and ability to relax." The motivational readiness to be hypnotized which S brings to the situation is a resultant of his particular complex life experiences and reflects such factors as the need to please authority figures, a wish for dependency relationships, the seeking of help for personal problems, etc. Individual differences are also prominent in the ability to relax—some Ss having successfully practiced self-relaxation in the past, others not. A consequence of E's introductory comments is the activation in S's Mental System of existing cognitive circuits representing cooperation and relaxation, designated for simplicity as one General Compliance (GC) network. At the same time, sensory inputs from physical aspects of the hypnotic setting—walls, ceiling, couch, presence of E, etc.—trigger appropriate circuits (labeled HS), so that connections are established by contiguity between GC and HS. Together these networks constitute the hypnotic context.

E proceeds to expedite a state of drowsiness in S and attempts to monopolize external sensory inputs to him. S is told to stare at the light and listen carefully to what E says. E keeps talking in soothing tones calculated to encourage further relaxation. Appropriate responses by S are commented upon favorably, and in general E tries

Phenomenological Aspects:

  1. E calls attention to necessary preconditions.
  2. E limits potential range of external sensory inputs to S.
  3. E assumes control, to fullest possible extent, of sensory inputs to S.
  4. S reaches desired state of low arousal (drowsiness).

Model Conceptualization:

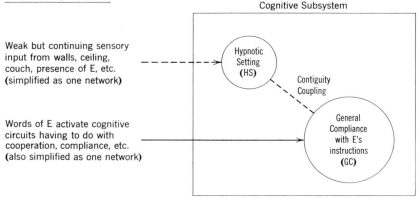

FIGURE 24.   Stages in hypnotic compliance: 1. Establishing the hypnotic context.

to keep S's attention focused on the induction task itself.*   After a while S, we assume, reaches the desired degree of low arousal which leads E to introduce a suggestion requiring compliance.

Figure 25 spells out the operations presumed to underlie S's narrowed range of attention and concentration, and the forceful build-up of the specific suggestion (SS). When E says "Your eyes will be glued shut," the cognitive SS network is triggered and connections begin to be formed to the hypnotic context networks, HS and GC. Since the SS signal discharges are the strongest, by virtue of that network's more intense sensory instigation, it rather than the others is amplified in the hyperfacilitation process. Reverberation of the boosted SS signals reactivates all the suggestion networks (SS, GC, and HS), providing extra facilitation to the SS one. The latter, on the second round, again dominates the cognitive scene, receiving still more amplification and perpetuating the chain reaction until interrupted eventually by a new input from E. Typically E repeats the suggestion one or more times, further adding to the SS build-up.

---

* Although there are many different induction procedures, all ultimately bring S to a narrowed state of concentration on E's instructions.

Phenomenological Aspects:

  S's narrowed range of attention in presumed low arousal state allows him to concentrate fully on
  E's specific suggestion (e.g., "Your eyes will be glued shut"), which acquires exceptional force.

Model Conceptualization:

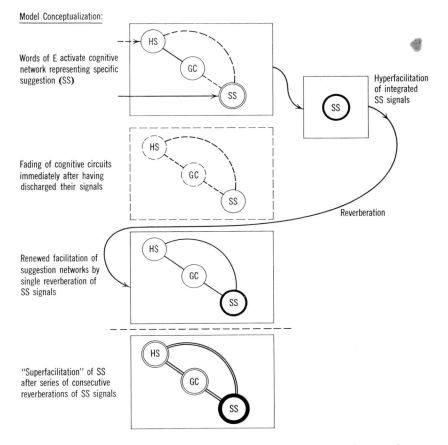

Words of E activate cognitive
network representing specific
suggestion (SS)

Hyperfacilitation
of integrated
SS signals

Fading of cognitive circuits
immediately after having
discharged their signals

Reverberation

Renewed facilitation of
suggestion networks by
single reverberation of
SS signals

"Superfacilitation" of SS
after series of consecutive
reverberations of SS signals

FIGURE 25.   Stages in hypnotic compliance.   2. E introduces the specific suggestion.   [*Note:* Strength of facilitation is indicated in ascending order by broken
lines, single solid lines, double solid lines, and thickness of blackened portions
of circles.]

In this way the suggestion networks are generally strengthened and
the SS one in particular becomes "superfacilitated." *

  * The term "superfacilitation" is employed to describe unusual strengthening
of connections between parts of the cognitive subsystem.   It should not be
confused with "hyperfacilitation," which refers specifically to the amplification
of integrated signals in the last phase of cognitive processing.

Thus, exceptionally potent reverberatory action is fostered by an externally manipulated reduction of irrelevant sensory input (S told to close eyes; distracting sounds minimized; etc.) and augmentation of relevant input provided by E (e.g., S instructed to pay close attention; E repeats suggestions). Also any extraneous network which gets activated in spite of the above precautions is likely to have its signals blocked by inhibition, triggered by the compliant S's set to attend *only* to E's words. Low arousal inherent in S's drowsiness contributes by weakening sensory input generally, which tends to filter out all but the strong E input even before the cognitive subsystem is put in motion. However, there must be an optimal stage of low arousal, inasmuch as sufficient nonspecific input is required to sustain an adequate degree of amplification during hyperfacilitation. The balance is a delicate one to achieve (White points to the role of E in arresting S at this level), since too much arousal will increase the likelihoood of successful competition and too little will not allow adequate boosting and reverberation.

Once the superfacilitation is accomplished, the compliant execution of the suggestion follows automatically, as shown in Figure 26. When E asks S to try to open his eyes, the immediately triggered cognitive SS network transmits signals of unusual intensity to its connected motoric circuits. The latter's action in turn produces decisive effector discharge preventing S from opening his eyes. Feedback of the motoric responses themselves also contributes to maintaining the strength of the SS network. In addition, E's subsequent expression of approval over S's obedience sets into motion a pleasure (PL) network, whose affective discharge feedback leads to increased facilitation of the coupled GC network. The hypnotic context is thereby strengthened with each successive compliance and the way is paved for progressively easier execution of later suggestions.

A compliant act ceases to be performed when the signal triggered by a *new* input wins out during hyperfacilitation and starts on its own reverberatory chain. Most often this occurs after E countermands the previous instruction, by saying "now you *can* open your eyes." In the absence of dominant new sensory input from E, it is possible that the behavior will drop out for other reasons. Prolonged muscular discomfort, for instance, can provide mounting proprioceptive feedback which will eventually outweigh the suggestion network in determining motoric output.

The notion of a superfacilitated cognitive network strengthened by uninterrupted reverberations can account for the carrying out of all kinds of suggestions—motoric, affective, or cognitive. In our own

Phenomenological Aspects:

1. E requests S to test force of suggestion ("Now try to open your eyes")
2. S complies with suggestion (unable to open eyes).
3. E expresses general approval over compliance.

Model Conceptualization:

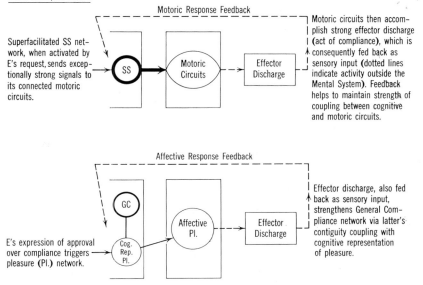

FIGURE 26. Stages in hypnotic compliance: 3. S executes the suggested act.

experiments such an interpretation holds equally well for the induction of a hand clench, the attachment of anxiety, or the evocation of a visual image. The following comments by Fred, made during his last hypnotic session in response to E's questions about the experience of being hypnotized, portray in words this pervasive state of superfacilitation:

You don't really feel asleep in the sense of not being aware of things the way you are in sleep. As a matter of fact it seems rather keyed up, sort of a superman-like being. You seem to be more keenly aware of things—you can do things that you normally can't. You're able to recall things and feelings that are ordinarily completely repressed and to experience them as if they were happening for the first time again—much as in waking moments sometimes you get the feeling that you've done something before and it seems very real and strong at the time. It doesn't just seem like a fleeting glance but rather that you're really in it again, feel yourself in it, see yourself in it . . . Emotions seem much sharper and finer than normally. I suppose that's because we're isolating them rather than going along in everyday life from one thing and switching right into something else. Here we're sort of stopping one moment, one emotion, and concentrating on it and bringing it to a real high pitch . . . You don't seem to drift off into something else the way you normally do. The attention span seems to be much longer, much deeper and sharper.

Harold, less eloquent, summarizes the hypnotic situation as one in which "it's easier to think, no outside thoughts interfere."

The posthypnotic feature of many of the experimental procedures is easily understood as a coupling of additional cognitive networks representing certain stimuli, such as Blacky pictures, to the suggestion network during hypnosis. Subsequent presentation of the stimulus in the waking state serves to trigger the still superfacilitated network.* With the passage of time, and assuming no intervening cues for mental rehearsal of the suggestion, the network probably grows gradually weaker to the point of unresponsiveness.

The so-called "transcendence" of S's voluntary capacity (as in extraordinary muscular feats like supporting the weight of several men on one's body outstretched across two separated chairs) supposedly achieved in hypnosis can also be viewed simply as the transmission of an abnormally strong set of signals from cognitive to motoric subsystems. The difference between performance during hypnotic and waking states is attributable to the superior setting in the former for the build-up of exceptional signal strength. Compatible with this interpretation is the fact that the limits of volitional control, though seemingly transcended, are nevertheless systematically related to hypnotic behavior. The further one gets from these limits, the smaller is the effect of hypnotic suggestion (48). In short, the same mechanisms are activated in hypnosis as in the waking state, only more so!

The influence of cognitive superfacilitation can extend not only to motoric and affective subsystems but also to the inhibition mechanism as well. The ease with which cognitions can be coupled with inhibition under hypnosis is quite striking. A common example is the induction of insensibility to painful stimulation, which we interpret to be the consequence of inhibitory action upon the cognitive representation and the cognitive label of physical pain inside the Mental

---

* The compelling quality of reactions to a posthypnotic cue is conveyed by Ned on an occasion when he had been previously instructed under hypnosis to speak into the telephone as soon as the lights in the room were made brighter: "The minute you turned up those lights I felt as if I had to do something and then right away the telephone pops into my mind . . . it seems like I was magically lifted up . . . a do-or-die situation."

System. The physical aspects of S's reaction to being pricked by a pin (bleeding, etc.) are the same as in the waking state—the *subjective experience* differs. Connections from cognitive circuits, which ordinarily lead to a variety of motoric (withdrawal, "ouch!") and affective (anger, fear) responses, are impeded and S remains in a seemingly analgesic condition. Another illustration is "rapport," a term used to describe the fact that S carries out the instruction to attend exclusively to E's words and no one else's. A general network "Not Words of E" is quickly and strongly linked to inhibition, so that any future activation of this newly established network by the words of another person automatically reduces the possibility of a response to that person.

It is natural to be misled into thinking that the phenomenon of rapport demonstrates a mysterious interpersonal quality inherent in the hypnotic relationship between E and S. We contend that a more parsimonious explanation for all hypnotic experience lies in the process of superfacilitation which, as we have discussed above, depends in turn upon restriction of sensory input and low arousal. A number of facts support the view that these determinants rather than E's mastery over S's "will" are the crucial elements: (1) the phenomenon of autohypnosis; (2) S's ability to execute suggestions which he gives to himself while E is supposedly directing the hypnotic session; and (3) the ease with which the hypnotized S can be transferred from one E to another.

Although it is true that autohypnosis is more successfully accomplished by persons previously trained as subjects, it is by no means incumbent upon us to ascribe magical significance to E's role in this regard. He serves to help S learn the desired point at which to arrest relaxation and S, having once acquired this skill, can practice it himself whenever he chooses. The stimulus can be one word from E, as in the instantaneous induction of a deep trance, or the same instruction self-applied. Again Fred's introspections are of interest: "I think that all the suggestions you've given me—I could follow them just by remaining relaxed and just sort of thinking about the suggestion itself, and I think I could produce just about anything that I've done." Similarly, Steve reports: "It just seems so easy—I guess most people consider this so occult and different, but it's really easily controllable."

In addition, several of our experimental Ss admitted in their final interview that they occasionally had resorted to autosuggestions completely unrelated to the task at hand. Laura, for example, narrated how she often became more comfortable under hypnosis by saying to herself things like "my foot will stop itching," "my hand doesn't feel tired," etc. The result was fully as effective as if E had given the instruction to her. Still another facet of hypnosis which leads us to discount the uniqueness of E's contribution is the ease of transferring the "power" of suggestion from one E to another. During the course of our experiments we sometimes instructed S to be responsive to another member of the research team and the transition always took place quickly and effortlessly. In other words, the inhibition network involved in the rapport phenomenon can readily be made inoperative by creating a new, more powerful network "Obey Instructions of New E."

By interpreting hypnotic compliance as the consequence of prolonged reverberation and superfacilitation of specific cognitive suggestion networks, it becomes simpler for us to comprehend the link between hypnosis and other states commonly assumed to be related—religious ecstasy, yoga, self-induced trances in primitive societies, etc. All require a certain degree of "concentration," whose antecedents we have spelled out to be an optimal combination of specific and nonspecific sensory inputs to the Mental System. Barber succinctly ties together the various manifestations of "detachment" in the following passage:

> This process of relative detachment from the environment . . . is often conceptualized as a mysterious entity called "trance." There is no objection to using the term "trance" to describe this process *if* (italics his) we remember that it is not an "entity" and that it is not "unusual." It is, in fact, a not too uncommon aspect of our daily life. An individual is reading a book when he suddenly realizes that he has no idea of what he has just been "reading." For a few moments he was "in trance"; he was not only unconcerned about the printed page, he was also not "thinking about anything" and not attending to and not perceiving his surroundings. We also experience this process of relative non-response to stimulation, this passive, relaxed, non-thinking attitude, as we become drowsy and sleepy. Leuba was justified in concluding from his extensive study of the "trance" of the yogi, the mystic, the shaman, and the hypnotic subject that: "Were it not customary to use the word trance only when the state . . . is produced under unusual or abnormal conditions, ordinary drowsy states and normal sleep would be called trances." (1, pp. 117–118)

By the same token our theoretical position can also encompass similar conditions with less striking effects than hypnosis itself, such as waking suggestibility, hypnoidal aspects of revery, drug-induced hypnagogic states, and so on. These represent points on the arousal continuum which approximate but do not reach the optimal hypnotic location. As a result, extraneous specific sensory inputs are sometimes processed and reverberation is interrupted; or the amount of nonspecific arousal is insufficient to maintain fully adequate amplification and reverberation is not sustained. But compliance under these conditions can often be accomplished quite effectively, as revealed in this description by Laura of her reactions to the initial suggestibility-screening session in which members of the group were asked to take turns "falling over backward":

> When you told me I was going to fall back, I thought "now I'm not going to do that—the other ones will, but I'll show them—this is just ridiculous." And so I waited and I was about the last to go up after I'd been watching everybody, and you hardly even said the first word and over I went. It was so funny I really laughed about it, because I was so determined that I wasn't going to do it.

MEMORY ALTERATIONS

Other major aspects of hypnosis, in addition to those directly manifested in compliance to suggestion, involve dramatic alterations of memory. In this section we shall take up three phenomena utilized in various stages of our hypnotic procedures: suggested posthypnotic amnesia; heightened ability to remember past occurrences (hypermnesia); and so-called "age regression."

The important consideration in attempting to understand such alterations is that events are imbedded in a *context*. The focus of attention always occurs, albeit unconsciously in many instances, within a surrounding environment of associations. Later recall is achieved by gaining access to the context, which then releases its encapsulated memory. Nowhere is this demonstrated more strikingly than in hypnosis. The highly trained S, accustomed to frequent excursions between hypnotic and waking states, acquires special sensitivity to contextual cues differentiating the two states. A host of experiences in one case are associated with lying drowsily on a couch in the laboratory with eyes closed, in the other with sitting up alertly and eyes open. The feeling of "detachment" is probably attributable to the sharpness of separation between the two settings. Continuity within a state seems to be greater from one session to the next, several days later, than from hypnosis to waking a few moments apart. Steve, for example, commented at the beginning of a period: "Hmmm, that's funny, I lie down and start picking up the conversation right where we left off last time—all of a sudden it pops into my mind!"

The phenomenon of suggested posthypnotic amnesia provides a

classic illustration.* E instructs S under hypnosis that, after awakening, he will be unable to remember anything that transpired while he was asleep. The trained S carries out this suggestion perfectly—drawing a complete blank when he tries to recall (either at E's instigation or his own) what had happened. Yet there are some curious aspects to this inability. The forgotten material still plays a very active part in waking cognition, as demonstrated by the paired-letter experiment (see Chapter 4) in which S could not remember having learned lists of paired letters but responded to stimuli in accordance with that learning. Also, S is somehow aware that the amnesia is in force and that only a thin wall is blocking recovery of the lost material. For instance, Steve, when requested to review all the events of a two-hour period just concluded, recounted everything that took place while he was awake and then added slyly: "The rest is your secret, you know but I don't—well, I know it but I can't think about it—I know what it is but I just kind of stop myself before I think of it."

Furthermore once the posthypnotic amnesia lifts, either due to spontaneous failure in the case of insufficient training or to a prearranged signal from E, the forgotten experiences suddenly appear in consciousness with amazing rapidity and vividness. During the night following his first session Ned found that all at once his "brains were going round and round, and more and more of the stuff that had happened came back—quite clear, not a fuzzy outline at all" (two days later his account of a very lengthy and involved hypnotic conversation held that first hour was practically verbatim!). Even more impressive evidence of this sudden on-off switching is contained in the following dialogue with Fred. In his final hypnotic session he was told that, upon awakening, he would be able to remember what had happened to him under hypnosis throughout the preceding weeks as soon as the light in the room was turned up:

E: (turns up light)
S: Umm, interesting! How about that!
E: What happened?
S: I can remember things now.

* It is not presently known whether there really is such a phenomenon as "spontaneous" posthypnotic amnesia, since it is virtually impossible to rule out implicit expectations of amnesia on S's part. Weitzenhoffer (47) offers the belief that spontaneous amnesia probably is a concomitant only of very deep hypnosis. In the latter event forgetting would be explainable, in terms of our model, as a consequence of greatly reduced amplification in the hyperfacilitation process. A stuporous condition, involving very low arousal, would not permit sufficient reverberation to consolidate cognitive networks.

E: What do you remember?
S: Just about everything. All those missing hours were filled in.
E: How did it happen?
S: Well, I don't know, I suppose the best way to describe it would be sort of a cloudy day and then all of a sudden the clouds disappear away from the sun and it sort of turns clear . . . like a rapid unfurling of everything there was . . . it was a little overwhelming.

Returning to our model, how are we to interpret such a phenomenon? Put most simply, there is inhibition of the connections between hypnotic context circuits and linked cognitive circuits of all kinds. We have already indicated, in the previous section on hypnotic compliance, that each specific suggestion network is hooked up to a context represented by hypnotic setting and general compliance. Also, we have stressed that during hypnosis the inhibition mechanism can be invoked immediately and effectively to increase resistance between coupled circuits. Thus E's amnesia instruction brings inhibition to bear on the connections between hypnotic context and specific events so that later, in the waking state, this strongly established network involving inhibition is triggered by E's request "try to remember" (see Figure 27) or by S's own cognitive initiation.

The instantaneous yet total nature of the amnesia effect is attributed to the fact that inhibition need be directed only to connections emanating from the hypnotic context circuits, which serve as a common mediating link to all the hypnotic networks. Blocking this general access prevents the specific memories from being reached.* Instead hyperfacilitation goes to the "Not Supposed to Remember" network, whose output corresponds to S's impression of knowing something is there but not wanting to make the effort to dredge it up. Disengagement of inhibition, either because of its own insufficient strength or from the creation of a stronger set of connections leading to the specific memories (e.g., the light signal given to Fred), results in the unimpeded flow of signals from the still highly facilitated cognitive content circuits. The latter process presumably underlies the outpouring of pent-up memories described by our Ss.

It has been noted that the circuits to which memory access is denied during posthypnotic amnesia are not inactive. If we ask S to associ-

---

* If by some chance the specific memories are reached by another route, their connections to hypnotic context, and consequently inhibition, will quickly cause them to be extinguished. Steve, for example, in the waking state once began to be reminded of some suggested amnesic material while listening to music previously paired with it under hypnosis. Immediately he reported feeling slightly ill and was unable to remember further.

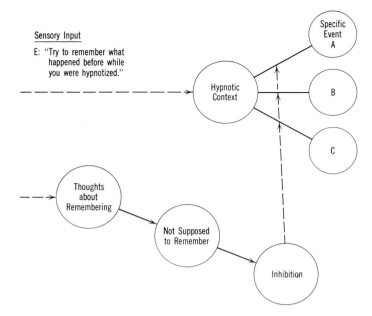

FIGURE 27. Networks representing posthypnotic amnesia. [*Note:* E's instruction activates Hypnotic Context networks and Thoughts about Remembering. The latter lead to the inhibition mechanism, which impedes the passage of signals from Hypnotic Context to Specific Events (A, B, C) previously having occurred under hypnosis.]

ate any letter with the combination W and K, he tends to respond "R," which had been paired with both W and K under hypnosis—in other words, the W-K-R network is able to discharge even though its context is blocked and S cannot remember the circumstance of having learned to pair letters. The reason is that an alternative access, not subject to inhibition, is provided for the W-K-R network by E's request to associate a letter with W and K. Any stimulus whose signals by-pass inhibition will trigger the suggestion networks to their existing intensity.

Just as in the case of compliance, S can bring posthypnotic amnesia under his own control without instruction from E. Indeed the amnesia itself represents compliance to suggestion, so we should expect it to obey the same rules. Steve gives us a very graphic description of this point when he tells about his reactions to the amnesia instruction:

E: In a little while now you're going to wake up. We're through for today—it's 3:25 P.M. When you wake up you won't remember what happened while you were asleep. Okay, wide awake!

S (awake): 3:25.

E: How did you know it was 3:25?

S: You told me.

E: Oh?

S: It seems like I have a discrimination of what's okay to remember and what's not.

E: How do you make that decision?

S: I don't know, it seems like this is a real conscious thing that I do. When you say "Don't remember" I suddenly sort through everything and then I remember a couple of little things that this doesn't apply to. As you said it, everything we did today seemed to run through my mind and I thought "Well I was awake and I was asleep and when I was awake it's okay to remember what happened." Then I just kind of juggle everything around to make sure what's what—the things I can remember and those I can't.

E: Everything that happened runs through your mind in that instant?

S: Well, just kind of a big overview, I guess. Not all the details, just a sort of check that everything is stored away in the right compartments.

E: How fast does that happen?

S: I'd say real fast—just like that! There's very little detail. It's like you've got all these little boxes sitting there in your mind and each one has got a lot of details in them of different little episodes. So then you just shove certain boxes back but if you specify to your mind that any of these boxes is okay to remember, then you can remember all the details inside of it.

E: How big is a box now for this session?

S: Well, I'd say they're fairly small today because there were a lot of switches from awake to asleep (S had been in and out of hypnosis several times for the particular experiments), but I suppose if it were one uninterrupted two-hour session I'd just throw everything into one big box.

A second type of memory alteration observed in hypnosis is hypermnesia, or better-than-normal memory for past events. Here too it is our opinion that context and superfacilitation are crucial. When the experiential setting is recaptured and superfacilitation of cognitive circuits is permitted to build up, latent memories are easily brought back into the focus of attention. Weakly connected circuits, ordinarily not activated, can suddenly be triggered by the exceptionally strong reverberatory signals of the suggestion network. Laura, for example, under hypnosis was once describing a photograph from the family album but could only recollect the circumstances partially. As she returned to the original event in her imagination, all the details began to be filled in. Below is the conversation as it took place:

S: That doghouse kind of reminded me of an outhouse. I remember in the family album we have this hilarious picture of an outhouse and my mother standing in front of it trying to get me to go in. I had my arms crossed in front of me, with a very stubborn look on my face, and I wasn't going in there. I don't remember why or anything. I know we were at somebody's house and I was probably around five or six. She wanted me to go to the bathroom before I went home and I know I wouldn't go in there, but I don't remember why. The only thing I know about it is what I've seen in this photograph and it's very funny because my mother has on real funny clothes that they used to wear —real short skirt and a funny hairdo and everything.

E: Do you remember who took the picture?

S: It seems as if maybe it was my aunt. I don't remember who took it but I know it was awfully funny. But I can't remember what the situation was or why, and I have no idea why I didn't want to go in there. Probably I just didn't have to go and she wanted me to before I went home because it was quite a long drive. But that's all I remember about it—that's the only thing I can think of.

E: Sometimes if you concentrate real hard on a particular experience which is very hazy it's easy to bring back more and more details. So let's try now to sort of relive that situation where you're standing with your mother in front of the outhouse. You can visualize the situation very clearly because you remember the photograph. Do you remember how your mother looked?

S: Yes.

E: Do you remember how you looked?

S: Yes.

E: All right, now put yourself back in that situation. There you are together with your mother—back together with your mother now. More and more of what happened will begin to come back to you. You're back in that situation and new things are occurring to you. Tell me what they are as you're back in that situation again. Can you see your mother now?

S: Yes.

E: Okay, you're back in that situation again as though it's happening now and you can see your mother very clearly. You've just said something. What is it that you just said to your mother?

S: I said "But I don't have to, I don't want to go in there."

E: And what did she say?

S: She said "Well you better go because it's such a long ride home." And I said "But I don't have to" and she said "Well you always do before you get home and then we have to stop somewhere." I remember

somebody was picking cherries—it was near a cherry orchard or something. It doesn't seem as if the outhouse had a door either. Maybe
that's why I didn't want to go in there.

E: What can you see as you visualize the outhouse?

S: Well I can just see this funny old place and then my mother standing
there trying to drag me in and I had my arms folded and was insisting
that I wasn't going in there. And now it seems as if it's because it
didn't have a door.

E: Okay, fine. Now who's taking the picture? Concentrate hard now.
Back in that situation again and somebody's got a camera. Who is it?

S: It's my mother's younger sister and she was with a whole bunch of
kids. They were in high school and they decided just for fun they'd
go somewhere and take a tent and go pick cherries. They had their
camera there because they lived about twenty miles away. They were
taking pictures of each other up in a tree and all sorts of things . . .

E: Can you visualize your aunt now?

S: Yes.

E: She has a camera and what is she wearing?

S: She had on slacks of some kind and an old man's shirt with the sleeves
rolled up and it seems as if they had on funny sailor hats or something
too, so all the twigs and stuff wouldn't get in their hair.

Recovery of the forgotten aspects was sufficiently startling to Laura
for her to want to check their accuracy. The next time she visited
her mother she asked the latter to supply the missing details without
any hint from S as to what they were. Lo and behold, her mother,
after struggling with her own memory for over an hour, came up
with precisely the same description!

When we consider more elaborate attempts to "age-regress" a hypnotized person, the accuracy of recall is more difficult to ascertain.
The interested reader is referred to a thorough treatise on this topic
by Reiff and Scheerer (41), who conclude from their experiments
that two forms of behavior, imagined and genuine, coexist in varying
degrees during every hypnotically regressed state. They also stress
the vital part in memory played by context, both the environmental
context of the original event and the experiential mode and functioning of the personality at that time. A few of our own forays into the
field of hypnotic age regression will be narrated later (Chapter 14)
in connection with the genesis of a psychological symptom in one of
our Ss.

In summary, this chapter has concerned itself with contributions
of the model to an understanding of the phenomena of hypnotic com-

pliance and memory, all of which are relevant to the series of experiments reported in Part B. Other aspects of hypnosis, including perceptual characteristics like hallucination and cognitive ones such as the absence of critical evaluation, will be discussed next in the context of "primary process" thinking.

"Primary process" thinking

13

Webster's Dictionary bears witness to the difficulty of separating perception from cognition in its definition of the latter as "the process of knowing; . . . also a product of this process, as a perception or notion." The differentiation which we find least objectionable hinges simply on the presence or absence of accompanying sensation. If the firing of sensory elements directly instigates a particular circuit's signal discharge, the output is classed as perception; if activation takes place via spread inside the Mental System, the output is labeled cognition. Inasmuch as all behavioral responses entail more than pure perception, one always deals in practice with a conglomerate of both processes. In the area of human thought, a variety of phenomena which offer real challenge to any theory of the mind grow out of Freud's distinction between "primary" and "secondary" modes of thinking.

DEDUCING PSYCHOANALYTIC OBSERVATIONS FROM THE MODEL

It is well-known that thinking tends to be bizarre under certain conditions. Nocturnal dreams are perhaps the most familiar example,

169

but peculiarities are sometimes also noted in free association, hypnosis, daydreaming, sensory deprivation experiments, psychosis, etc. Thoughts seem unaffected by demands of reality, time, order, or logic. Condensation and symbolism become prominent and, in general, there is an apparent discontinuity from one set of ideas to the next. How can such phenomena be accounted for? Freud (18) speaks of free-floating, mobile energy in the Unconscious, directing ideas only according to the possibilities for energy discharge—in contrast to the organized "secondary process" characteristic of the conscious part of the mind. For investigators committed to a search for underlying mechanisms, however, metaphorical interpretations of this sort are obviously unsatisfactory.

We approached the problem by seeking a common factor among the conditions giving rise to primary process thinking. The one that initially occurred to us was *reduced environmental sensory input.* All the conditions enumerated above are associated with at least some restriction of the senses, either by sleep, shutting the eyes, or otherwise limiting attentiveness to external sources. In pursuit of this hypothesis, we asked a group of six psychologists to rank-order the conditions first in terms of prevalence of primary process thinking, and second on a dimension of total amount of sensory input impinging from the environment. The consensus showed close agreement between the two lists: nocturnal dreams and extreme sensory deprivation experiments led both, and daydreaming appeared at the opposite end.

Encouraged by this congruence, we decided to plug "reduced sensory input" into the model and *deduce* its consequences in an effort to determine how many of the phenomenological aspects of primitive thought would follow logically. Figures 28 and 29 summarize the nonspecific and specific effects respectively. Broken-line boxes contain the phenomena which we had previously listed as pertinent, and solid-line boxes the intervening model deductions from the base of reduced environmental sensory input. From Figure 28 we see that a decrease in nonspecific arousal impedes cognitive reverberation, since amplification during the process of hyperfacilitation is cut down. Weaker reverberation in turn implies less spread in the cognitive subsystem, which has two main lines of effect.

First, the reverberatory action may not be strong enough to set in motion all the coupled circuits within a network. Given such partial activation among a number of contiguously discharging networks, the likelihood exists for breakdown in network differentiation. Hyperfacilitation will have more of a tendency than usual to occur se-

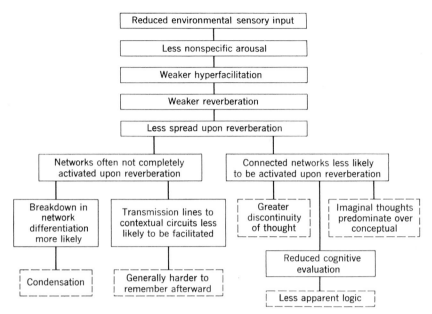

FIGURE 28. Relationship of reduced environmental sensory input to primary process thinking: 1. Nonspecific effects. [*Note:* Broken-line boxes contain various primary process phenomena, which are here deduced from the starting point of reduced environmental sensory input.]

quentially for circuit signals from *separate* networks, in contrast to the typical sequence of amplification of signals from the same network. Thus cognitive output, in which the identity of networks is ordinarily preserved in full, may now contain bizarre, abbreviated combinations of signal discharges—the phenomenon known as *condensation.* Incomplete reverberatory triggering of intranetwork circuits also means that *connections* between those circuits whose signals have been hyperfacilitated and other circuits representing the context in which the salient thoughts occurred are less likely to be facilitated. As a result it is more difficult afterward to remember the thoughts themselves, which are typically reached by way of their associated context (see pp. 161 f.) *

* The tendency to forget one's dreams is thus accountable *primarily* on the basis of generally weaker connections throughout the cognitive subsystem, plus the specific inaccessibility of contextual circuits—all stemming from restriction of sensory input during sleep. Inhibitory action triggered by anxiety

A second set of consequences of impaired spread has to do with the fact that *internetwork* connections tend to be traversed less by reverberating signals. Continuity of thought, which hinges upon the triggering of a chain of linked networks, obviously suffers. Cognitive evaluation, a reflective process of checking thoughts in terms of their present or past reality (to be discussed in detail later in the chapter), also makes use of spread for its execution. Reduction of this capacity is partly responsible for the seeming absence of logic inasmuch as judgment is notoriously deficient. Finally imaginal thoughts, tied closely to direct sensory referents and conveying concrete impressions, are likely to prevail over conceptual ones. The reason for this imbalance is that the latter, by their very nature (see pp. 119 f.), depend largely upon spread for activation. In contrast, sensory-instigated circuit discharges continue to take place to some extent, especially via interoceptive and proprioceptive sources, even when external sensory input is markedly decreased.

Figure 29 traces specific effects of reduced environmental input. Starting with the sequence of steps at the right-hand portion of the diagram, we note that the often lower intensity of arriving sensory signals makes for weaker cognitive activation, which may be insufficient to trigger networks in their entirety. Again the situation is ripe for a breakdown in network differentiation and subsequent condensation, just as it was with impeded reverberation described above. The middle portion records the fact that weaker sensory discharge accompanying cognitive output increases the possibility for confusion in subjective impressions of reality. On p. 118 it was pointed out that minimal sensations are sometimes mistakenly assumed to be a product of the imagination.

The left-hand section of Figure 29 elaborates the consequences occurring more or less by default from the restriction of externally induced cognition. Feedback of effector output becomes relatively more influential as a source of activation. Affective and motoric responses, via their sensory feedback, trigger networks containing circuits which represent those responses cognitively. In Chapter 8 we saw how the feedback of anxiety discharges led specifically to thoughts previously linked experimentally to anxiety. Cognitive mediation by affective- and motoric-based inputs heightens the apparent prelogical nature of primary process thinking, for the chains of association are

network discharge (corresponding roughly to repression of unacceptable ideas in the psychoanalytic frame of reference) presumably plays a more limited role in forgetting dreams.

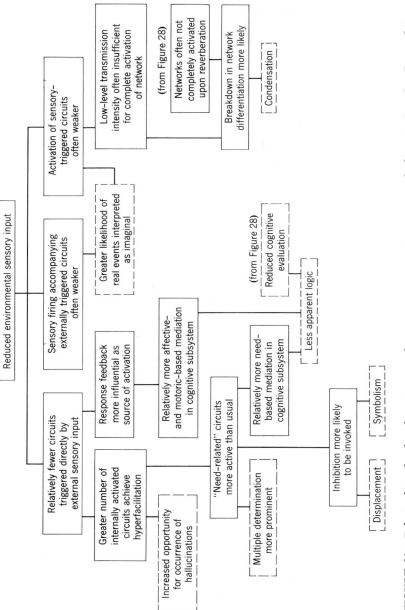

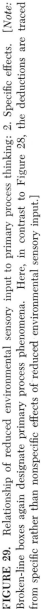

FIGURE 29. Relationship of reduced environmental sensory input to primary process thinking: 2. Specific effects. [*Note:* Broken-line boxes again designate primary process phenomena. Here, in contrast to Figure 28, the deductions are traced from specific rather than nonspecific effects of reduced environmental sensory input.]

not forged by their manifest content. A thread of "affective logic" has no obvious meaning to the observer.

By the same token a greater number of internally instigated circuit signals achieve hyperfacilitation than would otherwise be the case if environmental sensory input were maintained at a normally high level of frequency and intensity. If the signal discharge from a particular circuit is exceptionally strong and reverberates over and over in spite of the smaller amount of amplification, it is possible that a state of superfacilitation will develop to the point of creating hallucinatory output (see pp. 116–117). The absence of strong new, potentially competing sensory input favors such circumstances.*

Internal activation either stems directly from tissue needs, e.g., hunger and sex, transmitted by sensory signals to the Mental System, or indirectly from the high degree of facilitation existing between and within networks derived from and linked closely to primary needs. Mediation of thought sequences by such need-based inputs is a third factor contributing to the phenomenon of less apparent logic. Also *multiple determination*—referring to Freud's observation that cognitive output is often brought about by the convergence of two or more different associative paths—is apt to be more prominent with the greater emphasis on internal activation. Those "need-related" circuits possessing multiple connections from other circuits have a better chance of winning out in the competition for hyperfacilitation, in much the same fashion as letters with converging paired-associates were reported more than letters with only single pairings triggered by the stimulus (see experiment on facilitation in Chapter 4). Finally certain need-related circuits, particularly in the areas of sexuality and aggression, tend to be coupled with the anxiety network, whose activation invokes the inhibition mechanism. As a result hyperfacilitation is gained instead by signals from connected, substitute circuits not hooked up to anxiety—a process accounting for the phenomena of *displacement* and *symbolism.*†

Although all ten on our original list (see broken-line boxes in Figures 28 and 29) of primary process phenomena appear to follow from the starting-point of reduced environmental sensory input, it is improbable that we have exhausted the supply of influences. Nor do those influences spelled out above invariably produce primitive thinking; rather they make the setting relatively predisposed to its occur-

---

* Occasional superfacilitations of this sort probably underlie those especially vivid aspects of dreams which are remembered in detail after awakening.

† The topic of anxiety-laden needs and their derivatives has been discussed in detail in Chapter 11 (see pp. 143–150).

rence. Nevertheless it seems to us more than mere coincidence or twists of deduction that the initial premise led to so comprehensive and plausible a schematization. Clearly the formulation merits further exploratory work in the laboratory. For example, it would be of interest to manipulate degree of input restriction and note concomitant changes in the prevalence of various primary process characteristics.

Some illustrative material should provide welcome relief now to the reader who has conscientiously tracked the tortuous steps in Figures 28 and 29. In one hypnotic session Ned was asked to dream on three different occasions, while in a deep trance, of "a square with a circle inside." The first dream was not preceded by any special instructions; the second came at the peak of an induced anxiety mood; * and the third was in conjunction with a very happy mood.* His hypnotic reports immediately after each dream are given below:

1. (no special instruction) The square started turning slowly and kept going faster and faster and then it looked like a circle.
2. (anxiety mood) It was turned into a hammer or something and it kept coming toward me as if it were going to hit me. It never did—it would get close and then stop and then go away . . . come back at me again and keep getting closer and closer. And it kept doing that over and over again.
3. (happy mood) The circle came out of the square and seemed to be moving around the square in one direction and then it would stop and the square would start moving around the circle in the opposite direction and that was repeated over and over again. (Told with gestures as though describing a dance routine.)

These simple responses convey several primary process features. Dream #1 represents an imaginal condensation—the square and circle networks literally lose their individual identity as the former merges into the latter. The second and third demonstrate the cognitive repercussions of affective feedback. In #2 it is not too far-fetched to infer that the repeatedly menacing hammer stands for E's recital of the series of anxiety episodes, each more threatening than the one before, which S was required to relive during the mood induction. Displacement away from the original source of anxiety, E, and symbolic translation of the frightening situation into a hammer are both evident. (Doubltess the particular choice of a hammer was multiply determined, but without further inquiry it would be pointless to guess at the converging antecedents.) Dream #3, bizarre and illogical on the surface, reflects the mediation of pleasurable affect. Dancing

* See Chapter 8 for techniques used to induce affective moods.

(square-dancing and forming a circle?) likely has emotional connotations matching the joyful mood created by induction.

Another excerpt from Ned's verbatim transcripts poses some intriguing questions. The following dialogue took place in the midst
of his third hypnotic training session (S spoke in a low, halting,
almost dazed manner throughout; stomach gurgling was frequent):

E: Tell me how you feel now.
S: As if my whole body were fused into one lump of rock.
E: Is this a pleasant feeling?
S: Yes. And I feel very, very heavy.
E: Have you ever had this feeling before?
S: Yes, in dreams.
E: Try to think of one particular dream in which you had this feeling and
   tell me about it.
S: I haven't had a dream where I felt like that for a long time. I re-
   membered that once when I was really little I felt the same way.
E: Think back to that time and tell me about it. How old were you?
S: I was about four or five. I didn't want to wake up because it was so
   pleasant.
E: What thoughts went through your mind while you were dreaming?
S: I don't remember.
E: All right, now let's recapture that pleasant feeling you had a minute
   ago. Drifting and floating, feeling heavy, your whole body fused into
   one lump of rock, etc., etc. How are you feeling now?
S: As if I had my head bowed over against my chest . . . I'm dis-
   oriented . . . I feel as if my legs are raised up . . . still very heavy.
E: Tell me what thoughts are running through your mind.
S: It seems that I am twisting sideways. My head hurts. One spot at
   the back of my head hurts.
E: Have you changed your position?
S: I seem to be going head over heels . . . backwards.
E: Are you feeling any other sensations?
S: As if I'm jerking.
E: Tell me more about how you feel.
S (after 20-second pause): Everything is stopped.
E: And how do you feel now?
S: Not as heavy as I was but I still don't know which side is which . . .
   Everything seems quiet but my body still seems to be twisted.

A short while later he was instructed to dream for one minute, during
which time a loud noise was made by a door slamming (unsolicited!)
in the outer hall. The hypnotic dream turned out as follows:

There was a light flashing back and forth in front of my eyes . . . and
I seemed to be pushing, straining against something like a door and I
couldn't get through and the light kept flashing in front of my eyes. Then

I seemed to be going around in circles faster and faster . . . The light in my eyes bothered me and then I relaxed after I found that I got through the door.

Those of us in attendance at the time exchanged astonished glances over what could have been a script written by Otto Rank! Each had independently formed the opinion that S was more or less spontaneously undergoing a birth fantasy. As soon as the session was finished, we convened our entire research group and played the tape-recording for them without saying anything. Again the birth interpretation was unanimous. To remove any lingering doubt we played it back to S himself, under hypnosis, on his next appearance two days after. In reply to the question "What did that sound like?" he answered without hesitation: "A baby being born." The mystery was at least partly cleared up during the hypnotic inquiry which ensued.

It seems that about age 4 (approximately the period to which he had assigned the very pleasant dream) his mother showed him a picture of a baby at the moment of delivery, with its head "sticking halfway out." S reports only having thought to himself: "That sure is a silly picture." E, suspecting that the mother had been preparing him for the advent of a sibling, inquired if the episode happened near the time of his sister's birth. This seemed immediately to strike a responsive chord. S then added spontaneously that all his life he has had occasional thoughts about how "comfortable it must be inside the womb." In fact, he went on, every night he still goes to sleep curled up in a fetal posture.

What is one to make of this rather startling fantasy? Obviously it is not incumbent upon us to adopt the Rankian (39) view that such fantasies date directly from visual impressions registered originally at birth. More plausible is the interpretation that S's knowledge of the sequence of events at delivery was acquired much later and then superimposed upon an already existing, strong but vaguely formulated desire to recapture the fantasied security of the womb. Probably the network was established in childhood and ramified as he grew older. In the hypnotic session we are exposed to the elaboration which currently is most highly facilitated. Indirect stimuli for the quasi-hallucinatory experience seemed to be E's statements about recapturing the pleasant feeling, drifting and floating, and having an undifferentiated body image—together with the passive hypnotic context itself. At the very least, we are confronted with strikingly suggestive evidence that need-related circuits are formed very early in life and can persist enduringly and vitally thereafter, despite their apparent irrationality. (All of this comes as no surprise, of course, to the psychoanalytically oriented reader, but may give pause to opponents of such a deterministic outlook.)

The birth fantasy demonstrates the saliency, in the absence of well-defined sensory input, of signals whose hyperfacilitation is attributable in large measure to the internal state of facilitation among network connections. The other side of the coin is reflected by the hypnotically suggested dream which came right afterward. When external input is strong and unmistakably categorized, as in the case of the door slamming, it takes precedence over ongoing, internal activity. Though the birth theme is still reverberating ("pushing, straining against something"), the door had to be incorporated as a central symbolic element. We may speculate that the flashing light, in addition to its possible association with transition from darkness of the womb to brightness outside, is also determined by the laboratory light (shining through a glass with grooved circles) at which S was required to stare while the trance was being induced shortly before.

SOME CONSIDERATIONS RE LOGICAL THINKING

"Secondary process" refers to man's use of reflective thinking, by which cognitions are evaluated according to demands of reality and logic. Intelligence * and judgment assume special significance in this regard. Both past and present reality are factors in cognitive assessment. Also Freud's concept of *reality testing* falls within the evaluative domain. In our working model all such functions are accomplished by way of *reverberatory spread*, i.e., the action of hyperfacilitated signals upon connected circuits and networks, which makes checking possible.

Several considerations bear on the evaluative process. First, the strength of cognitive output is relevant. If output signals are very strong, they enhance a feeling of confidence that the phenomenon in question did really occur or that a particular solution to a problem is indeed correct. Steve provided us with clear illustrations during the paired-letter experiment (see pp. 35–37) when he apparently formed his impressions of rightness or wrongness of various responses

---

* Individual differences in intelligence are ascribed by us to genetic capacity for establishing connections in the cognitive subsystem. The ease with which circuits can be formed and hooked together into networks, especially those having to do with the evolution of concepts, is deemed crucial.

exclusively on the basis of comparative strength with which they popped into consciousness. Sudden insights, typically involving unique combinations of circuits, are another example of ideas represented by forceful emerging signals. The strength of these signals rests in part on a second consideration, the absence of competing thoughts. When hyperfacilitation is monopolized by particular circuit discharges, prolonged reverberation takes place in their networks. A subjective feeling of certainty, therefore, depends both upon degree of facilitation previously existing among connections and extent of uninterrupted reverberation at the moment.

A third, more obvious basis for judgment is specific past association with labels of truth or falsehood. If, upon reverberatory spread, a circuit standing for the designation "correct" is discharged, the ongoing cognitive operations will continue unimpeded until motoric responses appropriate to the approved thought are produced. These judgmental circuits may have been attached initially by inputs from others, e.g., teachers, or as a consequence of primarily internal chains of activity. On the other hand, if the circuit designating "incorrect" is triggered by spread, the operations will probably be subjected to inhibition and cut off prior to effector action. This coupling of "negative" discharge with the inhibition mechanism likely was mediated originally by the anxiety network. Disapproval expressed by parents, for instance, generates anxiety in the young child, whereupon inhibition is invoked and eventually paired by contiguity with the negative itself.

Logical thinking is hindered, as we have already mentioned (p. 172), by the reduction of environmental sensory input, which results in weaker reverberation and hence impaired cognitive evaluation. Another kind of interference is the reverberation of noise. Analogous to perceptual jamming described in Chapter 10 (see pp. 123–124), it is possible for cognitive incompatibility, or dissonance (16), also to produce noise during signal integration. If a person believed to be extremely prejudiced toward minority groups suddenly makes a sympathetic, understanding statement, the listener will have difficulty assimilating the contradiction and somewhere in the sequence of the latter's circuit discharges noise is apt to occur during integration. In those instances where the incompatible signals lead to sufficiently strong noise, its reverberation will trigger the inhibition mechanism directly and thus impede ongoing cognitive operations (dissonance reduction).

A more general condition creating noise is *input overload* (31)— sensory mechanisms are so flooded by diverse, concurrent stimuli that all inputs cannot be coded properly and the remainder bombard the Mental System in the form of noise. As in the case of jamming due to specific incompatibility, this type of noise reverberation also has the effect of hampering the secondary process by setting off inhibition.

In summary, the present chapter has applied the model to primitive and advanced modes of thinking. We have given special emphasis to the former as a means of demonstrating the heuristic value of our conceptualization in an area largely characterized by clinical description alone. The "primary process," replete with intriguing and complex phenomena, thereby emerges as a promising topic for systematic experimental study in its own right, rather than a casually noted by-product of research on sensory deprivation as before. The short section on "secondary process" was included chiefly to acquaint the reader with the model's potential for accommodating reflective thought in addition to prelogical. The path appears to be open for future extension of the functions, outlined in rudimentary fashion, to various aspects of decision making and problem solving. Next we shall pursue our "one world of psychology" theme by exploring implications of the model for the clinician's nearest and dearest domain—psychotherapy.

Therapeutic
intervention   14

Chapter 11 dealt with psychopathology in terms of pathogenic networks, entailing anxiety and inhibition, and the derivative networks
which subsequently evolve. In the last chapter the topic of "primary
process" thinking was considered in detail. But for readers chiefly
concerned with the applicability of theory to practical problems of
treating mental illness, such abstract reformulations are not likely to
generate much enthusiasm. Does the working model point to particular kinds of therapeutic approaches? Certainly some ingredients
for specification are present: major control over thoughts, feelings,
and action is assigned to the cognitive subsystem; inhibition is capable
of interfering with established connections and permitting new ones
to form; and hypnosis has been demonstrated to be a potent tool for
manipulating both inhibition and facilitation. Through an unfore-
seen circumstance, it was possible to try out these ideas while working with one of our experimental subjects. Joe's amazing plight, an
all-pervasive synesthesia, furnishes the setting for a discussion of
model and therapy.*

* We shall view our hypnosis efforts in this case mainly according to the
light they cast on propositions of the model rather than their relevance for the
vast field of hypnotherapy. Readers interested in the latter are referred to
such works as Wolberg (49) and Brenman and Gill (8).

181

THE CASE OF THE "YELLOW ROSE CATHEXIS"

A few unusual occurrences involving S's color imagery during the first six sessions prompted the following conversation immediately after the hypnotic induction in session #7:

E: Sleep more and more deeply now as we talk. I'd like to talk to you about colors and what meaning they have for you. I've noticed several times that colors have been important in things that you see while you're asleep here and colors are also important in your responses to words.

S: Yes. They seem to be present always every time I think of something. There are usually colors I see first and then the colors take the form of something.

E: When you're awake as well as when you're asleep?

S: Yes. It's just that when something is said, or I see something, or I'm asked to reply to something, a color or a series of colors will flash into my mind. Then, after concentrating on these colors, they take a form or a shape or spell out a word, and then this is what my reply comes from.

E: And this is true of all the thoughts you have while you're awake?

S: Yes.

E: Is it happening now as we talk?

S: Yes.

E: Tell me what colors are going through your mind now as we're talking.

S: Several shades of green and orange and a large block sort of between a red and a purple.

E: Is this distracting to you when you see these colors?

S: No, it's never distracting. It's very normal—or at least I never thought of it as being distracting. It always has been there.

E: When was the youngest period of your life that you remember having this?

S: As far as I know I've always remembered it. I could always picture things in color and remember things that were taking place. They always took the form of colors and then I could see what it was. It wasn't until high school that I was able to make the colors form words or letters. When I was asked to spell something I always spelled directly from the color to the word without seeing the letters or how the word was put together.

E: This happened in high school? Give me an example of what you're talking about.

S: It was the eleventh grade. I had an English instructor who was very much disturbed by the fact that I couldn't spell. So she asked me what came into my mind when she asked me to spell a word. She picked out a very simple word—RAN—and immediately red, darker red, and brown flashed into my mind and that stood for the RAN. The R was red, the deeper red became the A, and then the N turned to a brown, so there's a band of color that flashed through my mind. It was a continuum . . . She told me I should concentrate on making the color become the letter that it was supposed to represent and so I was trying to concentrate on that for a while. I could see the letter in the color that I had previously just seen the color.

E: After you learned to do this did the same color stand for the same letter?

S: The colors were basically the same, in other words all Rs were basically red, but the shade of red changed depending upon how the word was used or how the letter was used in the word. For example, in a word like RATHER the R in RA would be more toward the purple, and in the ER the E is green and the R very definitely red . . .

E: Are there other mental events that don't have the colors?

S: Whenever I'm asked a question and I don't know the answer, my mind turns black and white or gray and I see nothing . . . just free forms . . . sort of like a haze, looking through a cloud, and nothing comes to mind. Only when color enters into it do I think of something to say. When I am asked a question like those that you ask, there are just patches of color, many different colors, and they flash by in my mind very rapidly. Then one stops and becomes more stabilized . . . and when I concentrate on that one the color takes a form, either faces or people moving or things happening, and it becomes very vivid, just as I have seen them before . . .

E: Well, this must be fascinating for somebody in the field of architecture and design. Does it help in your work?

S: It doesn't seem to be of any advantage. Every time I feel it should be one color someone else feels it should be another. My colors seem to have different values than other people's. I feel very strongly that it has to be one color or another, it can't just be any old color.

E: Colors have connotations for most people—there are warm colors, soft colors—I wonder if you could tell me what connotations, what feelings various colors have for you.

S: There doesn't seem to be any particular emotional effect if a color is flashed. It doesn't necessarily make me feel a certain way. Light green and the yellows do give me a feeling of the outdoors and enable me to see pictures of being outdoors and feel as though I'm right there, but red doesn't seem to take either side. A little toward the purple, red could be very violent or it could be very depressing. When it's toward the yellow, it could be more gay and free. It can be many different things.

E: How about other colors?

S: Green more or less is always very pleasant—when it's very yellowish it becomes very bright sunlight and when it becomes deeper it's more like the shadows in a very dense forest. Bluish green feels like all outdoors—the sea, the trees, the sky—and becomes a very wonderful warm feeling. Blue is another color that's quite a bit like green, except royal blue has sort of a synthetic quality, never looks real. If it's a light blue it's more like the sky, and if it's a very dark blue it begins to take the form or the feeling of black or very deep and morbid colors. Brown is another color that I see very frequently and again it has a lot of mixed feelings depending upon what it's with. It can be very gay or very depressing. Sometimes when something is said that makes me very mad, everything I see is brown. Yet other times when something is very happy, I'll see brown and yellow and green all together.

E: How do you see the colors when they're all together?

S: They're not any definite form at first . . . the colors may be whirling in a sort of funnel form or they may be just drifting like clouds, or they're unusual free forms that have no definite meaning. When the moving patch of colors stops, then I can concentrate on it and make a face out of it or a person or some other object related to the color I was thinking about. Before it's more like a mist constantly changing, sort of like a steam bath where the steam is moving and changing shape.

By now those of us in attendance (E and two observers on the other side of the one-way vision screen) were sufficiently astonished and curious over the elaborate nature of the synesthesia symptoms that further detailed inquiries were made into their background. This was obviously not the simple association of color with tones, for example, that we had all read about in the textbooks! During the ensuing discussion S, still under hypnosis, revealed that he became quite concerned about his unusual imagery upon being made aware of its strangeness in high school. His vivid technicolor dreams were ridiculed by kids in the class and, feeling inferior, he soon decided to keep the whole matter to himself. But poor reading and spelling continued to plague him and eventually caused his academic failure at the U. S. Naval Academy after one year. This is the kind of difficulty he experienced:

S: I'd be writing a paper and I'd see everything in color. And the word MY or BY would be the same color. I would always interchange them and I'd go back and proofread and I would never catch it.

E: What was the color?

S: The Y was a yellow, the B was a yellowish brown, and the M was a brownish yellow. Although they were different, there was not enough difference.

E (convinced he had achieved a brilliant insight): So BM was brownish yellow. Does that bring any thought to mind?

S: Yes, the fact that BM and bowel movement were—not only the words are the same colors but also the actual object is the same color.

It turned out that he had first made the conscious connection in a
psychology course the previous semester, when he read Kenneth's
preoccupation with bowel movements in the book "One Little Boy,"
as he called it. However, the association was quite superficial—"I
merely noticed there was a relationship but didn't know whether this
was accidental or not."

Stuttering had also been a problem, especially in elementary school,
where he participated in speech correction classes. After the stuttering improved, he tended to mumble and not pronounce all the letters
in a word. Even now he still has to be careful not to talk or think too
fast.

Returning from Annapolis to a large midwestern state university, his
anxieties continued to mount:

I became very much concerned why I would set up a system by which
I would remember everything and spell and listen to music and everything
by color. I didn't know whether at first it was innate or whether it was
something I had established for lack of any other grounding in remembering and thinking . . . I had great difficulty in talking and in writing, getting my thoughts down in logical order. I became very much concerned
also that when I would read I would not see the words as I would gaze
along the page, but I would see what was happening. I merely saw the
activities that were taking place, I didn't see the words, and I began to
wonder that maybe this was the reason I was so slow at reading . . . I
tried to skim through a book, just look at words and see the words, but
then I got no meaning out of it. I couldn't figure out what was being
said . . . I became very depressed with myself over the fact that I sometimes could do it and sometimes couldn't and when I wanted to most, it
seemed I would have the greatest trouble in remembering facts.

During the next two years of college he ruminated more about the
possible origins of his trouble, read some psychology, and ended up
"pretty much confused—I could think of lots of things which might
have caused it but I didn't know whether they were true or not."

The remainder of the two-hour session was mostly devoted to having S "relive" episodes from his early life in an attempt to track down
the genesis of the colors (see p. 167 for discussion of hypnotic age
regression). The following was one of his recollections at age 3 or 4:

S: I see my father as he goes to the front door and leaves in the morning.
   I've either just gotten up or I'm usually sitting in the living room in
   my pajamas. He leaves and that's all I see of him until the next
   morning at the same time. He's very irritated, very grouchy, and I'm
   afraid of him. I don't dare say anything to him.

E: What do you think as you're sitting there in your pajamas? What thought crosses your mind?

S: I'm thinking why don't I stay in the bedroom until he leaves and then I don't ever have to see him.

E: And is this thought in picture form?

S: I just picture the fact that I stayed in the bedroom—in my bed or else I can stand around and look out the window or be getting dressed. I can hear my father stomp out of the house and then I can go out in the living room and he's gone, and everything is left to me and my mother.

E: Is the thought of yourself being in bed in color?

S: I can see the colors of everything as they are. The walls are sort of a purplish red color, more on a pink–lavender. My bed is natural finished wood, it's a reddish color. There's a crib on the other side which my sister is in and that's white enamel, very smooth finish. And then my brother's bed is above that one, it's a bunk bed and it's the same material. There's a quilt on my bed of all different colors and flower prints and all different colors sewed together. My brother has a maroon and cream color blanket with a plaid pattern to it and there's a yellow dresser.

E: What are the knobs like on the dresser?

S: They're sort of shaped like mushrooms. Little round knobs that are bigger at the one end and smaller at the other.

His mother appeared in quite another context:

E: Continue to sleep very, very deeply and now let's go back to a time when you were even younger. Let's go back to the first house you lived in. Tell me where you are and what's happening now.

S: It's late in the night and I'm sleeping on a mattress on the floor. I'm not quite three years old. I feel I have to go to the bathroom but I don't know to get up out of bed and go into the bathroom. I start urinating, or I've been urinating ever since I've been thinking that I have to go to the bathroom. And as I'm urinating I can see in my mind that on the bedsheet will be a large yellow rose. And I think to myself how pleased my mother will be to have this large yellow rose. And then I drift back into sleep.

E: Now, as you're still at this age in the same place, tell me what thoughts flash through your mind as I say "yellow."

S: I see this large yellow rose.

E: Now think of your father and tell me what thoughts go through your mind.

S: When I think of my father the color brown comes to mind.

E: What picture does it change into?

S: There is no picture. In fact I can't even picture my father. It's a very dark and gloomy brown, sort of a grayish brown. Everything seems to be brown . . . there's no shape or form, it's just like a mist and everything is brown in color.

E: All right, tell me now what colors come to mind as I mention different people. Remember you're still less than three years old. MOTHER –

S: Yellow

E: FATHER –

S: Brown

E: SISTER –

S: Blue

E: BROTHER –

S: Green

E: BROTHER –

S: Red

E: SISTER –

S: Blue

E: MOTHER –

S: Yellow

E: FATHER –

S: Brown

E: GRANDMOTHER –

S: Gray

E: GRANDFATHER –

S: Nothing comes to mind.

E: Did you know your grandfather?

S: No, he died before I was born.

E: Was this on your mother's side or your father's?

S: My father's.

E: How about on your mother's side?

S: I don't know my grandfather at that time.

E: All right, as we did this, describe how these colors came to mind that you reported.

S: When you mentioned mother, I could see my mother with a large yellow rose. It was bigger than she was or almost as big as she was. She could hold it in her hands. And I was lying on the couch—on the mattress rather—and she was saying how beautiful it was and how much she loved it, and I was so wonderful to give it to her.

E: How about your sister when you said "blue"?

S: I could see her all dressed in blue . . . with her big blue eyes . . . and she was in little baby clothes. A blue blanket wrapped around her and the little basket she's lying in is blue.

E: How much younger is your sister?

S: She's about six months old now.

E: Is this the basket you were in when you were younger?

S: Yes.

E: Is that why it's blue instead of pink?

S: Yes.

Several other impressions, presumably stemming from experiences at even younger ages than the above, were also re-created. Colors still pervaded his imagery, as in the following example:

S: I feel the cold wet . . . I feel that I'm trying to roll out of the wetness, but it stays right with me. I roll over to the side and feel the coldness of the sides of the bed. I still feel the cold and the wet all around my body and I roll back to the other side and the other side is better. It's not as wet on my body and the sides of the bed aren't as wet or as cold.
E: How old do you think you are now?
S: I'm a year old.
E: Can you stand up?
S: Yes.
E: Try to stand up now.
S: I can't. The blanket is all wrapped around my feet—I can't get my feet free to stand up.
E: What thought goes through your mind as the blanket is wrapped around your feet and you're trying to stand up?
S: Everything seems to be more gray—just plain colors flashing around, grays and colors.
E: What colors are flashing?
S: Reds and browns.
E: Are they flashing now?
S: They're whirling, just whirling around . . .
E: Can you talk?
S: No, I can't do anything.
E: Can you make sounds?
S: Yes.
E: What sounds can you make?
S: I can just open my mouth and just a continuous groan.
E: Now make that sound.
(At that point S emitted a weird, blood-curdling cry which startled everyone within earshot.)

One may justifiably question the authenticity of these very early recollections, but nonetheless they are a revealing product of S's cognitive processes. Our own queries were answered in this way:

E: How do you feel about going back to these early situations?
S: I keep thinking it's impossible—but suddenly there I am!
E: Do you really believe that you're back again in those situations?
S: They seem so real, but I don't know if it's true or not.

It is also clear that these "fantasies" cannot readily be dismissed as mere contemporary elaborations without any basis in fact. Witness the following conversation shortly thereafter at the close of the session:

E: Are you able to experience any sensations when somebody picks you up?

S: Yes.

E: All right, now your mother is picking you up. Your mother has just picked you up and she's playing with you. She throws you up into the air—out of her two hands into the air. How do you feel now as she throws you up into the air?

S: It's not my mother that's throwing me in the air.

E (taken aback): Who is it?

S: It's someone else.

E: Do you know who it is?

S: No.

E (as part of the waking instructions): As soon as you wake up you're going to say the name of the person that threw you into the air. After you're awake you won't remember what happened while you were asleep, etc. etc.

S (immediately upon opening his eyes): My Aunt G- - - - - .

E: Who's your Aunt G- - - - - ?

S: My father's sister.

E: What made you think of her when you woke up?

S: You got me. I don't know why I said it.

E: Did she use to play with you when you were little?

S: When I was very young she used to live with us at my grandmother's house. She was around most of the time.

E: How old were you then?

S: Well, we moved from there when I was about three. I must have been younger than three because I remember my brother had just started school at H. He was in kindergarten there and went to the first grade at W. after we moved.

The subsequent meeting of our research group resembled a clinical case conference. It was apparent that Joe, unconsciously at least, badly wanted our help in trying to alleviate his troublesome symptom. The clues available to us suggested that the key pathogenic and derivative networks were already close to identification: a basic hostility toward the father, provoking anal aggressive fantasies which evolved into the lasting association of father with the color brown; and an overwhelming desire, symbolized in the "yellow rose cathexis," for tenderness and love from the mother, who was paired with the color yellow. Admittedly theories of the genesis of synesthesia are not firmly established and the possibility of innate structural predisposition could not be ruled out. However, the particular manifestations of the symptom were apparently accountable in terms of his life experiences and therefore seemed amenable to change.

Following the model, we assumed that inhibition could be directed, via hypnosis, toward breaking the malignant cognitive connections and allowing new ones to take their place. Apart from the therapeutic uses to which hypnosis had been put by others, there was some indication in a brief excursion with another of our subjects that such an approach to reorganizing crucial cognitive networks might prove successful.* The chief reservation, contraindicating action on our part, concerned the obviously long-standing and extensive nature of the disorder. If we succeeded in eliminating only the symptom, and our cognitive probing misfired, might not a more disabling symptom turn up instead? The soul-searching was resolved in favor of a decision to begin the next session by exploring with Joe the seriousness of his motivation to get rid of the colors and, in the event of a jointly affirmative outcome, to proceed with utmost care at every step of the way.

This is what transpired right after the hypnotic induction on his regularly scheduled appointment (two days following the previous one):

E: What do you think about what we discussed last time while you were asleep?
S: I would like to find out what it is but other than that it makes no impression on my mind.
E: Do you have a strong desire to get rid of this seeing colors?
S: Not exactly to get rid of it—just to improve my ability to read and write and spell.
E: Well, if your improvement came with eliminating the colors, would you want that?

---

* In the course of describing under hypnosis personal experiences suggested by each of the Blacky pictures, Tom on Picture VI (Castration Anxiety) narrated an incident in which he and two adolescent friends were attacked and badly beaten by a gang. From that time on he experienced a panicky reaction whenever anything was put near his face, e.g., his young daughter reaching up to grab his glasses. During a later hypnotic session he was asked:

E: Would you like to get rid of this feeling?
S: Yes.
E: Okay, now we're going to get rid of the feeling. Whenever anything is around your face you won't have this feeling any more because you know what it's due to. It started with that frightening experience and is now left over from it. You will not have this feeling any more because you understand what caused it. You won't have this feeling any more whether you're awake or asleep because now you understand the origin and you're not going to be bothered by it any more.

Eleven days afterward, on his final appearance of the experimental series, a paper towel was placed over his face and he reported no reaction. Furthermore, he told of having been hit in the head accidentally by an umbrella a couple of days earlier—also with no consequent anxiety.

S: Yes.

E: So then you do want to get rid of the colors.

S: Yes.

E: Is that one of the reasons why you were interested in becoming a hypnotic subject?

S: Yes . . .

E: Had you intended to bring this up yourself?

S: No, I hadn't.

E: You were just hoping it would come out and then we would talk about it?

S: Not necessarily, I was thinking I'd gain some knowledge of what was taking place and then I would know more what to read on the subject —also to find out if it were really something I picked up in my childhood or not.

E: So you wanted to find out more about yourself.

S: That's right.

E: Were you pleased when we devoted a whole session to trying to find out about the colors?

S: Yes, I was.

E: It wasn't at all upsetting to you to dig back into those early experiences?

S: No, it wasn't.

After some rehashing of the material brought up the time before, E went on as follows:

E: I don't know that we can do anything to change this color problem because we don't know what it's really due to. In the medical field this is still pretty much of a mystery. All that's known is that some people do have this accompaniment of color to other kinds of things, but whether the cause is something physiological or whether it's learned early in life or what is still pretty much of a mystery. We might try to take one example of the colors and see if you can repeat it with the color being absent. Would you like to try that?

S: Yes.

E: All right, tell me what comes to mind when I say father.

S: Brown.

E: Tell me more about it.

S: When you mentioned father, the colors that were whirling around in my mind suddenly disappeared and everything turned brown in color. Then the word "father" was printed out in lower case letters across this brown background, and in the loop part of the F appeared my father's face. Then as the word "father" disappeared my father stood there all in the same colors of brown . . .

E: Now think of your father in two or three different situations and describe the colors.

S: Well, one that comes to mind is right after he had been fishing or hunting. He wears the same light brown sort of a tan coat and pair of trousers . . . and more of a yellowish brown hat . . . and his face is darker brown because of his whiskers and being tan from the sun . . . and he has a brown tackle box or brown case that his gun is in.

E: Now think of your father in another setting and tell me about it.

S: I see him in a brown topcoat, brown hat, brown suit. He's leaving for work. He just puts his coat on and walks out the door.

E: Now let's take a third setting.

S: I can see him out in the yard working in his garden. This time he has on gray clothes—gray trousers and a brown plaid shirt, but it's more gray than brown. He's digging in the ground, which is a dark brown. There's peat moss around which is a reddish brown. The shovel he's using is rusty color . . .

E: All right, now think of another picture, not involving your father this time, in which brown is the dominant color.

S: I just see a lot of general pictures—different things flashing in my mind . . . of the city . . . the brown telephone poles and the very dark, almost black railroad ties . . . brown fences and things of that sort.

E: What feeling does the color brown have for you? What is your emotional reaction when you see it?

S: It makes me feel as though it's drab, something I wouldn't want to wear.

E: Anything else?

S: I always associate it with bowel movement.

E: You made that association before you learned about the "anal period"?

S: Yes.

E: When did you first make it?

S: I recall that when I was quite young, about ten, I was playing with some clay. It was right after Christmas and my sister had gotten a set of oil base clays which we could make things out of. I had the brown piece and I was wadding it up in my hand and squeezing it. When I let go of it I noticed how it looked so much like a bowel movement, and I said something about it. Everyone yelled at me so I stopped and made something out of the clay instead.

E: Let's go back to that situation now and relive it. What's happening?

S (after describing physical setting in great detail): And my mother yelled at me not to talk that way. It isn't nice. And I said "But it does look like a bowel movement" and she yells at me again. Told me if I can't play with the rest of them like a nice boy, then I didn't have to play with them at all.

E: How are you feeling?

S: I don't see why she has to talk to me this way.

E: Are you angry?

S: Yes.

E: What do you want to do?

S: I'm just mad that people talk to me that way but I don't want to do anything.

E: You don't want to strike back, to get even?

S: No.

E: Have you ever wanted to strike back at others when they make you angry?

S: Not when they're present—only later.

E: In your imagination?

S: Yes. I recall the situation and then instead of acting as I did I would act as I felt I should have. Either tell them what I think, what they can do, and if they get mad, then I can hit them and do most anything to them.

E: All right, let's go back to your father and the color brown. You know the connotation that brown has—this is the connotation that brown tends to have for all children—it means feces. And feces are very important in the life of a young child. He has to learn to be toilet trained and sometimes parents get very concerned about this, so it becomes a central conflict between parents and children. The children are often frustrated and one of the ways they get back is through fantasies involving smearing. Does that make sense to you?

S: It seems to be very logical that this is the way a child would fight back against something.

E: So if you were mad at your father and couldn't fight back in any other way, you would fight back in your imagination.

S: Yes.

E: So you have some understanding of what might have been the relationship between the color brown and your father.

S: Yes.

By this stage the crucial cognitive networks were deemed to have been sufficiently re-activated, and E proceeded directly to mobilize inhibition against them:

E: Now that you have this understanding, we're going to try to make the association of brown with your father disappear, because we know that getting back to the roots of the problem often helps to clear it up. In a little while you're going to think of your father again and IT WON'T BE THE COLOR BROWN . . . IT WON'T BE THE COLOR BROWN. Think of your father now and tell me what you see.

S: I see my father standing alongside a road . . . it's out in the country . . . he's got on a green sweater and a red shirt and a pair of blue dungarees.

E (obviously pushing his luck): What color are his shoes?

S: They're an old beat up pair. They're brown with paint spots all over them.

E: What color are the paint spots?

S: It's hard to say—they're sort of white and off colors.

E: So there's almost no brown in this picture?

S: No.

E: Have you ever had a picture of your father like this before?

S: No, I haven't.

E: Are you surprised?

S: Somewhat, yes.

E: Are you pleased?

S: Yes.

E: All right, now the next picture of your father is not going to have any color in it—IT'S JUST GOING TO BE BLACK AND WHITE. Tell me about the next picture of your father.

S: All the color has left and I see everything in black and white now, but I can't get a picture of my father in black and white.

E: What do you see?

S: I just see a lot of clouds whirling around—all in black and white, all shades of gray. Every once in a while a face starts to appear but then it fades out again.

E: What color is the face as it starts to appear?

S: No color. Black and white, gray.

E: Now the face is going to become clearer and clearer. It's going to continue to be without color as it gets clearer and clearer. Describe it to me.

S: I still cannot distinguish what the features of the face are. I can see the outline of the head . . . I can see where the eyes are . . . and I can see the nose—it's my father's nose but it's very hazy.

E: Is there any color?

S: No, there isn't.

E: Continue to look at it. Stare at it hard. It's clearer and clearer. It's your father. You're completely NEUTRAL about this. It's a completely neutral face on your father. NO FEELINGS ATTACHED and NO COLOR. It's getting clearer all the time. Tell me what you see now.

S: I can see my father's face but it's flesh color, not black and white now.

E (suddenly reminded that it would have made more sense to have suggested "flesh color" in the first place): That's right—it's flesh color. That's the way it should appear, shouldn't it?

S: Yes.

E: And do you have any feelings about your father at this moment?

S: No.

E: Do you usually have feelings about your father when you visualize him?

S: Yes. Usually my feelings are why can't he participate in the family life instead of always being away from it. I always have the feeling, regardless of when I'm talking about him, why can't he become part of us instead of being so far away.

The next step was to extend the same process to another significant figure in his life:

E: You were just able to see your father in different colors than you've ever seen him before—the brown was gone and you saw him in green and red and so on. Then you were able to see him flesh colored, just as he ordinarily looks. Is that right?

S: Yes.

E: Let's see if we can go on from your father now to other objects. What is another association that you always make between a person and a color?

S: I always see my mother as being yellow.

E: And yellow is gay and happy, or not?

S: Mostly it is but not all the time.

E: Do you remember what you said last time that related yellow to mother?

S: Yes. You mentioned my mother twice. The first time I saw a very light and very gay yellow rose, and then afterwards I saw a very drab, sort of a brownish yellowish green color and exactly the opposite feeling.

E: Where did the yellow rose come from?

S: That was the yellow rose that was formed by my urine.

E: You said that the yellow rose was a present you had given to your mother. Why would a child have this kind of a fantasy—when he wets the bed, thinking that this is a present he's giving to his mother?

S: He would think that it was part of him . . . he's giving to his mother a part of himself.

E: All right, now we have some understanding of what meaning the association of yellow with your mother might have, don't we?

S: Yes.

E: Now that we have this understanding it should be very easy to change, so that yellow is no longer associated with your mother but instead you see her as she ordinarily is, true flesh colored just as you were able to see your father. NOW SEE YOUR MOTHER AS SHE REALLY IS. Tell me what you see.

S: I can see my mother wearing sort of a turquoise and aqua colored dress. It's a print of some sort—a summer print dress. And she has a hat on that matches and her red hair sticks out from around the hat. She's walking down the street.

E: Have you ever seen her in these colors?

S: Yes, she has a dress like this one she's wearing now.

E: Have you ever visualized her in that dress before?

S: No, I haven't.

E: How do you usually visualize your mother?

S: I can always visualize her face and then there's always the yellow rose. I can see nothing of her body or her dress or anything else.

E: So this was a very different image just now. Are you pleased to have a different one?

S: Yes.

E: Do you feel that we're making progress?

S: Yes.

With these mutual reassurances out of the way, E directed S's attention to the hazy background colors described earlier:

E: Now that we've understood the association of brown with your father and yellow with your mother, you should be able to generalize from these two associations, which are usually the important ones in a child's life. It may very well be that all of your use of colors grew out of your early association of these colors with your parents. Do you think that's possible?

S: Yes, it could be.

E: Are there certain dominant shades or colors that participate in the mist of whirling colors that you typically see?

S: They seem to be all sorts of colors. It seems as though there's in the background sort of a bright gay yellow and gay brown, not a drab brown, whirling around. Then in front are the truer colors—the bright reds and bright blues that flash by. They're very bright and just sort of whirl by and disappear.

E: Is this always the same?

S: Yes. It's not the same form but it takes about the same pattern.

E: So there's sort of a background set of colors and then foreground colors.

S: There seems to be a tremendous amount of depth to it, almost an infinite amount of depth.

E: And the background colors are always the bright yellows and the gay browns?

S: Yes.

E: And foreground colors are red, green, and blue. Is that right?

S: Yes.

E: Do the background colors tend to remain while the others go by?

S: The background colors sort of shimmer up and down and move sideways a little bit but they basically stay the same. The other colors flash by in front—they flash into view and then disappear. Then when I'm asked something, the colors in the foreground form an object which becomes the reply that I give.

E: So the background colors seem to be the primary ones?

S: Yes.

E: And the primary ones that you see are somehow related to the colors associated with mother and father, except they're much gayer and happier?

S: Right.

E: So this would seem to be a kind of fulfillment of relationships to mother and father. They're both gay and happy and this is the setting in which you like your thoughts to occur. Is that right?

S: Yes.

E: Now that you have some understanding of these primary colors, there's no need for them to be there any more. There's no need for them to be there any more because you know these are just remnants of some very early experiences that happened long, long ago and don't have any real bearing on your present situation. They've carried on through your life as vestiges of very early experiences which you've long since outgrown. They have no real meaning any more but yet you were never able to get rid of them. NOW YOU'RE GOING TO GET RID OF THEM. Tell me what thoughts are running through your mind and how you see them.

S: Right now there are no thoughts at all going through my mind. A dark black screen just came down over them. Now I just see these foreground colors flashing by and when I think of a word to say, it's formed on the screen.

Next the flashing foreground colors were made to disappear:

E: Now let's make the foreground colors disappear because those seem to be very secondary. It's just that you are used to seeing colors because of the yellow and brown, which were always in the background representing your mother and father. These others were the fleeting experiences and color really isn't important for them. It's just that you had the stage set in colors and they had to be consistent with it. Now that you don't need the background colors any more, you don't need the foreground ones either. Now the foreground colors are disappearing . . . they're disappearing too. YOU CAN SEE THINGS WITHOUT COLORS—NO COLORS FLASHING ANY MORE. Tell me what you see.

S: There doesn't seem to be anything. Every once in a while a piece of gray light flashes through and disappears—sort of like a straight line.

E: Now the colors have gone. Instead of the colors you're going to visualize things as they really are. So that if you want to visualize a page in a book you'll see the page just as it really is. You know that you have a rather remarkable facility for this—being able to look at a page and fix it in your mind—but in the past this gift has been somewhat detracted from by the colors, which have tended to interfere . . . How do you feel now as we're talking about these things?

S: I feel very strange.

E: Tell me more about that.

S: As I see things now, I see pictures that are more like photographs—colored photographs and black and white photographs. Everything is very sharp and clear. They don't move or dance around. A lot of things are going through my mind right now and some are dark and some are gay, but there's no emotional feeling toward them. They just seem to be pictures.

E: Have you seen the mist of colors at all?

S: No, I haven't.

E: The foreground colors haven't been going by?

S: No.

E: Do you like being able to see this way?
S: Yes.

After some additional practice in visualizing things that he had seen, e.g., a kitchen and a book, the relationship between colors and anxiety became more apparent. S was asked to bring back in his imagination a page of a book he had been reading earlier in the day, and to report its number at the top.

S: I can't find the page number.
E: Look hard all over the page until you find it, and then it will become clearer and clearer.
S: I found it now.
E: What is it?
S: It's blurred—I can't make it out.
E: It's getting clearer and clearer now. Look hard at it until you can make it out.
S: I can see that it's a three digit number but I can't make it out.
E: Where on the page is the number?
S: On the bottom.
E: All right, look hard at the bottom. The numbers are becoming clearer and clearer. The three digits are becoming clearer and clearer until you can make them out. What do you see?
S: I can make out the first number—it's one.
E: Now look hard at the second digit. What is it?
S: Now there's colors flashing all around.
E: The colors are flashing again?
S: Yes.
E: Now let's stop and think about what has just happened in this situation. You were trying to do something you couldn't do and you were feeling a little bit upset about it, is that right?
S: Yes.
E: When you began feeling upset, the colors came back.
S: Yes.
E: So you know not only the origins of the colors now, but why they come in at particular times when you're feeling upset. We're going to undo that association between feeling upset and seeing colors. From now on, even though you may be upset about something, the colors won't come back. You'll be able to think more clearly about what it is that's bothering you and you won't get that diffuse feeling of being upset with colors coming by. It won't be as disturbing without the colors because the colors add to the feeling of being upset, since they interfere with and disrupt your thoughts.

Further efforts were then directed toward preventing the colors from coming back in anxiety-laden situations. The session was concluded in the following manner:

E: We've made a lot of progress today in eliminating the colors. They may stay away now and you'll be completely free of them. This won't seem at all strange to you. You'll be glad the colors aren't there to disrupt your thoughts. Your thoughts will come more clearly and more directly. But if the colors should come back, this won't bother you because you know that it's hard to undo a lifetime's practice all at once. We've made a very good start today, haven't we?

S: Yes.

E: And you won't think about this after the session is over. You won't remember what we've talked about, but the progress we've made will continue to hold while you're awake. You'll be able to think this way while you're awake. Then next time, when you're asleep again, we'll talk about what happened in the meantime. When you're awake, thoughts won't seem strange without colors and you just won't think about it—it will be as though you've been thinking this way all along. So whatever happens, one way or the other, it won't be disturbing to you. Do you understand?

S: Yes.

E: Is there anything else you want to say now before you wake up?

S: No.

E (still hedging cautiously): You also know that after you're awake, if any thoughts do trouble you—and I'm sure they won't—you can always call me up before the next session . . .

The invited phone call did not materialize that evening or all the next day. Our suspense was at fever pitch when Joe practically bounded into the lab right on schedule for his regular appointment. He gave this account, in the waking state, of what had transpired:

S: The first strange thing that I noticed the evening after our last session, when I went to my meal job, was that I seemed to be taller in relationship to the group of fellows I was standing with. This was sort of an unusual feeling at first but I didn't think much about it. That night, when I started to go to sleep, nothing went on in my mind at all—I didn't see the colors. The next morning I was aware of the fact that I didn't wake up to the montage of colors. There was just nothing there. The only thing I heard was the alarm clock when it went off.

E: Was this disturbing to you?

S: It was, yes. I felt very lonely, as though nothing was around. I felt that my mind was completely blank and became very much concerned about it. Then I felt oh, what happened last time [the previous session]? So I started trying to think of everything that took place and recalled most of it. Then this feeling of loneliness pretty much left . . .

E: How about the colors?

S: I see colors differently in my mind's eye now. They're completely different in quality. Before I had been seeing extremes in colors and not the middle hues and tones. At first it was disturbing to see the middle ones but after I'd been able to recall what happened, then I was rather pleased with what was taking place.

E: Has the absence of the flashing colors made any difference in your speech or spelling or anything?

S: I can think quicker. I was typing a paper I had already written and I did catch spelling errors I was making, but I still made errors in leaving out a word or turning letters around. For the first time, and I thought this was kind of important, I could look at an entire line and then type it. Before I would get confused and forget which word was which. There have been other things but I don't know if they're really related or not.

E: What kinds of things?

S: Well, one thing that happened yesterday morning which I thought was unusual. Afterwards I wondered whether it was related. I work at a sorority for a meal job, scrubbing floors, and the cook came dashing out of the kitchen. The dishwasher had caught fire so I dashed into the kitchen. It was a gas dishwasher and my first impression was that the gas had caught fire. But then very quickly, without any real reflecting at all, I knew that it wasn't gas because there wasn't an odor of gas. I could smell ozone burning so I knew it was an electrical fire and merely turned the switch off. Normally I just don't think that fast. I was very much pleased by that . . .

E: How about your feeling of being taller?

S: One of the fellows that works in the kitchen is from Germany and he's not in with the group. He tries to act as though he knows something and then he's usually wrong. Instead of keeping quiet he tries to talk his way out and he gets in more trouble. I noticed that I was pitching in with the rest of them that evening in calling his bluffs and poking fun at him. Suddenly I looked around at the fellows and I felt taller than I had previously. It stopped me cold and I didn't say anything more. I was actually kind of afraid. Then the next day I remembered what we had talked about and that I didn't feel apart from the group any more. I didn't feel humble or small or inferior.

E: So the fact that you no longer felt inferior about the colors somehow made you feel physically taller?

S: Yes . . .

E: Well, on the whole what's your impression? Are you glad about what's taken place or not?

S: I'm very pleased as to the progress it's made. At first I felt that this isn't the purpose of the experiments. It should be for your benefit and not mine.

E: So you were feeling guilty that we were doing things which were not exactly what we wanted to do to begin with.

S: Right.

E: Of course there's no need for that because we are going to do all of our experiments too. Anything we can do to help you in the meantime, we'll gladly do.

S: I deeply appreciate it. I feel very pleased. In fact all day today and most of yesterday I've been very eager to see how I would react to different situations. I've been much more alert to what's going on around me. If I walk down the street, instead of being completely involved in my own thinking, I'm aware of the houses, the trees, the grass—and after I walk a block I can almost recall everything I just passed. It's been quite exciting actually.

E: You seemed excited when you came in today. Of course this excitement will wear off. It's like a blind person who suddenly is able to see again. It's all very exciting and exhilarating at first but it shouldn't stay that way.

Shortly thereafter, S was hypnotized and one of the experiments was carried out. However, E did want to clear the air first (under hypnosis) with respect to the failure of S's suggested posthypnotic amnesia:

E: I want to tell you now that it was all right for you to have remembered what happened last time. The reason I suggested that you wouldn't remember was that I thought it might be less disturbing to have the change come about first and then all the connections follow afterward. But I intended for you to be aware of them in the waking state eventually anyway, and as long as you've done it yourself, that's fine. Once you did remember, the lonely feeling disappeared, so you've already made that connection, haven't you?

S: Yes.

E: All right, is there anything else you're thinking about now?

S: No.

Casual inquiries during the next week of sessions disclosed that the colors had not returned and everything was going well. In the final meeting, sixteen days after the therapy period, a significant item was noted. S had generalized the solution of his color problem to another context never before discussed:

Something happened just yesterday. Whenever I had seen a person from India previous to these sessions, I became very upset and annoyed. I usually went out of my way to avoid them so as not to have to look at them. After the color problem was worked out I noticed that I was no longer bothered by them. So I spent some time early one morning just going over what had happened and I began to realize that the brown color of the skin was the annoying factor—from the association with brown, father, and bowel movement.

At the conclusion of feedback concerning the series of experiments, E mentioned that he would like to be kept informed of S's progress in the future.*

ANALYSIS IN TERMS OF THE MODEL

Viewed from the standpoint of the model, Joe's pervasive synesthesia symptom may have had its origin in a very early coupling of the anxiety network to misty, whirling colors. Figure 30 depicts this hypothetical association. Whatever the reason, either innate or learned, for the existence of the color networks, it appears that they were sufficiently active contiguously with strong anxiety discharges to establish a highly facilitated connection to the inhibition mechanism. The assumption of frequent activation of the anxiety circuits, in magnitudes exceeding the upper limit of inhibitory effectiveness, helps to understand why the ongoing color discharges may have been linked especially to anxiety in this formative stage of development. The consequences of such a hookup were probably twofold: (1) colors could themselves trigger inhibition and thereby assist in cutting

---

* One year later a letter was received from Joe following an invitation, extended to him by a member of the research group, for him to write. Below are relevant excerpts from that letter:

"I am pleased to report that I have had for the most part no recurrence of the color impressions we talked about last Spring. There have been a few isolated incidents in which the colors have occurred. Once last summer when I was playing poker, I had a color response to a penny, a nickel, and a dime. The penny was red, the nickel was dark brown to blue green, and the dime was deep blue to tan. I do not picture the colors now. I was not able to remove the colors altogether. Instead I shifted the colors to correspond to the respective colors of the poker chips: white—penny, red—nickel, blue—dime. This impression occurs only when I play poker and not in relation to the three coins when used in any other situation.

. . . The only other incident occurs when I read. Before my mind is a background of tan color with an undefinable object in front. It appears after I have read for 15 or 20 minutes. I have not been able to identify the object or to remove the impression.

. . . As I mentioned to ——— the other night when he called, I got thinking about the experiments of last year after attending the May Festival concerts this time. Last year the concerts took place a week or so before the experiments started. I had a very colorful and picturesque experience. The visual impression was primary and the music secondary. This year the concerts were an entirely new experience. I was more aware of the music . . . more interested in the instrumentation. There was never a color response.

Color has also been absent from my dreams. I still have visual impressions of the dream but they appear in black and white. I also have fewer dreams . . ."

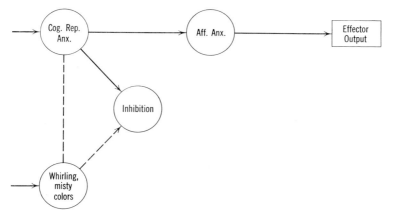

FIGURE 30. Early association of anxiety network with colors. [*Note:* As a consequence of contiguous activation the whirling, misty colors acquire connections to the anxiety network, so that colors become capable of triggering inhibition directly.]

down further anxiety output at the effectors; and (2) at the same time they contributed to general cognitive blocking, indirectly by monopolizing the hyperfacilitation process as well as directly by their inhibitory action. Thus, colors came to play a dual role of anxiety reduction and cognitive interference.

In the course of evolution of cognitive networks from childhood experiences, the colors likely changed from an undifferentiated state to a characteristic series of content relationships. Joe's verbal reports under hypnosis enable us to reconstruct some of these mental events with a fair degree of confidence. On pp. 183–184 he describes the connotations of greens, blues, blacks, browns, and yellows. We know that letters of the alphabet acquired specific color associations, though sometimes not separate enough to avoid confusion. Most interesting, of course, were the connections between father and brown, mother and yellow. Also, somewhere along the line the misty, whirling colors lastingly assumed a cast of bright gay yellows and browns (see p. 196). We shall return to a possible explanation for their gay quality after reviewing the pathogenic and derivative networks built around the parents.

Figure 31 illustrates pathogenic and derivative networks involving the father. Probably as a result of a variety of contributing factors, including the neglect aspect singled out for mention, S harbored deep-seated resentment toward his father from an early age. This hostile

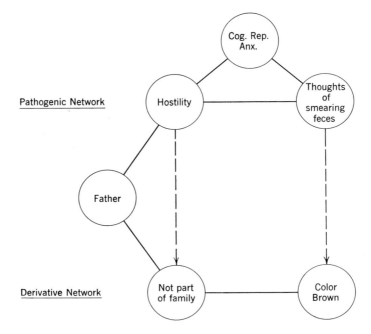

FIGURE 31. Pathogenic and derivative networks involving father.

attitude, along with the smearing fantasies appropriate to his matura-
tional level at that time, soon became linked to the anxiety network
as a result of social disapproval of aggressive behavior. The triggering of inhibition then prevented such thoughts from achieving dominance among cognitive outputs. That S generally felt constraints
against any expression of hostility is revealed in the narration of the
clay episode (pp. 192–193)—only later in his imagination could he
fight back. In regard to his father, even those belated thoughts seem
to have been hindered and we see only the emerging derivatives stressing regret over father's lack of participation in the family life. Similarly, the smearing was replaced by the "drab" color brown to complete a derivative network with remote, if any, connections to anxiety.
The independent fact of prominent ongoing color discharges predisposed coupling with some kind of color, and the selection of brown
in particular arose from its obvious content relevance.

    In like fashion the mother-yellow derivative evolved from anxiety
over early interpersonal relationships, the yellow rose fantasy connoting unsatisfied yearning for maternal indulgence. The gay quality

of the yellows and browns as they typically appeared in the background haze can be attributed to a wish-fulfilling representation of the parents. We have already observed (p. 148) that positively toned daydreams are selectively retained and strengthened over the years by virtue of their concomitant affects, whereas negative ones tend to be nullified by inhibition.

The breaking of color connections was brought about by triggering S's inhibition mechanism from an external source. Since S already had extensive practice, under hypnosis, in manipulating inhibition during the course of experiments, it was easy for E to supply instructions that S could carry out effectively. The father-brown sequence (pp. 193–194) deserves special attention in this regard. Once the pathogenic and derivative networks were reactivated (and therefore rendered susceptible to change by contiguous forces), E began by directing S's inhibitory action toward the specific color association. It was no problem for the brown to be replaced subsequently by a variety of other colors not subjected to inhibition. But the simple cognitive realignment ran afoul when E then suggested that the next mental picture of father would have *no* colors in it, just black and white. Father's face could not be made to appear clearly! In retrospect it appears likely that the inhibition, instigated by E, of all colors removed the anxiety-reducing function of colors described above and permitted the recently revitalized pathogenic network to emit strong anxiety discharges again. The latter in turn produced frequent and protracted inhibitory action sufficient to abort ongoing imaginal processes.*

The remedy, which E seized upon more or less intuitively, was to bolster inhibition of the troublesome anxiety (and the hostile thoughts giving rise to it) by suggesting "no feelings" attached to the forthcoming visualization. By blocking the connections of father's face to hostility and anxiety, further disruption was avoided and the flesh-colored face emerged readily. The remaining therapeutic interventions of E, dealing with the mother-yellow coupling (p. 195) and the background (pp. 196–197) and foreground colors (p. 197), all proceeded smoothly. Not long thereafter, though, anxiety reared its ugly head once more.

The great strain, involved in S's frustrated attempt to recapture a

---

* In an earlier incident (pp. 186–187) S also experienced difficulty in visualizing his father. There he was asked to tell what thoughts went through his mind as he thought of his father, whereupon everything turned brown. Apparently the reactivated pathogenic network's discharge caused the picture of father to be blocked and in its place appeared the relatively anxiety-free derivative, brown.

particular page number in a book he had been reading, caused a relapse into flashing colors (p. 198). From the relationships portrayed in Figure 30 we would expect just such a reinstatement of colors in the event of unusually strong anxiety discharge, which would set off the color network by spread. Earlier in the session any feelings of anxiety S may have experienced were insufficient for the colors to revert, so it seems the page-number struggle (in which he was unable to perform as E requested, in addition to failing to demonstrate his photographic memory prowess) was abnormally intense.* E was subsequently successful in breaking the anxiety-whirling colors connection by the same technique employed in the other interventions.

S's failure, the morning after the therapy session, to obey the posthypnotic amnesia instruction is also obviously related to potent anxiety discharge. His deep concern over the feeling of loneliness upon awakening (p. 199) was sufficient to overcome the barrier to recall. Perhaps a similarity of sensory context cues between the hypnagogic half-asleep condition and actual hypnosis (see Chapter 12) paved the way, for the amnesic inhibition is linked by instruction solely to the waking state. If indeed there existed such a predisposition for amnesia to be circumvented, then the anxiety discharge readily accounts for the cognitive contents recovered. Effector output in general provides, via response feedback, stronger input to the cognitive subsystem (and hence more spread) than does internal activation. In the present instance the anxiety input quickly triggered the highly facilitated hookup of networks recently formed under hypnosis. Interestingly, the flashing colors did not themselves return—in accord with the training of the previous session—but rather the whole exchange popped back and allayed anxiety in the process.

The Indian episode (p. 201) disclosed in the final meeting is even more intriguing in its implications. Merely the sight of brown-skinned people used to suffice to discharge a hostility-anxiety network, resulting in S feeling "very upset and annoyed." The later hypnotic manipulation of inhibition, carried out specifically in connection with pathogenic circuits involving the father, simultaneously weakened those affective associations of brown generally, as evidenced by the fact that negative reactions were *automatically* removed from the Hindus as well. Father and Hindus had apparently shared the same network of color and affects through a curious set of mediations.

---

* It is plausible to conjecture that the later relapses during poker games (see footnote on p. 202) were also occasioned by very strong anxiety inherent in those situations. The fact that S was able, all by himself, to reassign the colors appropriately to the chips is especially worthy of note.

SOME REFLECTIONS ON THE THERAPEUTIC PROCESS

In answer to the question raised at the beginning of this chapter, we can conclude that our conceptual framework, as buttressed by events in the case just presented, does lend itself solidly to a specific therapeutic orientation. The seemingly extensive changes wrought in Joe's personality within a few hours' time pose a real challenge for any theory of therapy. Not only did his lifelong and pervasive color symptoms disappear, but his emergency reactions quickened, he became more perceptive of his surroundings, feelings of inferiority abated, and in general his cognitive efficiency improved. These major alterations cannot be shrugged off as illusory or evanescent. How did they come about? To say merely, in the psychoanalytic tradition, that they were somehow brought about by a transference relationship is obviously incomplete and unsatisfactory as an explanation.

In our view, the reorganization, accompanying E's intervention, centered largely inside the cognitive subsystem. Key pathogenic and derivative networks were isolated and the powerful force of inhibition was brought to bear upon them.* Old connections were reactivated, deliberately weakened, and replaced by new ones. All these acts were made possible through the techniques of hypnosis. By having S "regress" to early childhood, the crucial dynamic factors were uncovered in short order. The exceptional potency, inherent in the hypnotic setting (see Chapter 12), of subsequent manipulations enabled the realignments to be accomplished effectively.

It must be stressed that we are dealing with much more than either plain symptom removal or substitution of alternative, competing responses. The psychological "sectioning" was performed on those connections *responsible* for the symptom. For example, viewing the derivative equation of brown with anger as one of S's symptoms, it would have been possible no doubt to break only that association. However, there would be every reason to suspect that the underlying pathogenic network entailing the father might create the troublesome tie again in the future as it had in the past. Cutting the father-brown

---

* The widespread consequences of therapeutic concentration on relatively few networks (e.g., origins of the father-brown connection and the yellow rose episode) supports the contention that these were indeed "key" samples from S's cognitive subsystem. Effects of the experimental manipulations were probably ramified in many networks coupled with these few.

link, and neutralizing the coupled hostility and anxiety circuits, reduced this likelihood of a "spontaneous" recurrence of the symptom
at a later date. The other extreme—providing a new, stronger response without first inhibiting the old one—also runs the risk of failure
if the balance of strength should for some reason shift back.

From this case one is tempted to wonder about the therapeutic
necessity for deep emotional involvement with content on the part
of the patient, as well as for elaborate "working through" of personality problems in the conscious waking state. Joe was able, under
hypnosis, to recapture seemingly traumatic childhood episodes at a
cognitive level, without experiencing the strong affective reactions
which must have accompanied them originally (see p. 191). Whenever anxiety did begin to manifest itself during the therapy session, it
was easily dispelled by instruction from E and then incorporated
within the cognitive reorganization. Perhaps the real function served
by a patient's emotional involvement is to help the psychotherapist
identify key pathogenic networks rather than to contribute materially
to the treatment process. If the diagnosis can be made more expe-
ditiously, as in the use of hypnosis, without resorting to the tags provided by anxiety discharge, then the patient can be spared considerable anguish. Similarly, we are led to doubt the necessity for the
patient's conscious understanding, in the waking state, of the roots
and ramifications of his difficulties in order to achieve beneficial results. Our therapeutic efforts were carried out while S remained in a
deep trance. Supporting this view, the insight which he gained into
his reaction to Hindus (realized in a half-asleep condition, it should
be noted), *followed* the actual change itself, which had already occurred automatically as a by-product of the father-brown discussion.

Admittedly there are many reasons why it is imprudent to generalize from results with an N of 1 to the whole field of psychotherapy.
A further caution derives from the fact that our particular S was
deeply susceptible to hypnotic techniques and had already been given
a dozen hours of training prior to E's intervention. Also, the synesthesia symptom itself was unusually clear and readily relatable to S's
early experiences. Nonetheless we raise these issues concerning the
therapeutic process deliberately in the hope of provoking more widespread recognition of the need for rigorous, detailed theorizing in a
vital area of human transaction. The currently controversial status of
various types of treatment eloquently testifies to this need. We
submit, in conclusion, that conceptual approaches of the kind generated by the working model are prerequisite to eventual improvement in the practice of psychotherapy.

Epilogue
to
Part C

In a literal sense the term "epilogue" is a misnomer, for these con-cluding remarks do not "serve to complete the plan of the work." The plan is only partially unfolded up to this point and much work remains to be done. But just as we attempted to set in perspective (pp. 103–107) the experiments reported in Part B, we shall try here to summarize the effort to "psychologize" the model and "remodel" the psychology.

The grand goal set for our program of investigation is the develop-ment of a *comprehensive* yet *detailed* theory of thought, feeling, and action—a theory not only capable of integrating phenomena all along psychology's broad spectrum, but also leading ultimately to discovery of the intricate underlying mechanisms by which the human mind operates. The laboratory research sought to demonstrate the suscep-tibility of our working model to empirical scrutiny. Techniques of hypnosis and physiological recording were called upon to assist in the tracking of mental events as they occur *between* stimulus and response. Part C witnessed a tentative rapprochement of the con-ceptual framework with diverse fields of psychology, the topics chosen for discussion hopefully sampling in fairly representative fashion the vast pool of psychodynamic phenomena. A brief chapter-by-chapter review may enable the reader in retrospect to focus more sharply upon the overall success or failure of this phase of the venture.

We began in Chapter 10 with further details of the model itself, relating to evolution and function of the cognitive subsystem. These elaborations provided the background for discussion of organizational phenomena of perception; properties of percepts and images, including hallucinations; and sources of perceptual interference, with emphasis upon notions of jamming and direct inhibitory action. Points of contact between the model and the area of learning were established in passages on reinforcement, expectancy, extinction and spontaneous recovery, generalization and discrimination, and finally retention.

Chapter 11 first treated topics in motivation and emotion, setting the stage for a more thorough analysis of the operation of anxiety and inhibition in the Mental System. Next these concepts were utilized to explain the defenses of denial, repression, suppression, and isolation; and the evolution of derivative networks from pathogenic ones. Psychopathological symptoms, fantasies, fixation, and regression all were shown to be generally encompassed by the working model, though the predisposing influences of past experience in a particular individual's life history necessarily remain to be elucidated.

Chapter 12 dealt with certain key hypnotic phenomena, since it is incumbent upon any theory which makes use of a specialized technique in its methodology to provide some understanding of that technique. Starting with the premise that existing viewpoints tend to be largely descriptive, an extended molecular analysis of hypnotic compliance was spelled out. Memory phenomena were also considered in terms of the working model.

"Primary" and "secondary" modes of thinking were the subject of Chapter 13. The capacity of the model to clarify fuzzy formulations was demonstrated in its application to the bizarre, prelogical nature of thought in dreams, psychoses, conditions of sensory deprivation, and the like. By deducing the consequences, according to the model, of reduced environmental sensory input, it was possible to arrive at the various phenomenological attributes of Freud's "primary process." The conceptual framework's potential for handling reflective or evaluative aspects of cognition was explored briefly.

The last chapter completed our running of the psychodynamic gamut by offering implications of the model for the practice of psychotherapy. This exercise in versatility was abetted by the existence in an experimental subject of a remarkably pervasive synesthesia symptom, which proved to be amenable under hypnosis to a form of treatment compatible with the model's assumptions.

With this summation we now rest our case for a conceptual model of the mind. The laboratory already beckons with dozens of tempting problems and, in the resumption of our research efforts, the familiar cry "Back to the drawing board!" will no doubt soon be heard again. In truth this epilogue is little more than a prologue. Who would have it any other way?

Initial hypnotic induction procedure

You know that your ability to be hypnotized depends entirely on your willingness to cooperate because if you didn't want to be hypnotized we wouldn't be able to do it . . . but if you do pay close attention to what I say and follow what I tell you it will be very easy for you to learn to fall into a fairly deep hypnotic sleep . . . and as I said before all of our subjects are preselected so that we're confident of your ability to do this . . . now just relax . . . make yourself entirely comfortable . . . keep your eyes on that spot . . . just keep staring at it all the time . . . keep staring as hard as you can and as long as you can . . . completely relaxed . . . relax all the muscles of your body . . . relax the muscles of your legs . . . relax the muscles in your arms . . . make yourself completely comfortable . . . that's fine . . . just let yourself be limp . . . limp . . . limp . . . just relax more and more . . . more and more . . . completely relaxed . . . completely relaxed . . . fine . . . legs beginning to feel heavy and limp . . . arms feeling heavier and heavier . . . heavier and heavier . . . feeling heavy as lead now . . . whole body is now feeling heavy . . . heavier . . . heavier . . . feeling tired and sleepy now . . . tired and sleepy . . . drowsy . . . sleepy . . . drowsy . . . sleepy . . . that's fine . . . completely relaxed now . . .

213

completely relaxed . . . breathing now slow . . . regular . . . slow
regular . . . that's fine . . . eyes are getting tired from staring now
. . . blinking a little . . . more and more tired . . . the strain in your
eyes is getting greater and greater . . . greater and greater . . . you
want to close your eyes and relax completely . . . you want to close
them and relax . . . but keep them open a little while longer . . .
keep them open a little longer and soon you'll reach your limit and
the strain will be so great your eyes will be so tired . . . your lids
will become so heavy that your eyes will just close by themselves . . .
they'll just close by themselves when you reach your limit and then
you'll be completely relaxed . . . completely relaxed . . . warm . . .
comfortable . . . tired and drowsy . . . tired and sleepy . . . tired
and sleepy . . . paying attention only to the sound of my voice . . .
eyes getting more and more tired . . . they're closing . . . feel
heavier and heavier . . . blinking a lot now and you want to close
them . . . keep them open a little longer . . . a little longer . . .
your lids are feeling heavier now . . . heavier . . . heavier . . . eyes
more and more strained . . . more and more strained now . . . feeling wet and uncomfortable . . . more and more strained now . . .
feeling wet and uncomfortable . . . more and more strained now . . .
your lids are getting heavier . . . pushing down more and more . . .
heavy as lead . . . and your eyes now are blinking and closing . . .
blinking and closing . . . and now you're reaching your limit and
your eyes will close as they get heavier and heavier . . . that's fine
. . . close your eyes now and relax . . . that's fine . . . completely
relaxed . . . and now I'm going to begin counting to five and at each
count you'll feel yourself going more and more deeply asleep . . . at
each count go more and more deeply asleep . . . all right . . . 1 . . .
sleeping more deeply now . . . 2 . . . more and more deeply asleep
. . . more and more . . . that's fine . . . completely relaxed . . . 3
. . . sleeping still more deeply now . . . sleeping still more deeply
. . . 4 . . . sinking into a deeper and deeper sleep . . . deeper and
deeper sleep . . . 5 . . . more and more deeply asleep . . . that's
fine . . . sleeping deeply . . . completely relaxed . . . not thinking
of a thing . . . that's fine . . . that's fine . . . now your eyes are
tightly shut and your lids are glued together . . . your lids are glued
together . . . tightly shut . . . and no matter how hard you try you
cannot open your eyes . . . you're struggling but you cannot open
them . . . that's fine . . . now relax . . . relax . . . completely relaxed . . . you tried to open your eyes but you couldn't get them open
—your eyes were closed so tightly that you couldn't open them and
this shows that you're in a hypnotic sleep now and you know what

it feels like . . . there's nothing strange about it . . . it's as though you're asleep but still you can hear clearly what I'm saying and you can follow instructions that I give you very easily . . . that's right . . . just relax and now put your arms down by your side . . . arms by your side . . . fine . . . completely relaxed . . . sleeping deeply now . . . now your right arm is getting heavier and heavier . . . your right arm is heavier and heavier . . . now it's as heavy as lead and you cannot raise your right arm . . . it's so heavy you cannot raise it . . . try to raise it but you won't be able to . . . all right now relax . . . that's fine . . . everything's going well now . . . you struggled to raise your right arm but you couldn't . . . it was so heavy . . . now your arm isn't heavy any more . . . it's getting lighter and lighter and now you can raise it without any difficulty . . . raise your right arm now . . . that's fine . . . good . . . all right just sleep deeply now . . . not thinking of a thing . . . completely relaxed . . . finding out more and more what it's like to be hypnotized and you know there's really not much to it . . . it's a very simple thing . . . it's easy to go into a deep sleep . . . all right sleep more and more deeply . . . and now you cannot say your name . . . you cannot say your name . . . no matter how hard you try you cannot say your name . . . try to say your name but you won't be able to . . . try . . . all right now relax . . . relax completely and now you can say your name very clearly . . . say your name (S says name) . . . that's right . . . fine . . . and now you know that it's possible for you to talk even while you're asleep . . . you'll be able to talk very distinctly and still stay asleep . . . this is different from usual nighttime sleep . . . this is one of the different things about hypnosis . . . you can talk . . . you can open your eyes and see when I tell you to . . . you'll even be able to get up and walk around and still stay deeply asleep . . . all right relax completely now . . . relax completely and now you're going to be able to open your eyes and still stay deeply asleep . . . that's fine . . . can you see now? (S says "yes") . . . and are you still asleep? (S says "I don't know") . . . it's hard to tell, isn't it? . . . that's right . . . actually you still are asleep . . . you can close your eyes now and sleep deeply . . . this is the different part about hypnosis . . . you can still be asleep and open your eyes and see . . . and you can talk and all the time you're deeply asleep . . . deeply asleep . . . that's fine . . . now close your eyes again and keep them closed . . . now keep your eyes closed and sleep deeply . . . sleep deeply . . . all right what we're doing now is just practice . . . we're giving you practice in going to sleep and you've done exceptionally well this first time . . . there's no doubt but what

you're going to be a good subject and you want to cooperate . . .
this is obvious and that's fine . . . in a little while I'm going to wake
you up by counting to five . . . when I get to four you'll open your
eyes and at five you'll be wide awake . . . and after you awaken
right after you wake up you'll hear someone calling your name . . .
after you wake up you'll hear someone calling your name . . . all
right sleep deeply . . . sleep deeply . . . completely relaxed . . .
and after you're awake you won't remember what we talked about
. . . what happened while you were asleep . . . and this won't seem
strange to you because you know that this is the instruction that I'm
giving you . . . after you wake up you won't remember what happened and you won't struggle to remember . . . it will all seem perfectly natural to you because this is the instruction I'm giving you
now . . . all right . . . completely relaxed . . . now I'm going to
count to five and you'll wake up . . . 1 . . . waking up a little now
. . . 2 . . . waking up more and more . . . 3 . . . more and more
awake . . . getting ready to open your eyes when I say 4 . . . 4 . . .
5 . . . wide awake!

Policy regarding the research use of hypnosis*

Appendix B

1. *Selection of subject participants will exclude those with known past or present cardiac illnesses or severe nervous disorders.* Pre-experimental physical examinations do not appear to be feasible, partly because of the expense involved, partly because of the possible psychological implications of such examinations for the research data obtained, and partly because even such examinations do not provide infallible safeguards against sudden cardiac attacks in the absence of a history of heart pathology. In dealing with subjects of college age and older, it would seem reasonable to screen out cardiac risks on the basis of specific interview questions. It should be noted that we are concerned here not with the danger of attacks brought on by the use of hypnosis, but with the possibility that such an attack could conceivably occur coincidentally with a subject's participation.

The matter of excluding persons with severe nervous disorders poses some problems of definition. For one thing, it is assumed that research groups will have available one or more members who will be clinically competent to screen out grossly psychopathological subjects. Also, information concerning the psychiatric history may also be ob-

* Department of Psychology, University of Michigan. (Approved March 25, 1958.)

217

tained from an initial interview. However, the question of where to draw the line between severe disorder and mild emotional difficulties, for our present purposes, is first of all a matter of judgment and secondly would seem to depend upon the nature of the experiment itself. It is conceivable that, with proper controls, one may want to study emotionally disturbed individuals hypnotically.

2. *An "agreement to participate" will be signed by each subject, or, if he is under 21, his parent or legal guardian.* The chairman advises that, in the opinion of the University's legal staff, a waiver or release has no protective function in such instances as we are concerned with, since an individual cannot legally sign away the rights in question. However, the agreement form merely serves to indicate that the subject is voluntarily engaging in the experiment.

3. *Hypnotic induction and suggestion will be carried out only by qualified personnel, upon authorization by the Chairman of the Department.* Regarding the definition of the term "qualified," Weitzenhoffer writes as follows in his book, *General Techniques of Hypnotism:* "A sound grounding in the behavioral sciences as well as in hypnotism is a minimum requirement, clinical orientation and training is much to be desired—only then is a hypnotist fully equipped to handle hypnotic phenomena." It is suggested that the authorization of the Chairman be restricted to those faculty members and graduate students who meet the above requirements, with the exception that special authorization may be given for others to work under the direct and immediate supervision of qualified personnel.

4. *A physician must be "on call" and available in cases of emergency.* The literature indicates that there are occasional transitory somatic sequelae to hypnotic induction, such as mild nausea, headache and dizziness. Good practice requires that the experimenter ascertain the physical and emotional condition of the subject before the latter departs from the session, and that he also assume responsibility for symptoms which may arise subsequent to the subject's departure. In extreme cases the presence of a physician may be required, although such instances would be rare. In any case, from the standpoint of legal protection, the safeguard of having a physician on call would appear to be warranted.

5. *All sessions will be conducted in the presence of a non-participant witness.* In addition to the obvious value that the testimony of such a witness would have in litigation, it is felt that the mere presence of a witness serves to discourage the development of a class of fan-

tasies which contains the seeds of lawsuits. Again, the practical neces-
sities of research would seem to require a somewhat broad definition
of "non-participant," and this requirement could probably be met by
having present another member of the research team whose function
was not that of conducting the hypnotic aspects of the experiment.

6. *All sessions will be completely tape-recorded, and the tapes are
to be preserved intact for a period of three months after the conclusion of each subject's participation.* After this three-month period,
the tapes may be replaced by complete verbatim typescripts, which
are to be retained for a period of time consistent with existing statutes
of limitations. Preservation of the tapes themselves for the entire
statutory period would, of course, be preferable, but the above solution is offered as a compromise between research budget limitations
and the requirements of legal protection.

7. *Experiments will be conducted in accordance with the principles
embodied in Ethical Standards for Psychologists, 1953.* In addition,
the experimental situation should be characterized throughout by a
professional atmosphere such that subjects are given no reason to feel
imposed upon. It should be pointed out that the best hypnotic practice is that in which the hypnotist works actively with rather than
against the will of the subject.

References

1. Barber, T. X. The concept of "hypnosis." *J. Psychol.*, 1958, **45**, 115–131.
2. Blum, G. S. Psychoanalytic behavior theory: a conceptual framework for research. *Perspectives in personality research* (H. P. David and J. C. Brengelmann, Eds.). New York: Springer, 1960.
3. ———. An investigation of perceptual defense in Italy. *Psychol. Rep.*, 1957, **3**, 169–175.
4. ———. Defense preferences in four countries. *J. Proj. Tech.*, 1956, **20**, 33–41.
5. ———. Perceptual defense revisited. *J. Abnorm. Soc. Psychol.*, 1955, **51**, 24–29.
6. ———. An experimental reunion of psychoanalytic theory with perceptual vigilance and defense. *J. Abnorm. Soc. Psychol.*, 1954, **49**, 94–98.
7. ———. *The Blacky Pictures: a technique for the exploration of personality dynamics.* New York: Psychological Corporation, 1950.
8. Brenman, M., and Gill, M. M. *Hypnotherapy.* New York: International Universities Press, 1947.
9. Bruner, J. S., and Postman, L. On the perception of incongruity: a paradigm. *J. Personal.*, 1949, **18**, 206–223.
10. Bullock, T. H. Neuron doctrine and electrophysiology. *Science*, 1959, **129**, 997–1002.
11. Cheatham, P. G. Visual perceptual latency as a function of stimulus brightness and contour shape. *J. Exp. Psychol.*, 1952, **43**, 369–380.
12. Clapp, C. D. *Two levels of unconscious awareness.* Ph.D. dissertation, University of Michigan, 1951.
13. Colby, K. *Energy and structure in psychoanalysis.* New York: Ronald, 1955.

14. Duke-Elder, W. S. *Textbook of ophthalmology* (Vol. IV). London: Kimpton, 1949.

15. Fenichel, O. *The psychoanalytic theory of neurosis.* New York: Norton, 1945.

16. Festinger, L. *A theory of cognitive dissonance.* Evanston: Row Peterson, 1957.

17. Freud, S. A note upon the mystic-writing pad. *Collected papers* (Vol. V). London: Hogarth, 1948 (translated under supervision of Joan Riviere).

18. ———. The unconscious. *Collected papers* (Vol. IV). London: Hogarth, 1948 (translated under supervision of Joan Riviere).

19. ———. *The problem of anxiety.* New York: Norton, 1936.

20. Friedlander, J. W., and Sarbin, T. R. The depth of hypnosis. *J. Abnorm. Soc. Psychol.*, 1938, **33**, 281–294.

21. Goldstein, R. H. *Behavioral effects of psychological stress.* Ph.D. dissertation, University of Michigan, 1958.

22. Hebb, D. O. The American revolution. *Amer. Psychol.*, 1960, **15**, 735–745.

23. ———. *Organization of behavior.* New York: Wiley, 1949.

24. Hull, C. L. *Hypnosis and suggestibility.* New York: Appleton-Century, 1933.

25. Jasper, H. Reticular-cortical systems and theories of the integrative action of the brain. *Biological and biochemical bases of behavior* (H. F. Harlow and C. N. Woolsey, Eds.). Madison: University of Wisconsin Press, 1958.

26. Jones, E. *The life and work of Sigmund Freud.* New York: Basic Books, 1953.

27. Kety, S. S. A biologist examines the mind and behavior. *Science*, 1960, **132**, 1861–1870.

28. Magoun, H. W. Non-specific brain mechanisms. *Biological and biochemical bases of behavior* (H. F. Harlow and C. N. Woolsey, Eds.). Madison: University of Wisconsin Press, 1958.

29. McCulloch, W. "On reliable circuits of unreliable components." Address delivered at Department of Psychiatry, University of Michigan, Ann Arbor, Michigan, 1958.

30. Miller, G. A., Galanter, E., and Pribram, K. H. *Plans and the structure of behavior.* New York: Holt, 1960.

31. Miller, J. G. Information input overload and psychopathology. *Am. J. Psychiat.*, 1960, **116**, 695–704.

32. Minkowich, A. *Correlates of superego functions.* Ph.D. dissertation, University of Michigan, 1958.

33. Nelson, S. E. Psychosexual conflicts and defenses in visual perception. *J. Abnorm. Soc. Psychol.*, 1955, **51**, 427–433.

34. Orne, M. T. The nature of hypnosis: artifact and essence. *J. Abnorm. Soc. Psychol.*, 1959, **58**, 277–299.

35. Osgood, C. E. *Method and theory in experimental psychology.* New York: Oxford University Press, 1953.

36. Perky, C. W. An experimental study of imagination. *Amer. J. Psychol.*, 1910, **21**, 422–452.

37. Perloe, S. I. Inhibition as a determinant of perceptual defense. *Perc. and Mot. Skills*, 1960, **11**, 59–66.

38. ———. *An experimental test of two theories of perceptual defense.* Ph.D. dissertation, University of Michigan, 1958.

39. Rank, O. *The trauma of birth.* New York: Harcourt, Brace, 1929.
40. Rapaport, D. The conceptual model of psychoanalysis. *J. Personal.,* 1951, **20,** 56–81.
41. Reiff, R., and Scheerer, M. *Memory and hypnotic age regression.* New York: International Universities Press, 1959.
42. Sarbin, T. R. Contributions to role-taking theory: I. Hypnotic behavior. *Psychol. Rev.,* 1950, **57,** 255–270.
43. Spence, K. W. *Behavior theory and learning: selected papers.* Englewood Cliffs, New Jersey: Prentice-Hall, 1960.
44. Tolman, E. C. Performance vectors: a theoretical and experimental attack upon emphasis, effect, and repression. *Amer. Psychol.,* 1959, **14,** 1–7.
45. Troland, L. T. *The fundamentals of human motivation.* New York: Van Nostrand, 1928.
46. Weitzenhoffer, A. M., and Hilgard, E. R. *Stanford Hypnotic Susceptibility Scale, Forms A and B.* Palo Alto: Consulting Psychologists Press, 1959.
47. ———. *Hypnotism: an objective study in suggestibility.* New York: Wiley, 1953.
48. White, R. W. A preface to the theory of hypnotism. *J. Abnorm. Soc. Psychol.,* 1941, **36,** 477–505.
49. Wolberg, L. R. *Hypnoanalysis.* New York: Grune and Stratton, 1945.

Index

225